The Numismatourist

*The Only Worldwide Travel Guide to Museums, Mints,
and Other Places of Interest for the Numismatist*

by

Howard M. Berlin

The Numismatourist

by

Howard M. Berlin

Cover design by Jess

ISBN-10: 1-933990-29-5
ISBN-13: 978-1-933990-29-3

Published by:
Zyrus Press, Inc.
P.O. Box 17810
Irvine, CA 92623

Printed in the United States of America

Table of Contents

In Memory of Richard G. Doty, Ph.D., 1942-2013
Senior numismatic curator, National Numismatic Collection of the
Smithsonian Institution's National Museum of American History

Foreword

As a museum enthusiast and numismatic curator, I thought I had visited more than my fair share of exhibitions featuring coin collections. But then I took a look at *The Numismatourist*: The only world-wide travel guide to museums, mints and other places of interest to the numismatist. Just the name conjures images of far-flung adventure—and Howard Berlin's treatment delivers it with an introduction to over seventy countries boasting numismatic exhibitions. Even readers with a smidge of reluctance (perhaps because a certain family member unendingly encourages you to marvel at these miniature masterpieces?) will enjoy traipsing across the globe whilst thumbing through these pages. But, if like me, you seek out numismatic displays whenever possible, get ready for a treat because more than one-hundred and seventy-five destinations await.

Chock-full of information about venues on and off the beaten path, The Numismatourist is a clever resource. Reading it is fun and enlightening—yet the book also illustrates how coin collections matter, as much as ever, in the United States and around the world. What started as Berlin's straight forward idea to build a list of places with numismatic exhibitions evolved into a significant contribution to the world of museums. This massive compilation, and Berlin has only scratched the surface, reflects the educational value people feel for coins. Whether it's a curator who devotes a lifetime to unlocking the mysteries of these tiny objects or a visitor who volunteers their time in pursuit of a personal experience with them, people do care about coins. And it is this shared interest—in coins as history teachers, cultural treasures, political statements and technological wonders—that coalesces when you take stock of just how many places around world display coins. But also, in the unique way that guide books are destinations in themselves, we needn't visit each display to become more well-informed.

So whether you pick this book up while planning a travel adventure or because you're simply curious about where in the world all these coin collections reside, your interest will be rewarded. A numismatic expedition lies ahead—and with Howard Berlin's voracious travel schedule—we can look forward to future volumes about all those future coin displays just now in the making.

Karen M. Lee
Curator, National Numismatic Collection
National Museum of American History

Preface

I feel that a country's history is perhaps best exhibited by the evolution of its money, which both represents an intrinsic component of its heritage and mirrors its socioeconomic history. Also, the national legal tender is considered one of the leading symbols of that country's identity and autonomy. What better way to educate the public about its monetary heritage than that of showcasing its numismatic treasures in an exhibition in a museum, the nation's central bank, or a mint?

This book was born from my "World Destinations" column that appeared in *WorldWide Coins* about my travels to places that feature various fascinating exhibits about coins and currency. The column had won the Numismatic Literary Guild's "Best Column" award for world commercial numismatic magazines for two consecutive years. To my knowledge, this is first book of its kind and combines three of my favorite pastimes: numismatics, travel, and writing.

This is intended to be a worldwide travel guide for the numismatist, those whose hobby or profession is about coins and paper money. Inside you will find its contents to be a reference catalog of numismatic collections of exhibits in museums, banks, mints, and libraries around the world that are open to the general public. It is for the numismatist who is traveling, either on vacation or business, and wishes to visit places of interest.

Following my retirement as a college educator, I have had both the time and good fortune to travel. I have visited more than 50 countries, averaging about 75,000 miles annually—as the extra-page inserts and immigration stamps in my passport will verify. Some of these destinations, which had numismatic institutions of one kind or another, were first chronicled in my semi-monthly column. Prior to the column's debut, Wayne Homren, the editor of the Numismatic Bibliomania Society's electronic newsletter, *The E-Sylum*, dubbed me, the "Numismatourist." I'm quite sure that there are many other travel writers that log more miles than I do, but I'm probably one of a very few with this peculiar niche—writing solely about visiting numismatic exhibits in museums, central banks, and mints.

For me, such an amount of frequent traveling has had its benefits. The obvious ones are the perks from accumulating frequent traveler air miles and hotel upgrades. Another benefit allows me to experience other monetary systems besides the British pound and the ubiquitous euro. The third and most important is that I've been able to personally meet many of the museum's directors and curators, who behind the scenes make their institutions into an enjoyable educational experience. Many times they personally escorted me on guided tours through their "home," providing me with insights and experiences regular visitors do not experience. This often entails a visit to the museum's vault where the most prized specimens are kept. For those museums that have an admission fee, I am frequently given the privilege of free entry.

As one who has many times competitively exhibited parts of my own collection, I also have become interested in the various techniques museum curators use to display their numismatic possessions. These range from the mounting of coins, paper money, and medals to the use of various materials, lighting, mirrors, lenses for magnification, and the incorporation of text material. I would photograph some of the more interesting of these techniques and share them with curators stateside.

Peter Greenberg, an American TV and radio personality and author of *The Travel Detective*, writes, "Most of us love to travel. That's the good news. The bad news: We hate the process of travel." While I can't do anything about finding the best airfares and hotel rooms, I can tell you where most of the public numismatic exhibits are located around the world. Instead of hunting the internet with multiple keywords searches, I have already done the research for many of the most popular spots worldwide in one handy book.

As a result of my travels and experience, my research notes are compiled into a single numismatic travel guide, listing over 175 places in 75 countries spread over North, Central and South America, the Caribbean, Europe (divided into Western and Eastern European regions), Asia, the Middle East, Africa, and Oceania-Pacific. My selection criterion was a simple one. The institution, whether it is a museum, mint, or central bank, had to be open to the general public. With this single restriction, there are a number of well-known institutions that were not included. These generally included central bank museums, as their admission is restricted to school group class visits.

Of the 175 places included in this book, there are 75 institutions representing 42 countries which are known to have numismatic exhibitions of varying degrees but only a minimal amount of information is provided. These institutions are included in the "additional museums" portion at the end of each section because sufficient information could not either: (1) be obtained about the museum, (2) be verified from other sources, (3) the museum did not respond to repeated requests for information, (4) the exhibition was closed due to long-term renovation of the building or other reasons, or (5) I learned about the institution just before the manuscript was to go to the publisher and a detailed entry could not be included.

There is one important point that I have discovered repeatedly to my frustration. Just because an institution, even a well-known one, reportedly has a numismatic collection does not mean they exhibit any part of it. This is particularly true of many university library collections, which are often bequeathed by alumni and secluded from the public, only for the eyes of researchers. So, some of you might question why a well-known museum's collection is not included in this book (university or otherwise). It may be because it does not publicly exhibit its collection for a number of reasons, some of which may be security and cost.

Despite the more than 175 places listed with about 100 of these described in detail with pictures, this book is not meant to be an all-inclusive, worldwide compilation of places hosting a numismatic exhibition of one kind or another. However, this book does cover a wide variety of venues, ranging from well-known, premier public and private institutions, like the museums of the American Numismatic Association and London's venerable British Museum, to those concentrating on currency of their own country or city, like the Banknote Museum of Ionian Bank at Corfu. There are even those that cater to the unusual. Several museums showcase only counterfeits, and there is even a museum for wooden nickels. Some museums, like the Numismatic Museum Athens, are entirely numismatic in scope. Others have either one or more rooms set aside for their numismatic exhibits, or have its numismatic specimens integrated among the historical items throughout the museum.

While one might expect renowned institutions to possess nearly complete collections of a given series, and for them to display specimens of the highest grades and rarity, those at the local level, often with lesser financial support, sometimes have exhibitions featuring less spectacular displays with reduced grade material. Nonetheless, these institutions are just as proud of their exhibitions. In these situations, I encourage visitors to focus more on the interesting stories and associated backstories they tell about the specimens rather than the quality of the material.

The organization of this book is by continent or geographical region, further subdivided by country. For the United States, division is by region: Northeast, South, Midwest, and West, and is further subdivided by states—14 in all, including Washington, D.C. For Europe, the division is between Western and Eastern European countries.

My intent is to provide information about each institution that is useful for the visitor. Whenever possible, each entry includes a picture of the building, so visitors will be able to recognize it from the street. In addition, there is usually a scene of the gallery or one or more of the exhibition's numismatic highlights. There also is a background description of the museum and of the contents of the exhibition and what visitors would expect to see. Like traditional travel guides, there is additional information that includes the street address, telephone numbers, e-mail contact address, the English version of the official website (if there is one) or an alternate but unofficial website, hours of operation, days/holidays closed, and nearby public transportation stops (for metro/subway, bus, tram). Most of the institutions listed in this book are located in major cities and are on or nearby public transportation routes.

Also included are icons representing information about whether or not the institution is wheelchair/handicap accessible, permits cell phone use, permits photography/video recording, charges an admission fee, has multi-language audio guides, a library, a cafeteria or food court, and a souvenir gift shop. If an English language website is not available, as is often the case with many French- and Spanish-speaking countries, cut and pasting the foreign language text into either Google's multiple language translation engine (translate.google.com) or Microsoft's Bing translator (www.bing.com/translator) works reasonably well.

Another helpful feature is the inclusion of maps of the continents and geographical areas, with those cities included in this book indicated. For certain countries, like those in Europe that generally have four or more cities with numismatic venues, I have added separate maps. This is done to gain a better idea as to the geographical relationship of these cities and countries when planning trips.

The reader is cautioned that even the contents of permanent exhibits are sometimes an evolutionary process, possibly changing over time. Any facts, accurate in this book at the time of printing, may be slightly outdated later. This applies to internet URLs, museum opening and closing times, and even telephone numbers. Because admission fees are also subject to change, prices are not specifically mentioned. Readers are therefore encouraged to check the institution's official website (if available), or call ahead to confirm opening and closing times and days of operation.

There are several additional points worth mentioning, which might seem trivial for the experienced international traveler. First, museums are generally closed on Mondays, particularly true in Europe and many parts of the world outside the United States and Canada. For Americans who haven't traveled internationally to any extent, most of the world operates on a *24-hour clock*—what we would call "military time"—so that when reading international websites, a time expressed as 17:30, is 5:30 p.m. Also, Europeans and much of the rest of the world express dates compactly in the dd/mm/yy(yy) format where the day of the month is given first, then the number of the month, so that 06/07/13 is *6 July 2013*, not June 7, 2013. To eliminate confusion, all dates given in this book have the month spelled out. Lastly, the floors of buildings, especially in Europe, are usually numbered starting with the first floor above the ground floor (which is zero).

A final word is in order about visiting these institutions. Many are comprehensive art or history museums whose numismatic exhibition is but a small part of the overall scheme of things. If you have the time, I strongly encourage you to seek out its other well-known priceless treasures on display, many of which are from antiquity, a favorite interest of mine, and probably yours as well. The British Museum has the Rosetta Stone that unlocked the secrets of Egyptian hieroglyphs; the Israel Museum in its Archaeology Wing contains the world's finest collection of Holy Land archaeology while the nearby Shrine of the Book houses the priceless Dead Sea Scrolls found in the Qumran caves. And you should be able find many things of interest once you exit the National Numismatic Collection in the National Museum of American History—just one of the many museums of the Smithsonian Institution complex.

No travel guide is ever perfect. Try hard as I may, errors will inevitably find their way into the final manuscript. Any errors or omissions are my own and are purely unintentional. If I have overlooked some important detail, including your favorite place, feel free to let me know about it. I welcome your comments and experiences by email at numismatourist@yahoo.com or on my website at www.numismatourist.com. It's possible your suggestions will be addressed in a future edition. Happy travels.

Howard M. Berlin
Wilmington, Delaware

Acknowledgements

Being the first book of its kind to my knowledge, I would first like to thank the people at Zyrus Press for their faith in undertaking such a project. One book such as this with a contracted focus decreases the successful odds. However, the support of Zyrus Press, the interest from a number of individuals, and several professional organizations has made me very optimistic that this was a worthwhile project worth pursuing.

There are so many people, who over the years have been so gracious in sharing their "home" with me so I could both write my columns and gather material for this book. Generally, most of my visits to the museums, central banks, libraries, and mints were coordinated several months in advance with the directors and curators. However, a few visits were made without appointments, only when I found there was such a museum after I arrived in a particular city. Showing up at the museum unannounced, with no appointment, and myself very embarrassed, museum directors or curators were always very obliging to put aside their busy schedule and were quite hospitable to meet with me.

I would like to thank the directors, curators, and staffs of the following institutions and individuals for their assistance in the preparation of both my past magazine columns and for this book. To those persons employed by the institutions that answered my e-mails, letters and telephone calls, providing helpful information when requested and whose names I may never know, I also extend my deep-felt thanks. Without all their invaluable help, this book would not have been possible.

Altes Museum (Berlin, Germany)
American Friends of the Shanghai Museum (New York, NY)
American Numismatic Association (Colorado Springs, CO)
American Numismatic Society (New York, NY)
Yigal Arkin (Jerusalem, Israel)
Ashmolean Museum, University of Oxford (Oxford, England)
A.H. Baldwin & Sons, Ltd. (London, England)
Balzekas Museum of Lithuanian Culture (Chicago, IL)
Banco de la República (Bogota, Colombia)
Bank Al-Maghrib Museum (Rabat, Morocco)
Bank of Canada Currency Museum (Ottawa, Canada)
Bank of England Museum (London, England)
Bank of Estonia Museum (Tallinn, Estonia)
Bank of Finland Museum (Helsinki, Finland)
Bank of Israel Visitor Center (Jerusalem, Israel)
Bank of Japan Currency Museum (Tokyo, Japan)
Bank of Montreal Museum (Montreal, Canada)
Basel Historical Museum Coin Cabinet (Basel, Switzerland)
Bernisches Historisches Museums (Berne, Switzerland)
Bode-museum Münzkabinet (Berlin, Germany)
British Museum (London, England)
Bulgarian National Bank Museum (Sofia, Bulgaria)
Cabinet de médaille du Musée d'art et d'histoire (Geneva,
    Switzerland)
Central Bank of Brazil Museum of Money (Brasília, Brazil)
Central Bank of Jordan Currency Museum (Amman, Jordan)
CoinsWeekly/MünzenWoche (Lörrach, Germany)
Coin World (Sidney, OH)
Correr Museum (Venice, Italy)
Deutsche Bundesbank Money Museum (Frankfurt am Main,
    Germany)
Deutsches Historisches Museum (Berlin, Germany)
Federal Reserve Bank of Atlanta Visitors Center & Monetary
    Museum (Atlanta, GA)
Federal Reserve Bank of Chicago Money Museum
    (Chicago, IL)
Federal Reserve Bank of Kansas City - The Money Museum
    (Kansas City, MO)
Federal Reserve Bank of New York (New York, NY)

Federal Reserve Bank of Philadelphia (Philadelphia, PA)
Federal Reserve Bank of San Francisco (San Francisco, CA)
Federal Reserve Bank of San Francisco, Los Angeles Branch
(Los Angeles, CA)
Fitzwilliam Museum, University of Cambridge
(Cambridge, England)
German Technical Museum Berlin (Berlin, Germany)
Germanisches Nationalmuseum (Nuremberg, Germany)
Hamburg History Museum (Hamburg, Germany)
Heritage Auctions (Dallas, TX)
Hunterian Museum, University of Glasgow (Glasgow, Scotland)
International Council of Museums (ICOM)
International Committee of Money and Banking Museums
(ICOMON)
Israel Museum (Jerusalem, Israel)
Japan Mint and Museum (Osaka, Japan)
Kadman Museum (Tel Aviv, Israel)
Korea Tourism Organization (New York, NY)
Fritz Rudolf Künker GmbH & Co. KG (Osnabrück, Germany)
Kunsthistorisches Museum Coin Cabinet (Vienna, Austria)
Owen W. Linzmayer, BanknoteNews.com (San Francisco, CA)
Louisiana State Museum (New Orleans, LA)
Magyar Nemzeti Bank (Budapest, Hungary)
Manchester Museum, Manchester University
(Manchester, England)
MoneyMuseum (Zurich, Switzerland)
Money Museum Bangko Sentral ng Pilipinas
(Manila, Philippines)
Money Museum of the National Bank of Slovakia
(Kremnica, Slovakia)
Musée monétaire du canton de Vaud (Lausanne, Switzerland)
Musée National d'Histoire et d'Art Luxembourg
(Luxembourg City, Luxembourg)
Museum Bank Indonesia (West Jakarta, Indonesia)
Museum of Stamps and Coins (Monte Carlo, Monaco)
Museum of the Bank of Lithuania (Vilnius, Lithuania)
Museum on the Mound, Lloyds Banking Group
(Edinburgh, Scotland)
Museum of National Bank of Belgium (Brussels, Belgium)

Nationalmuseet, Royal Collection of Coins and Medals
(Copenhagen, Denmark)
National Museum Cardiff (Cardiff, Wales)
National Bank of Denmark (Copenhagen, Denmark)
National Bank of Serbia Museum (Belgrade, Serbia)
National Museum of Finland (Helsinki, Finland)
National Museum of Ireland, Collins Barracks (Dublin, Ireland)
National Museum, The Royal Coin Cabinet
(Stockholm, Sweden)
National Numismatic Collection of the Smithsonian Institution
(Washington, DC)
Newman Money Museum (St. Louis, MO)
Numismatic Museum of the Centrale Bank van Suriname
(Paramaribo, Suriname)
Numismatic Museum Athens (Athens, Greece)
Palazzo Doria Tursi Museum (Genoa, Italy)
The Perth Mint (Perth, Australia)
Princeton University Numismatic Collection (Princeton, NJ)
Reserve Bank of India Monetary Museum (Mumbai, India)
Reserve Bank of New Zealand Museum
(Wellington, New Zealand)
Royal Castle Museum Coin Cabinet (Warsaw, Poland)
Royal Mint (Llantrisant, Wales)
Shanghai Museum (Shanghai, China)
Staatliche Kunstsammlungen Dresden-Münzkabinett
(Dresden, Germany)
Staatlichen Münzsammlung München/State Coin Collection
Munich (Munich, Germany)
State Museum of San Marino (San Marino, San Marino)
Swiss National Museum (Zurich, Switzerland)
Teylers Museum Coin Cabinet (Haarlem, The Netherlands)
United States Mint (Denver, CO)
United States Mint (Philadelphia, PA)
Uppsala University Coin Cabinet (Uppsala, Sweden)
Ömer Yalçinkaya (Almaty, Kazakhstan)
Zagreb Archaeological Museum (Zagreb, Croatia)

H.M.B.

Symbols

○ Open times/dates. You should be aware that most countries use the 24-hour time clock (e.g. 17:30 is 5:30 p.m.) and dates are written as dd/mm/yyyy (e.g. 06/07/2013 or 6/7/2013 is 6 July 2013, not June 7, 2013).

● Closed days/dates

ⓘ Information, including printed guides

℃ Museum telephone number

✋ No admission fee; however donations are usually sought, but not required

✋ Admission fee; others such as seniors or retired persons may receive free admission with proof of age

🪪 Photo ID required and/or security screening. For federal venues in the U.S., foreign nationals are required to show their passport. Large backpacks or packages may have to be checked in a locker before entry.

📷 Photography or video permitted, usually without flash and without tripods and generally for non-commercial purposes. In some cases, a fee for a separate ticket may be charged for the privilege of taking pictures or videos.

🚫📷 No video or photography permitted. This includes picture taking using cellphones/mobiles.

🚫 Cellphones/mobile phones are to be turned off. If not specified, it is usually a good courtesy to others to either turn your cellphone/mobile off or set to the vibrate mode while in the museum.

📚 Museum library

♿ Wheelchair access available/handicap accessible

🎧 Audio-guide available, usually for a rental fee

🛒 Souvenir/gift shop

🍴 Food court/restaurant

Public Transportation

The information given is for the closest stop/station, generally within several blocks. In most instances for metro/subway, bus, and tram lines, the name or number (and/or color) of the line is given first followed by the station or stop name, if applicable, in parenthesis.

Metro/Subway

 German S-Bahn

 German U-Bahn

 London Underground

 All other cities

Bus

 London

 All other cities

Tram/Trolley/Light Rail

 All cities

Internet

✉ e-Mail or online contact form

🌐 Numismatic website – the English language version is specified unless indicated otherwise.

North America

United States

Even before its founding in 1776, the United States' numismatic legacy was rich in the coinage from its colonial rulers and the barter systems of the indigenous peoples that inhabited the lands before the arrival of the colonists and the Spanish conquerors.

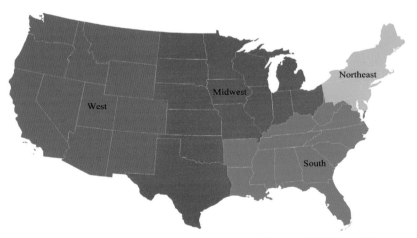

Map highlighting the four regions of the contiguous 48 states of the United States plus the District of Columbia used for this travel guide.

The following four sections have the United States divided by region: Northeast, South, Midwest, and West, and are further subdivided by states to make it easier for the traveler. The four regions, with their corresponding states, are listed below. States marked with an asterisk (*) indicate that there are numismatic venues listed in this book.

Northeast

Connecticut

Delaware

Destrict of Columbia*

Maine

Maryland

Massachusetts*

New Hamshire

New Jersey*

New York*

Pennsylvania*

Rhode Island

Vermont

South

Alabama

Arkansas

Georgia*

Florida

Kentucky

Louisiana*

Mississippi

North Carolina

South Carolina

Tennessee

Virginia*

West Virginia

Midwest

Illinois*

Indiana

Iowa

Kansas

Michigan

Minnesota

Missouri*

Nebraska

North Dakota

Ohio*

Oklahoma

South Dakota

Texas*

Wisconsin

West

Arizona

California*

Colorado*

Idaho

Oregon

Montana

Nevada

New Mexico

Utah

Washington

Wyoming

Geographically, each region has its own characteristics. In some cases this could be also said of the numismatic history for each region. Each has its share of numismatic venues, although some more than others. Throughout the country, this ranges from two United States Mints that still function to produce coins to one that was decommissioned long ago; the Bureau of Engraving and Printing which prints the nation's paper money; museums of eight Federal Reserve Banks representing six of the twelve Federal Reserve districts; and museums, big and small, some with specialized themes.

From top to bottom, left to right: the Philadelphia skyline, a statue of Benjamin Franklin, the Liberty Bell, the Philadelphia Museum of Art, Philadelphia City Hall, and Independence Hall.

United States

Northeast Region

The northeast region is subdivided into the six New England states and the five mid-Atlantic states plus the District of Columbia, the nation's capital.

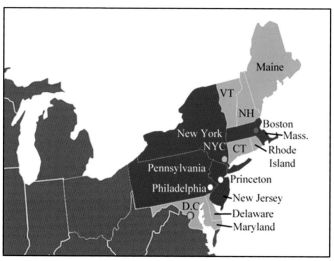

Map highlighting the 11 states plus the District of Columbia that comprise the northeastern United States. The states having numismatic venues with detailed descriptions are shown in dark blue and their cities indicated by a white dot. A red dot represents cities with limited information while a green dot indicates cities having venues with both detailed and limited information.

All of these states were part of the original 13 colonies that formed the United States in its 1776 declaration of independence from Great Britain. Because these states are the nation's oldest, it is rich in numismatic history. The 1652 Massachusetts Pine Tree shilling, considered colonial America's most famous coin, was struck at a Boston mint when England was not inclined to send coins to the colonies. Philadelphia, the birthplace of the nation and home of the first United States Mint, is also the birthplace of some of the nation's early Continental coins and paper money, thanks to Benjamin Franklin, who designed the fugio cent and Continental currency bearing his "Mind Your Business" quotation.

In this region, visitors will find in the nation's capital the world's largest numismatic collection housed at the National Numismatic Collection of the Smithsonian Institution, although there is but only a tiny fraction of it on display. Nearby, one can watch paper money being printed at the Department of the Treasury's Bureau of Engraving and Printing. The lead bank of the Federal Reserve System in New York City has an exhibition highlighted by a visit to the world's largest gold depository. The Federal Reserve Bank of Philadelphia's Money in Motion interactive exhibit features 17 stations and is just one block away from the Philadelphia Mint, currently at its fourth location. The Firestone Library on the campus of Princeton University offers periodic exhibitions from their collection, much of which has been contributed by its alumni.

Washington, DC	• National Numismatic Collection of the Smithsonian Institution
New York, NY	• American Numismatic Society
	• Federal Reserve Bank of New York
Philadelphia, PA	• Federal Reserve Bank of Philadelphia, Money in Motion
	• Philadelphia Mint

Additional institutions with limited information:

Washington, DC
- Department of the Treasury, Bureau of Engraving and Printing
- Dumbarton Oaks Research Library and Collection, Coins & Seals Collection

New York, NY
- Museum of American Finance

Boston, MA
- Museum of Fine Arts, Boston – Michael C. Ruettgers Gallery for Ancient Coins

The National Numismatic Collection, Smithsonian Institution
Stories on Money
Washington, District of Columbia

Housed in the National Museum of American History of the famed Smithsonian Institution, "Stories on Money" draws from a tiny fraction of the National Numismatic Collection's more than 1.5 million objects that preserve the role of America's money in economic history.

Entering the gallery, the introductory display explains that money preserves the stories of American history and reflects the birth of nations. Shown is a stater coin from Lydia (652-615 BC) and a 1652 Pine Tree Shilling from the Massachusetts Bay Colony, which is perhaps America's most famous colonial coin.

Main entrance of the National Museum of American History as seen from Constitution Avenue.

1607-1765: Making Do in Colonial America

The first settlers in the colonies found little precious metal in which to mint coins. Initially wampum shells, tobacco, and "ten penny" nails like those on display were used as barter. The lack of sufficient gold or silver for coins led to the creation of the first paper money by a government outside China. There is a 1690/1 Massachusetts 20-shillings note—the first paper money in the Western hemisphere.

1776-1861: Money for a New Nation

Following the Revolutionary War, the U.S. Mint, and other entities began to issue their own forms of paper money, many with unusual denominations. There are examples of Revolutionary War currency such as a 1776 United States dollar banknote. Also shown are 1779 U.S. $65- and 1779 South Carolina $90-notes.

1825-1875: Gold!

Gold was first discovered in the Carolinas and Georgia prior to 1800 and provided the first gold coins such as the North Carolina1834 Christopher Betchler $5-specimen. After gold was discovered in California in 1848, many private gold coin coins were issued, like the $20 1853 Moffat & Co. Also on exhibit are several coins of this era issued by the U.S. Mint.

1861-Present: Rebuilding America's Money

This section illustrates the major change in America's money—the Greenback, the first national paper money since the Revolutionary War. Besides paper money, coins were also redesigned. On display is a virtual 20th-century type set from one cent to $20, including the 1909S VDB penny.

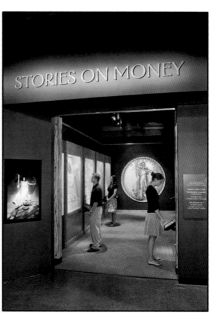

A Penny for Your Thoughts?

Examples of the penny, or cent, are shown, which have been minted since 1793. It is no longer as it once was, and it now costs more than a cent to make one. Here, visitors can cast their vote about the future of the most-produced coin in the world.

America's Legendary Coins

It would be impossible to display even a modest portion of the National Numismatic Collection in this gallery. Nevertheless, on one display are 18 of America's legendary coins that are favorites of the Museum staff. Among those shown are: three classes of the 1804 dollar, the 1787 gold Brasher doubloon, one of five known 1913 Liberty nickel specimens, and a $20 1933 St. Gaudens gold piece, of which fewer than 20 pieces were not melted down.

Power of Liberty

The gallery's final section, called "The Power of Liberty," presents coins from the United States and the world depicting Liberty, the feminine personification of freedom, also featuring real and mythological women. George Washington, rejecting the tradition of displaying images of men or women who held power, chose Lady Liberty on the

1793 large cent so that Americans could be inspired by the power of liberty, not the power of a president.

Visitor's Checklist
National Museum of American History, Kenneth E. Behring Center, National Mall, 14th Street and Constitution Avenue, N.W., Washington, DC 20560
Stories on Money Exhibit – 1st Floor East, Transportation & Technology

ⓘ ℂ (202) 633-1000

○ Daily: 10 a.m.-5:30 p.m.; extended hours: 7:30 p.m. December 26-30. Check website for other dates as they vary, depending on the calendar year

● December 25

✋ ♿ 📷 🎧 🛒 🍴

The obverse of an 1849 double eagle—the first federal $20 gold coin made.

Public Transportation

Ⓜ Blue/Orange (Federal Triangle or Smithsonian Metro)

🚌 52/63/64

Internet

✉ info@si.edu, or use contact form at:

🌐 americanhistory.si.edu/about/contactform.cfm?key=88&contactkey=17
americanhistory.si.edu/exhibitions/exhibition.cfm?key=38&exkey=1327

Princeton University Numismatic Collection
Princeton, New Jersey

Going back at least to 1849 when alumni donated over 5,000 sulfur casts of Greek and Roman coins to what was then incorporated as the College of New Jersey, Princeton University's collection is the oldest continuously curated numismatic collection in the United States. Located in the Firestone Library, Princeton University maintains a comprehensive numismatic collection for use in research, teaching, and exhibits. It shares exhibit space with other departments of the library's Department of Rare Books and Special Collections.

Major Exhibitions

The Department of Rare Books and Special Collections sponsors four major exhibitions annually: two in the library's main gallery on the first floor and two in the Milberg Gallery on the second floor. The Cotsen Children's Library includes an interactive exhibition gallery for children. In addition, materials from the collections are displayed in various lobby cases, in online galleries, and in the exhibition gallery of the Seeley G. Mudd Manuscript Library at 65 Olden Street.

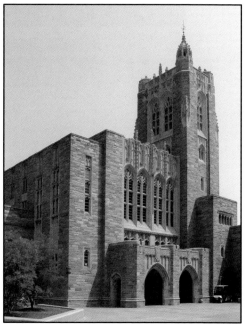

The Firestone Library, home to the Princeton University Numismatic Collection.

The general collection has grown to more than 60,000 specimens, often due to generous gifts of numismatic collections from alumni and faculty. The archaeological aspect of University's collection centers on 40,000 Greek, Roman, Byzantine and Muslim coins excavated before 1939 at Syrian Antioch. By category, the collection contains over 3,000 coins from the Classical and Hellenistic periods, as well as the "pseudo-autonomous" coins issued by Greek cities under the Roman Empire. Coins issued by Greek cities in the names of Roman emperors however, are housed with the Roman material. The most notable single group consists of 314 silver staters and their fractions from Tarentum.

There are about 6,000 Roman coins, including the "Greek imperials" – 650 of which were struck during the Republican era, plus there is a considerable holding in the coinage of Roman Corinth.

A view of the Leonard L. Milberg Gallery for the exhibition, "Capping Liberty: The Invention of a Numismatic Iconography for the New American Republic," one of several major exhibits held each year.

From the Byzantine era, there are over 500 gold, silver, and bronze coins. Medieval European coins number about 275, the largest are those from the Italian states, England, and France (52). From Southeast Asia, the University has a considerable collection of Chinese coins, especially the donated collection in 2006 of more than 2,000 coins of Souheng Wu by the Wu family. The collection is rich in round copper coins with square holes from the 9th through 19th centuries, which nicely complements the Museum's other holdings of ancient issues of China in the shape of knives and spades.

The remainder of the collection consists of about 2,000 items of the United States, including the Colonial, Continental, and Confederate periods, particularly paper money of these periods. Also included are New Jersey items and "Rosa Americana" series and over 770 aviation medals on subjects from ballooning to space travel.

Visitor's Checklist

Princeton University Numismatic Collection, Department of Rare Books and Special Collections, Firestone Library, One Washington Road, Princeton, NJ 08544

- ❶ ℂ (609) 258-9127 – the curator, Dr. Alan Stahl
- ◯ Tuesday, Wednesday and Thursday: 9:30 a.m.-4:30 p.m. (Numismatic Research Collection)
- ⬤ January 1, December 24-26
- ♨ ⓑ 📷 (In the research collection) 📷 (In the exhibits)

The obverse of a rare 1792 silver half disme.

Public Transportation

- 🚌 606 (NJ Transit)

Internet

- ✉ rbsc@princeton.edu
- 🌐 www.princeton.edu/~rbsc/department/numismatics/ (department main page)
- 🌐 www.princeton.edu/~rbsc/department/numismatics/exhibits.html (current exhibit)

A Confederate States of America $1,000-note from Montgomery, Alabama.

American Numismatic Society
New York, New York

Organized in 1858, the American Numismatic Society (ANS) is a museum and research institute devoted to the study of coins from all periods and cultures. Originally at 155th Street and Broadway, it has been at its current location in lower Manhattan since October 2008.

The numismatic collection, currently estimated at approximately 800,000 coins and related objects, is of international caliber, rivaled only by the largest European state collections. The ANS's numismatic cabinets are divided into the following departments:

- Greek: a major world collection of ancient Greek coinage, where the Hellenistic section is particularly notable (100,000 coins).
- Roman: includes all coins of Republican and Imperial Rome, the silver coins of the imperial provinces, and coins of Roman Alexandria. The single greatest strength are the aes grave and the early heavy copper coinage of Rome.
- Byzantine: comprises approximately 13,000 coins struck at Byzantium and at the regional mints from the reign of Anastasius I, 419-518 AD (13,000 coins).
- Islamic: comprises coins and other objects from North Africa, the Middle East, and as far as Afghanistan and Central Asia from the Islamic conquests of the 7th and 8th centuries to the present day (60,000 objects).
- East Asian: comprises coins and other objects produced in the area of modern China, Korea, Japan, and Vietnam. Also included are all coins struck in these regions from the beginning of coinage in the 7th century BC to the modern day. It also includes paper money (50,000 objects).
- South Asian: consisting of the coins and paper money of all periods from three principal regions: the Indian subcontinent, Southeast Asia, and ancient Central Asia (50,000 objects).
- Medieval: from Latin Europe from the fall of the Roman Empire down to the end of hammer-struck coinage during the 17th century (50,000 coins).
- United States: includes all coins issued in and for the British North American plantations until 1783 and for the United States thereafter, including Alaska and Hawaii.

Highlights include one of four known Confederate half dollars, an 1804 dollar, and a 1933 double eagle on loan (32,000 objects).

- Latin America: (20,000 coins).
- Modern: includes all coins minted by minting machinery - the screw press and the roller press — struck in Europe, Canada, Oceania and sub-Saharan Africa (100,000 coins).
- Medals and Decorations: contains more than 50,000 medals from around the world of all varieties, including commemorative medals, art medals and society medals. It also includes decorations issued in the United States.

The ANS maintains several exhibits which are changed periodically.

ANS Headquarters located at the corner of Canal and Varik Streets in lower Manhattan.

The Harry W. Bass Jr. Library is the ANS library, which houses one of the world's most comprehensive collections of numismatic literature, and presently numbers approximately 100,000 items. These include cataloged books, periodicals, manuscripts, photographs, pamphlets, auction catalogs, and microforms. Much of the library material is arranged on open stacks as non-circulating collections and all materials must be used within the ANS premises.

The Federal Reserve Bank of New York at 33 Liberty Street is a short distance away by subway, and a visit there is highly recommended. Advance registration, however, is required for tours.

The Harry W. Bass Jr. Library.

Visitor's Checklist
American Numismatic Society, 75 Varick Street, 11th floor, New York, NY 10013
- ❶ ⓒ (212) 571-4470
- ◯ Monday-Friday: 9:30 a.m.-4:30 p.m.; open on Columbus Day
- ● Saturday and Sunday; bank holidays, in addition to the days after Thanksgiving and Christmas
- ♿ ⧯ Visitors wishing to use the library should contact: library@numismatics.org

Public Transportation
Ⓜ 1/2/A/C/E (Canal Street)
🚍 M20 (Varick Street at Watts Street)

Internet
🌐 isaac@numismatics.org
🌐 numismatics.org

Federal Reserve Bank of New York

New York, New York

The Federal Reserve Bank of New York is by far the largest, most active, and most influential of the 12 regional Federal Reserve Banks. The New York Fed moved to its current location on Liberty Street in 1924 and is perhaps best known for its vault 80 feet underground and built on bedrock in order to hold the large amount of gold stored in its chambers.

The Gold Vault

For many, the New York Fed's gold vault is perhaps the highlight of the guided tour. This is currently assumed to be the world's largest gold repository, containing even more gold than is stored at Ft. Knox. Approximately 98 percent of the gold stored is owned by 36 foreign governments, and central banks, while the remainder is the property of the United States and the International Monetary Fund. The bullion is stored in 122 separate compartments in the main and auxiliary vaults. It is largely a relic of an era when the gold standard and gold exchange standard were used to establish the relative values of national currencies, and gold itself was used to meet international payments.

Liberty Street entrance of the Federal Reserve Bank of New York.

Foreign governments and official international organizations store their gold at the Federal Reserve Bank of New York because of their confidence in its safety, the convenient services the Bank offers, and its location in one of the world's leading financial capitals.

There are no doors into the gold vault. Entry is through a narrow 10-foot passageway cut in a delicately balanced, nine-foot-tall, 90-ton steel cylinder that revolves vertically in a

140-ton, steel-and-concrete frame. The vault is opened and closed by rotating the cylinder 90 degrees.

Tours

Visitors to the New York Fed have the option of taking either a self-guided or a guided tour. However, visitors taking the self-guided tour will not be able to see the gold vault. With either tour, visitors learn about the role of the New York Fed and the wider Federal Reserve System, as the nation's central bank, in setting monetary policy, promoting financial stability to support the flow of credit to families and businesses, and serving communities to advance broad-based economic growth in the region and nation. Also, visitors learn about the central banking functions of the Federal Reserve System through an interactive, multimedia exhibit that allows visitors to participate in a monetary policy simulation and to learn about the Fed's role in the economy.

Entrance to the New York Fed's gold vault, built on bedrock in order to hold the large amount of gold stored in its chambers.

Registration and Arrival

For either type tour, advance registration is required via the New York Fed's on-line form, which may be booked up to three months in advance. Available starting times currently are: 10 a.m., 11 a.m., 12 p.m., 1 p.m., 2 p.m. and 3 p.m. with guided tour lasting approximately 45 minutes. A government-issued photo ID is required and all visitors and bags will be screened. There are no storage lockers available and visitors should bring only essential items with them; no packages and large bags will be permitted inside.

Visitor's Checklist

The Federal Reserve Bank of New York, 33 Liberty Street, New York, NY 10045. Visitors are to enter at 44 Maiden Lane (one block north of Liberty Street).

- ❶ ℂ (212) 720-6130 or (646) 720-6130
- ○ Monday-Friday: 10 a.m.-5 p.m.
- ● Weekends; public holidays.
- ✋ ♿ ♿ (government-issued photo ID) 🚫 🚫

A view of one of gold vault's chambers with stacked 27-pound gold bricks.

Public Transportation

Ⓜ 2/3 (Wall Street); 4/5 (Fulton Street), J/Z (Broad Street, Fulton Street)

Internet

✉ general.info@ny.frb.org, frbnytours@ny.frb.org (tours); use the on-line registration form at: www.newyorkfed.org/aboutthefed/visiting.html

🌐 www.newyorkfed.org/aboutthefed/visiting.html#tabs-1

Federal Reserve Bank of Philadelphia
Money in Motion
Philadelphia, Pennsylvania

Money in Motion is a 3,500-square foot exhibit located inside the Federal Reserve Bank of Philadelphia, highlighting money, banking, and the Federal Reserve System. This interactive exhibit features 17 stations, which is updated with a new station each year—evolving just as the Federal Reserve's role evolves.

The 6th Street front entrance of the Federal Reserve Bank of Philadelphia.

Treasure Trove

Visitors will marvel at the "Treasure Trove," a collection of the earliest form of money starting with wampum shells to an array of unique and rarely seen currency issued after the Federal Reserve System was founded in 1913. There is a colorful collection of paper money from the original 13 colonies and the Continental Congress along with many coins that circulated in the 1700s. Money and tokens used during the Civil War are on display. Notable pieces include three 1934 gold certificates, an extremely rare $100,000 banknote, and a $20 Saint-Gaudens double eagle coin.

The newest security features on the United States currency are shown and visitors are allowed to test their skill at detecting counterfeits using an interactive element called "True or False."

Then, the "Eye on the Money" exhibit takes visitors inside the vault to show how the Federal Reserve manages $100 billion dollars of cash each year, distributing it to its customers, and processing transactions using highly sophisticated machines to see if it is fit, unfit, or counterfeit. The unfit currency is shredded for visitors to witness. A currency cart holding $1,350,000 in $5-bills is on display along with a 25-foot tower of shredded bills totaling $100 million.

Match Wits with Ben

One of the most popular elements is "Match Wits with Ben," a timed interactive game that pits visitors against Benjamin Franklin to test their knowledge of money, banking, and the Federal Reserve.

At another station, visitors may also try their hand at operating a bank that advances players from a trainee to investment manager—if they answer the questions correctly. Still another display lets visitors experience what's ahead in the payments system as they interact with a futuristic teller.

Federal Reserve Monetary Policy

For those who want to better understand the Federal Reserve's monetary policy's role in managing economic growth, inflation, and unemployment from the 1950s to the 1990s, the element "Monitoring Monetary Policy" explains it all.

"Match Wits with Ben" exhibit challenges visitors about their knowledge of money and central banking.

Visitors can relive each decade with videos describing the economic, social, and cultural environment that set the stage for how the economy fared during that time. For anyone interested in understanding more about inflation and why it's important, there's another exhibit station to explore.

Before leaving, visitors can learn about the Fed's vital role in maintaining the nation's financial stability in a short video depicting the Fed's role in the days following the terrorist attack on September 11, 2001.

For coin collectors, the "Change for America" display allows visitors to put a quarter in a machine and get the latest addition to the America the Beautiful Quarters series, which honors the national parks and monuments in the 50 states.

The United States Philadelphia Mint is one block away at 151 North Independence Mall East (5th and Arch Streets) and a visit there is highly recommended.

Visitor's Checklist
The Federal Reserve Bank of Philadelphia, 100 N. 6th Street, Philadelphia, PA 19106. Visitors use the 6th Street entrance for the "Money in Motion" exhibit.

ⓘ ⓒ (866) 574-3727 (toll-free)

○ Monday-Friday (January and February): 10 a.m.-2 p.m.; Monday-Friday (March-December): 9:30 a.m.-4:30 p.m.; also during June-August Saturday: 9 a.m.-3 p.m., Sunday: 11 a.m.-3 p.m.

● All federal and bank holidays.

✋ ⓖ ⚑ ◉ ⊘

⚑ (by appointment only) ⓒ (215) 574-6540 ○ Monday-Friday: 9 a.m.-4 p.m.; 4th floor

A 1934 series $10,000-gold certificate, the second highest denomination U.S. banknote, is one of the many banknotes on display.

Public Transportation
Ⓜ SEPTA Market-Frankford Line (8th and Market, 5th and Market); Broad Street Line (Chinatown)

🚌 46 (Arch and 6th Streets), 47/48 (Arch and 7th Streets), 47/47M/61 (8th and Race Streets)

Internet
🌐 www.philadelphiafed.org/education/money-in-motion

United States Philadelphia Mint
Philadelphia, Pennsylvania

Since 1969, the current location of the United States Philadelphia Mint is its fourth site since the original Mint's founding in 1792. The Mint's interactive, self-guided tour is divided into seven color-coded areas enabling visitors to better understand the process for the production of its proof, uncirculated and commemorative coins, Congressional gold medals, silver, gold, and platinum bullion coins.

At the start of the gallery, visitors are guided by special images and colors to help distinguish the seven different coin design and manufacturing areas.

Art

The United States Philadelphia Mint at the corner of 5th and Arch Streets.

Visitors see how the striking of a coin begins with artistry and design. Current law mandates that the following inscriptions appear on all circulating coins: "Liberty," "In God We Trust," "United States of America," and "E Pluribus Unum," as well as each coin's denomination and the year of issuance. Also, it takes an official act of Congress to create a coin.

Die Making

In the die shop, visitors see how thousands of working dies are created with painstaking precision in which to strike millions of coins. Making perfect dies is a complex process, but it's necessary as every coin must be perfect or they won't be accepted by vending machines.

Blanking

At 40 feet above the factory floor visitors now see how the Mint makes up to 60 million coins daily. Copper and nickel ribbons, which are about 13 inches wide and 1,500 feet long, are fed through a blanking press, like a giant cookie-cutter, punching out round, plain-surfaced disks called *blanks*. The leftover strip, called *webbing*, is chopped and recycled.

Annealing & Upsetting

The blanks are heated in an annealing furnace to soften the metal of the blank and are then poured through a huge washer and dryer. Finally, shiny blanks are rolled through an upsetting mill, which raises a smooth, hard edge around each blank. This rim helps with the striking process and also allows stacking of coins. After spinning out of the upsetting mill, the blank is called a *planche*.

Exhibit that demonstrates how coin blanks are created from huge rolls of metal strips.

Striking

Two dies—obverse and reverse, or heads and tails—are placed into the coining press. With one mighty strike, the designs from the steel dies are transferred to the planchet, creating a genuine coin.

Inspecting

After striking, visitors see press operators using magnifying glasses to spot check each batch of new coins to be sure that they meet the Mint's strict quality standards. If a flaw is spotted, all of the coins in the trap are scrapped and sent to a coin destruction machine called a *waffler*.

Bagging

After the coins have been inspected, they travel to the automated counting machines. All coins, except pennies, which are bagged and shipped by weight, are counted and poured into giant bulk bags. The filled bags are weighed, sealed shut, loaded onto pallets, and taken by forklift to the Mint's vaults. New coins are then shipped to Federal Reserve Banks.

Some of the many tour highlights are: the first coining press used to strike America's first coins in 1792, the key to the first Mint, the Mint deed signed by President Andrew Jackson, and Peter the Mint Eagle, a real bald eagle who made the First United States Mint his home.

The Federal Reserve Bank of Philadelphia Mint's "Money in Motion" exhibit is one block away at 100 N. 6th Street and a visit there is highly recommended.

One of several interactive exhibits that invite children to trace the route of coins in the monetary system as they "send" coins into circulation through financial institutions and businesses.

Visitor's Checklist

United States Philadelphia Mint, 151 North Independence Mall East, Philadelphia, PA 19106. It is located on 5th Street between Arch and Race Streets.

- ℹ ☏ (215) 408-0112
- ○ Monday-Friday: 9 a.m.-4:30 p.m.; weekend and holiday hours are offered during the summer.
- ♨ ⑤ ♿ (photo ID 18+) ⊗ ⛟

Public Transportation

Ⓜ SEPTA Market-Frankford Line (5th & Market Streets)

🚌 48 (Arch and 5th Streets), 57 (4th and Race Streets)

Internet

⊕ www.usmint.gov/mint_tours/?action=philadelphia

Additional Institutions, Northeast Region

The following institutions in the Northeast Region of the United States are known to have numismatic exhibitions of varying degrees that are open to the public. These are listed here, either because sufficient information could not (1) be obtained about the museum, (2) be verified from other sources, (3) the museum did not respond to repeated requests for information, (4) the exhibition is closed due to long-term renovation of the building or other reasons, (5) or I learned about this venue just before the manuscript was to go to the publisher and complete information could not be included.

Museum of Fine Arts, Boston, MA.

Bureau of Engraving and Printing, Department of the Treasury, Bureau of Engraving and Printing

14th and C Streets, SW, Washington, DC 20228

ⓘ Ⓒ (877) 874-4114 (General Inquiries, toll free), (866) 874-2330 (Public Tours, toll free); (202) 874-2330

✉ moneyfactory.info@bep.gov

🌐 www.moneyfactory.gov

Dumbarton Oaks Research Library and Collection, Coins & Seals Collection
1703 32nd Street, NW, Washington, DC 20007
ⓘ ⓒ (202) 339-6401
✉ museum@doaks.org
🌐 www.doaks.org/museum/collection/byzantine/coins_seals_collection.html

Museum of American Finance
48 Wall Street, New York, New York 10005
ⓘ ⓒ (212) 908 4110
🌐 www.moaf.org/exhibits/money_history/index

Museum of Fine Arts, Boston – Michael C. Ruettgers Gallery for Ancient Coins
Gallery 212C, 465 Huntington Avenue, Boston, MA 02115
ⓘ ⓒ (617) 267 9300
🌐 www.mfa.org/collections/featured-galleries/michael-c-ruettgers-gallery-ancient-coins

A photomontage of iconic scenes of Atlanta, located in the South region of the United States. From top to bottom, left to right: Atlanta skyline, the Fox Theatre, the Georgia State Capitol, Centennial Olympic Park, Millennium Gate, the Canopy Walk, the Georgia Aquarium, The Phoenix statue, and the Midtown skyline.

United States

South Region

The 12 states of the United States' South Region included in the section of this book depart from the Census Bureau's definition somewhat, essentially confining itself to the country's southeastern quarter.

Map highlighting the 12 states that comprise the Southeastern United States. The states with numismatic venues are shown in dark blue and their cities indicated by a white dot. A red dot represents cities with limited information.

The numismatic history of this region includes Spanish America where the silver Spanish dollar–pieces of eight–was the forerunner of the U.S. silver dollar and legal tender in the United States until the Coinage Act of 1857. The region also included two United States Mints specifically for the minting of gold coins–one at Charlotte, North Carolina and another at Dahlonega, Georgia. A third mint at New Orleans, Louisiana struck silver and gold coinage.

In this region, one finds the Federal Reserve Bank of Atlanta's Monetary Museum with its "Story of Money" exhibit where millions of dollars are counted, sorted, or shredded daily. The restored New Orleans Mint, the only mint to have produced both American and Confederate coinage, displays the Eureka Bar–the heaviest known gold bar from the days of the California Gold Rush in addition to coins that were struck at the mint.

Atlanta, GA • Federal Reserve Bank of Atlanta
Visitors Center & Monetary Museum
— The Story of Money

New Orleans, LA • New Orleans Mint Museum

Additional institutions with limited information:

Fredericksburg, VA • National Bank Museum

Federal Reserve Bank of Atlanta Monetary Museum

Atlanta, Georgia

The Federal Reserve Bank of Atlanta's Monetary Museum uses historical artifacts, rare coins, currency, videos, multimedia, and interactive exhibits to assist visitors learning about the Federal Reserve System and its role in the economy.

The Atlanta Fed is one of 12 regional Reserve Banks in the United States that, together with the Board of Governors in Washington, D.C., make up the Federal Reserve System—the nation's central bank. Since the Federal Reserve System was established by an act of Congress in 1913, its primary role has been to maintain a sound financial system and a healthy economy.

The Federal Reserve Bank of Atlanta on Peachtree Street.

The Story of Money

The Museum, whose theme is "The Story of Money," is contained entirely on the Bank's first floor. Coins and banknotes are interspersed with other items throughout the Museum.

Within the main Museum area, visitors can explore the story of money, from barter to modern times, as told through an exhibit of artifacts, coins, and currency notes in 16 display cases. With gold nuggets, wampum, and much more, visitors trace the evolution of money from barter to modern currency along with the story of banking and money in America right up to the founding of the Federal Reserve System in 1913.

Monetary Policy and Payment Services

The main area of the Museum also houses exhibits that explore two of the Fed's three main functions: monetary policy and payments services. Visitors learn how and why the Federal Reserve conducts monetary policy and how its actions affect their lives. They also learn about the many ways the Fed provides payments system services to help the nation's economy run smoothly and maintain the stability of the financial system through exhibits that explore the evolution of payment methods.

Ring cases: The story of money as a medium of exchange.

Walking down the corridor of the Museum, guests can learn about counterfeiting measures, view a gold bar, large denomination notes, and see rare gold coins, including a complete collection of the gold coins minted at the Dahlonega mint in northern Georgia.

Automated Vault

The Museum also gives visitors a opportunity to a look at the Bank's cash-processing operations where millions of dollars are counted, sorted, or shredded daily. They also get a glimpse into the Bank's automated vault and see the robotic transports that do the heavy lifting. Interactive wayside stations in the "cash overlook" area not only detail the Bank's cash operations, but also allow visitors to view the Bank's night-time check processing operations.

Within the Museum's pocket theater, visitors learn about the Fed's third main function: banking supervision and regulation. By playing the "Banker's Challenge" game, visitors have a chance to manage a bank's risk. The theater also offers two short movies about the Federal Reserve: *The Fed Today* and *Monetary Policy: Part Art, Part Science.*

Visitor's Checklist

Federal Reserve Bank of Atlanta, 1000 Peachtree Street, N.E., Atlanta, GA 30309

- ❶ ℂ (404)-498-8777
- ○ Monday-Friday: 9 a.m.-4 p.m.
- ● Saturday and Sunday; January 1, Martin Luther King Jr. Day*, Washington's Birthday*, Memorial Day*, July 4, Labor Day*, Columbus Day*, Veterans Day*, Thanksgiving Day*, December 25. When holidays fall on Saturday, the Museum will be open the preceding Friday. For holidays falling on Sunday, the Museum will be closed the following Monday. An asterisk (*) denotes a movable date.
- ✋ ♿ ♿ (photo ID/driver's license18+ for U.S. citizens; passports for international visitors) 📷 🚫 (must be locked in lockers provided)

Unbroken money trees were good luck, like those of 17th-century Japan. Bronze coins were cast in "trees" of different sizes.

Public Transportation

- Ⓜ Gold/Red (MARTA Midtown Station)
- 🚌 110 (Peachtree NE and 10th/11th); 27 (Peachtree NE and 11th); 36/99 (Juniper NE and 10th)

Internet

- ✉ Use the on-line contact form at: www.frbatlanta.org/fedfaq/search/contacts.cfm
- 🌐 www.frbatlanta.org/about/tours/virtual/money/

New Orleans Mint Museum
New Orleans, Louisiana

The United States Mint at New Orleans, built in 1835 on the site of Fort St. Charles, is currently the oldest surviving structure to have served as a U.S. Mint. It also holds the distinction of being the only mint to have produced both American and Confederate coinage. The first coins were minted, starting in 1838, and when Louisiana seceded from the Union in 1861, it then struck coins for the Confederacy and also housed Confederate troops. After the Civil War, the Mint resumed full operations by 1879 and was the only southern mint to reopen after the war. In 1909, minting ceased and the building was used for a number of official purposes until it was transferred to the state in 1966. In 1981, the Mint was opened to the public as a state museum site. Damaged by Hurricane Katrina in 2005 and after over two years of closure for repairs and renovation, the Museum reopened in October 2007.

The front façade of the Old New Orleans Mint.

Numismatic Heritage

As a branch mint of the United States Mint, the New Orleans Mint has an outstanding numismatic heritage with some designs having very short runs—as little as one or two years. Some of the more notable coins struck at the New Orleans Mint are:

- 1838-O Three-cent silver. This was the only year a silver three-cent coin was struck by a branch mint and was also the smallest denomination silver coin.

- 1838-O and 1839-O 50-cent silver capped bust and quarter eagle gold. These were the only two years the "O" mint mark appeared on the obverse—also the first time in American numismatic history that mintmarks appeared on the obverse. Starting with 1840, mintmarks generally were on the reverse, with the exception of the Lincoln cents beginning 1909 until 1968.
- 1854-O $3-gold. This is the only year the $3-gold piece was struck at the New Orleans Mint.

The Mint Museum has a number of interesting exhibits which include coins, machinery, documents, and relics relating to the daily operations of the coining department. A number of coins on display are on loan from the Federal Reserve Bank of Atlanta and a few local collectors.

The Eureka Bar

On display is the "Eureka Bar"—the heaviest known gold bar from the days of the California Gold Rush. It is made of 0.903 fine gold, weighing 933.94 ounces (about 80 lbs). The Eureka Bar, lost in the 1857 shipwreck of the S.S. Central America about 160 miles off the coast of Charleston, South Carolina, was discovered in 1987.

Counterfeits

There is a section devoted to counterfeit coins. The highlight is an 1857 counterfeiting device

An 1868 coin press manufactured by Morgan Orr & Co. of Philadelphia that was used at the Mint.

used to produce phony half dollars. A small coin press thought to have been sold by the Mint and later owned by the Mardi Gras doubloon maker Alvin Sharp, is on display.

In 1975, the New Orleans Mint was designated a National Historic Landmark by the National Park Service U.S. Department of the Interior. The plaque reads: *This site possesses national significance in commemorating the history of the United States of America.*

Visitor's Checklist

The Old Mint (New Orleans Mint), 400 Esplanade Avenue, New Orleans, LA 70116. Enter either on Esplanade Avenue or Barracks Street.

- **ⓘ** Ⓒ (504) 568-6968 or (800) 568-6968 (toll free)
- ◯ Tuesday-Sunday: 10 a.m.-4:30 p.m.
- ● Monday; January 1, Mardi Gras (Tuesday before Ash Wednesday)*, Good Friday*, July 4, Elections Day (1st Tuesday in November in even-numbered years)*, Thanksgiving*, and December 25. An asterisk (*) denotes a movable holiday date.

An 1839-O gold quarter eagle ($2½) showing the mint mark on the obverse – one of two years this occurred on U.S. coins.

Public Transportation

- 🚌 5/55 (Decatur & Barracks Sts.; N. Peters St. and Esplanade Ave.)
- 🚊 Riverfront (French Market Station)

Internet

- 🌐 www.crt.state.la.us/museum/properties/usmint/

Additional Institutions, South Region

The following institution in the South Region of the United States is known to have a numismatic exhibition of varying degree that is open to the public. This is listed here, either because sufficient information could not (1) be obtained about the museum, (2) be verified from other sources, (3) the museum did not respond to repeated requests for information, (4) the exhibition is closed due to long-term renovation of the building or other reasons, (5) or I learned about this venue just before the manuscript was to go to the publisher and complete information could not be included.

National Bank Museum
900 Princess Anne Street, Fredericksburg, VA 22401
ⓘ ℂ (540) 899-3243
✉ Fburg@Illuminet.Net
🌐 www.epodunk.com/cgi-bin/genInfo.php?locIndex=55074 (unofficial site)

A photomontage of iconic scenes of Chicago, located in the Midwest region of the United States. Clockwise from top: Downtown Chicago, the Chicago Theatre, the Chicago 'L,' the Navy Pier, Millennium Park, the Field Museum, and the Willis (formerly Sears) Tower.

United States

Midwest Region

The 14 states of the United States' Midwest Region represent the vertical center of the county–the nation's heartland which is nearly one-third of the country by area.

Map highlighting the 14 states that comprise the Midwestern United States. The states having numismatic venues are shown in dark blue and their cities indicated by a white dot. A red dot represents cities with limited information.

In this region, one finds the money museums of three Federal Reserve Banks: Chicago, Kansas City (Missouri), and Cleveland. Also in Chicago within the Balzekas Museum of Lithuanian Culture, there is an exhibition gallery of Lithuanian coins, banknotes, tokens, orders and decorations. Selected items of the collection of the well-known numismatic collector and writer Eric P. Newman are on display at the Newman Money Museum on the campus of Washington University in St. Louis. When visiting Texas, be sure to drop by the Treasury's Western Currency Facility of the Bureau of Engraving and Printing in Ft. Worth, one of two sites where the nation's currency is printed. For collectors of wooden nickels, stopping by the Wooden Nickel Historical Museum outside San Antonio might be a treat.

Chicago, IL • Balzekas Museum of Lithuanian Culture
• Federal Reserve Bank Chicago Money Museum

Kansas City, MO • Federal Reserve Bank of Kansas City, The Money Museum

St. Louis, MO • Newman Money Museum

Additional institutions with limited information:

Fort Worth, TX • Bureau of Engraving and Printing, Western Currency Facility Tour and Visitor Center

Cleveland, OH • Federal Reserve Bank of Cleveland Learning Center and Money Museum

San Antonio, TX • Wooden Nickel Historical Museum

Balzekas Museum of Lithuanian Culture
Chicago, Illinois

The Balzekas Museum of Lithuanian Culture is the creation of Stanley Balzekas, Jr. who founded the Museum in 1966 in a building next to his car dealership, and has been at its current location since 1986. Of the exhibits relating to Lithuanian coins and stamps, many were acquired from the collection of Dr. Alexander M. Rackus (1893-1965), a well-known local physician and historian.

The Balzekas Museum of Lithuanian Culture on S. Pulaski Avenue.

Coins

This covers Lithuania's history, first as part of Poland from as early as 1492 with the half-grašis of Grand Duke Aleksandras minted in Vilnius plus other specimens from the 16th century. Mint sets and commemorative coins from both pre- and post-Soviet independent Lithuania are included.

Paper Money

Exhibits relating to the history of Lithuanian paper money are shown. One is about the notgeld from the port city of Kaipeda, also known as Memel (Memelburg), which was part of Prussia from the 15th century until 1919. Specimens are shown of the first independent Lithuanian banknotes dated 1922 in both the temporary series printed in Berlin and the permanent series, although initially printed in Prague, but were later printed in England.

One of the Museum's display cases in the numismatic gallery.

During World War II when Germany invaded Lithuania, ration paper money, denominated in punkte, was used. Many Lithuanians were in displaced prison camps such as Augsburg and Scheinfeld after the war, which had their own coupons for purchasing goods at the camp canteen, some of which are on display.

Gaining independence in 1991 from the breakup of the Soviet bloc, Lithuania issued temporary "talonas" notes at par with the Russian ruble for the transition from the ruble to the litas monetary system. There are examples of 0.10-, 0.20-, 0.50-, and 1-talonas notes. Also on display are the first 1991 series of banknotes printed under the litas monetary system placed into circulation in 1993.

Lottery Tickets, Tokens, and Medals

There is a nice display of lottery tickets, starting with Lithuanian tickets from the early 1930s. During their wartime occupation of Lithuania, the Germans also issued lottery tickets, in Reichmarks with the 1944 date. Also shown are Soviet Union lottery tickets during the 1960s denominated in kopecks.

With churches as the cornerstone of the Lithuanian community, ethnic organizations such as the Society of St. Stephen or the Society of All Saints issued tokens, often 5¢, which were good for a purchase.

One display case is devoted to the medals of Petras Rimša (1881-1961), Lithuania's most outstanding medalist whose many designs reflect patriotic themes.

A 15th anniversary wooden nickel issued by the Museum in 1981.

Lithuanian Orders and Decorations

Examples of all three of Lithuania's orders and decorations are exhibited. The Order of the Cross of Vytis is the highest military decoration for valor. The Order of Vytautas the Great is given for outstanding civil or military merit but has not been restored in present-day Lithuania. The example of the 3rd Class Order on display was awarded to Dr. Rackus for his contribution to Lithuanian culture. The Order of Grand Duke Gediminas is awarded for outstanding civil merit. In recognition of his work on behalf of Chicago's Lithuanian community, Balzekas, the Museum's founder, was awarded the 3rd Class Order of Grand Duke Gediminas personally by the Lithuanian President Algirdas Brazauskas in 1996 and both the badge and neck ribbon are on display.

Victor David Brenner

One display is devoted to a Lithuanian who has had a lasting impact on United States numismatics—Victor David Brenner. Easily recognized by his initials V.D.B., Brenner, a Jewish immigrant, designed Lincoln's bust for the 1909 penny at the request of President Teddy Roosevelt, which has remained with us for more than 100 years.

Visitor's Checklist

Balzekas Museum of Lithuanian Culture, 6500 S. Pulaski Rd., Chicago IL 60629

  🛈 ℂ (773) 582-6500

  ◯ Daily: 10 a.m.-4 p.m.

  ● January 1, Easter*, December 25. An asterisk (*) denotes a movable date.

  ✸ ⓑ ⬥ (by appointment only) 📷 🛒

Public Transportation

  Ⓜ Orange (Pulaski)

  🚌 3A (Pulaski and 65th Street)

Internet

  ✉ info@balzekasmuseum.org

  🌐 www.balzekasmuseum.org

Money Museum of the Federal Reserve Bank of Chicago

Chicago, Illinois

Chicago is home to the head of the Federal Reserve Bank's Seventh District. Visiting the Money Museum can be done either with a guided tour or on your own. The guided tour lasts about 45 minutes, starts at 1 p.m. daily, and includes a short video in the theater about the Federal Reserve System.

The main entrance of the Chicago Federal Reserve Bank at 230 South LaSalle St. in the heart of Chicago's financial district.

Story of America's Money

The story of America's money with appropriate specimens starts with the "Colonial America" period from 1620 to 1789, when silver and gold were the money of choice, but they were also in short supply and bartering was a common practice.

The next period, "Experiments In Banking 1789-1860," was the period between the Revolutionary and Civil Wars when the government went through a trial and error period of developing its financial system. It twice tried unsuccessfully to establish a central bank. In its place, up to 10,000 private state-chartered banks filled the void.

"Financing a Civil War 1860-1865" is next when the banking legislation of the 1860s provided for the national banking system and a uniform currency. The National Banking Act of 1863 created a system of federally-chartered but privately-owned banks to issue a national currency primarily backed by government bonds.

On display is an 1861 $10-demand note, called a "greenback" because of the green color on the reverse, which began the tradition of printing money in green ink on a cotton-linen paper blend.

Following the Civil War, "An Era of Silver and Gold 1865-1900" was the period of tight money. The major issue was how much money should be created and how it should be backed. Some wanted gold as the best means to stabilize the economy; others wanted silver to be used to raise prices and wages.

A display explaining the creation of the Federal Reserve System in 1913 and its 12 districts.

Federal Reserve Notes

"A New Central Bank 1900-1918" is the era of the creation of the Federal Reserve System in 1913. A new currency appeared for the first time—the Federal Reserve Note (Series of 1914). Among those shown are the 1918 $5,000- and $10,000-Federal Reserve Notes.

The "Depression and War 1918-1945" period has the nation dropping the gold standard in 1933 and coming out of the depression. The Fed assumed the primary responsibility for influencing the supply of money in the economy

Other Notes on Display

One section of the Museum has a display titled, "Money in America," whereby a number of the more interesting examples of America's currency are showcased. Included are: an 1875 $2-National Banknote, aka the "Lazy Two"; an 1875 $10-U.S. note—aka the "Jackass note"; a 1901 $10-U.S. note—aka the "Bison note"; the back of an 1890 $1,000-U.S. Treasury note—aka the "Grand Watermelon"; and a 1905 $20-Gold Certificate—aka the "Technicolor" note.

Know Your Money: Find the Fake

The paper money contains various security features, to help prevent it from being copied: a large portrait, watermark, security thread, fine line printing patterns, microprinting, and color-shifting ink. However, that still hasn't stopped those from trying to counterfeit the nation's currency.

One million dollars is nestled underneath a clear dome consisting of straps of $20 bills.

There are specimens of $5-, $10-, $20-, $50-, and $100-notes where the face side of each is shown and you have try to decide if that note is genuine or counterfeit.

One Million Dollar Displays

There are three $1-million displays. One is a $1-million cube made up of $1-bills that weighs over 2,000 pounds. Another display has a suitcase filled with 10,000 $100-bills. With a 10-second time delay after pushing a button, visitors can have their picture taken as a free souvenir standing next to the suitcase with the $1 million!

Visitor's Checklist

Money Museum of the Federal Reserve Bank of Chicago, 230 South LaSalle Street, Chicago, IL 60604 (corner of South LaSalle St. and W. Jackson Blvd.)

- ❶ ⓒ (312) 322-2400
- ○ Monday-Friday 8:30 a.m.-5 p.m.; 1 pm for tours
- ● Saturday and Sunday; all bank holidays.
- ✋ ⑤ ⌕ (photo ID 18+) 📷

Public Transportation

Ⓜ Brown/Purple/Orange/Pink lines (Quincy/Wells); Blue lines (Jackson)

🚍 11 (Wells and Jackson); 134/135/136/156 (LaSalle and Quincy)

Internet

✉ tours.chi@chi.frb.org (pre-registration for tours)

🌐 www.chicagofed.org/webpages/education/money_museum/index.cfm

Federal Reserve Bank of Kansas City
The Money Museum
Kansas City, Missouri

The Money Museum at the Federal Reserve Bank of Kansas City is a unique experience offering a free, up-close look at the nation's financial system in action. At the Money Museum, visitors can learn more about the Federal Reserve System through interactive exhibits that explore banking, how people pay for things and how monetary policy decisions impact their family's bottom line.

The Truman Coin Collection

The Truman Coin Collection contains more than 450 coins on loan from the Truman Presidential Library and Museum. The collection consists of examples of coins produced by the U.S. Mint during every presidential administration.

The Truman Coin Collection also includes a double eagle ($20) coin minted during President Teddy Roosevelt's administration. Roosevelt had commissioned Augustus Saint-Gaudens to redesign the 1907 double eagle, but when Saint-Gaudens' health deteriorated, his then-assistant, Henry Hering, completed the project.

Kansas City Federal Reserve Bank building as seen from the Liberty Memorial Mall.

The collection is located along with other historical exhibits in the front lobby of the Federal Reserve Bank of Kansas City.

In addition to the Truman Coin Collection, the Money Museum contains numerous other currency specimens, tracing the nation's history from the Free Banking Era to the Civil War to the founding of the Federal Reserve.

Lifting a Gold Bar

Think you can lift nearly 27 pounds? One of the Museum's highlights is that visitors will have a chance to find out, trying their hand at lifting a solid gold bar. On display a unique gold bar weighing 389.27 troy ounces (27.4 lbs, or 12.1 kg) that was cast at the San Francisco Mint in 1959. At $1,590 an ounce on May 9, 2012, the bar was worth almost $619,000 and is one of many that once filled the vault at the Federal Reserve Bank of Kansas City. Although the bar's weight remains constant, its value fluctuates daily according to the market price of gold. A screen near the bar calculates its value based on the changing market price of gold.

Truman Coin Collection exhibit.

Designing Your Own Money

Ever wondered how a cowboy would look on a $10-bill? How about a $10,000-bill with the motto "The buck stops here?" The Money Museum will provide the supplies and visitors supply the ideas. The look of the currency in your wallet has been changing over the last several years. Now visitors can give the nation's currency their own redesign with an exhibit designed specifically for the Money Museum.

Other Interactive Exhibits

The Money Museum includes several exhibits explaining the role of the Federal Reserve, some of which are interactive. Visitors can peek inside the Kansas City Fed's vault and cash processing area, which handles millions of dollars a day, and see what $40-million in cash really looks like. Step into the shoes of a bank examiner and try to spot a counterfeit bill. Other exhibits explain banking, the economy and how the Fed works.

A special Legacy Exhibit traces the history of the Federal Reserve System and the Kansas City Fed from its beginnings to today. A number of artifacts, including a rare Thompson machine gun once used by Bank guards, are available for viewing.

Interactive exhibit: "Can You Detect a Counterfeit?"

Visitor's Checklist

Federal Reserve Bank of Kansas City, 1 Memorial Drive, Kansas City, MO 64108. Enter the Bank's entrance on Memorial Drive.

- ❶ ℂ (816) 881-2683 or (800) 333-1010, ext. 2683 (toll free)
- ○ Monday-Friday: 8:30 a.m.-4:30 p.m.; 1-hour tours at 9:30 a.m. and 1:30 p.m. (requires 15-day advanced registration)
- ● Saturday and Sunday; bank holidays
- ♨ ⑤ 🖼 (photo ID/driver's license18+ U.S. citizens; passports for international visitors) 📷
- 📷 (bank vault, security officers) 🛒

Public Transportation
- 🚌 57 (Grand Blvd. and Main St.)

Internet
- ✉ KCtours@kc.frb.org
- 🌐 kansascityfed.org/moneymuseum/includes/index.cfm
- 🌐 https://kansascityfed.org/moneymuseum/includes/tourReg.cfm (tour registration form)

Newman Money Museum
St. Louis, Missouri

The Newman Money Museum houses exhibits from the collection of the local well-known collector and prolific numismatic author, Eric P. Newman. Opened in 2006, it is located on the campus of Washington University in the lower level of the Mildred Lane Kemper Art Museum.

Benjamin Franklin

Visitors are first met by a seated mannequin of Benjamin Franklin, whose animated face starts talking when activated via a motion detector. Wearing his trademarked bifocals—one of his notable inventions—Franklin's voice greets visitors to the Museum and introduces them to several related displays behind him on the wall.

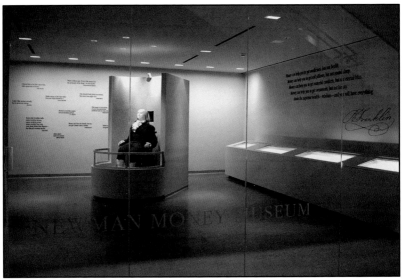

Entrance to the Newman Money Museum showcases a mannequin of Benjamin Franklin.

One display is devoted to Franklin's portrait on banknotes and coins including the Franklin half dollar (1948-1963), a 1914 $100-Federal Reserve Note, a Series 1878 $50-Legal Tender Note, a $2-obsolete note from the Franklin Bank of New York, and a

$10-obsolete note from the Franklin Bank of Boston. Others show his influence on the design of Colonial coin and paper money, like the 1787 Fugio cent he designed with its "Mind Your Business" motto.

Topical exhibits cover varied subjects—all supplemented with specimens from Newman's own collection. At one time Newman briefly owned all five 1913 Liberty head nickels.

One exhibit shows more than a dozen money changers and money counters manufactured from different parts of the world while another shows many antique balance scales and weights used for weighing small quantities of silver and gold, while answering the question: "Is it worth its weight?"

Show Me the Money

Creating an exhibit about the "Show Me" state, Newman honors his Missouri roots, having been born and raised in St. Louis. Nearby are various types of numismatic errors that can occur with coins and notes, in addition to counterfeits and counterfeit detectors, play money, the art of paper money is displayed by a fractional currency shield. Another case shows African Americans on money and women on money under the title, "Not Just a Pretty Face."

A clever use of multiple $1-bills folded to create a shirt to illustrate the theme, "Don't Lose Your Shirt to Inflation."

Inflation

Always a popular theme, numerous large-denomination banknotes that countries printed in response to the declining worth of their currency are displayed. As a warning, "Don't Lose Your Shirt to Inflation," a novel item on display is made of several $1-bills folded to create a shirt, with collar, sleeves, and red buttons added.

Phony as a $3-Bill

The display with its large number "3" explains the three-dollar bill was legitimate and circulated widely, with 25 examples, many of which were issued by private and Confederate banks. Although no legal $3-bill was ever issued by the U.S. Treasury, there are several $3-gold coins shown that were minted from 1854 to 1889.

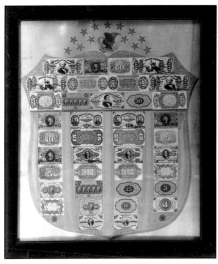

A fractional currency shield, containing 41 notes as an example of how the art of paper money requires a complex set of skills. To quote Andy Warhol (albeit out of context): "Making money is art."

Native Americans

The American Indian is often displayed on America's money. Examples shown are the Indian Head cent, Buffalo nickel, $2½, $5, and $10 Indian Head gold pieces. The $5 1899 "Running Antelope" silver certificate showing the vignette of Ta-to-ka-in-yan-ka, Chief of the Oncpapa Band of Sioux Indians is also included.

The "End of the Money Trail" is a fitting, concluding exhibit, showing what happens to money when it is worn out. It can become recycled paper for envelopes, note pads, and the creation of novelties like souvenir bags, pens, and paperweights filled with shredded money.

Visitor's Checklist

Newman Money Museum, Mildred Lane Kemper Art Museum at the Sam Fox Arts Center (lower level), Washington University, 1 Brookings Drive, St. Louis, MO 63130

- ❶ ⓒ (314) 935-9595
- ◯ Monday, Wednesday, Thursday, Saturday, and Sunday: 11 a.m.-6 p.m.; Friday: 11 a.m.-8 p.m.
- ● Tuesday
- ≋ (available by reservation only to accredited researchers)
- ✋ ⓖ 📷 (Money Museum only)

Public Transportation

- Ⓜ Skinker Metrolink Station
- 🚌 1-Gold (Skinker and Brookings)

Internet

- 🌐 www.newmanmoneymuseum.org

Additional Insititutions, Midwest Region

The following institutions in the Midwest Region of the United States are known to have numismatic exhibitions of varying degrees that are open to the public. These are listed here, either because sufficient information could not (1) be obtained about the museum, (2) be verified from other sources, (3) the museum did not respond to repeated requests for information, (4) the exhibition is closed due to long-term renovation of the building or other reasons, (5) or I learned about this venue just before the manuscript was to go to the publisher and complete information could not be included.

One of two sculptures by Henry Hering flanking the west entrance of the Federal Reserve Bank of Cleveland.

Bureau of Engraving and Printing, Department of the Treasury, Western Currency Facility Tour and Visitor Center

9000 Blue Mound Road, Fort Worth, Texas 76131

ⓘ ⓒ (817) 231-4000 or (866) 865-1194 (toll free)

✉ moneyfactory.info@bep.gov

🌐 www.moneyfactory.gov/tours/fortworthtxtours.html

Federal Reserve Bank of Cleveland Learning Center and Money Museum

1455 East Sixth Street, Cleveland, Ohio 44114

ⓘ ⓒ (216) 579-2000

✉ learningcenter@clev.frb.org

🌐 www.clevelandfed.org/for_the_public/tours/learning_center/

Wooden Nickel Historical Museum

345 Austin Road, San Antonio, Texas 78209

ⓘ ⓒ (210) 829-1291

✉ Use the on-line contact form at: www.wooden-nickel.net/contact/

🌐 www.wooden-nickel.net

United States

West Region

The 11 states of the West Region of the United States represent the western third of the county. With much of the region originally inhabited by various American Indian tribes, barter and wampum were the primary forms of payment.

Map highlighting the 11 states that comprise the Western United States. The states having numismatic venues are shown in dark blue and their cities indicated by a white dot.

In those states originally part of Mexico, Spanish coins were legal tender. When gold was discovered in California, creating the California Gold Rush of 1849, gold dust and nuggets soon became the accepted currency. Eventually private firms minted their own coins and tokens, many of which were in fractional amounts.

A photomontage of iconic scenes of Los Angeles, located in the West region of the United States. From top to bottom, left to right: Los Angeles skyline and San Gabriel Mountains, Venice Beach lifeguard tower, Griffith observatory, and Hollywood sign.

In this region, one finds the well-known Edward C. Rochette Museum of the American Numismatic Association on the campus of Colorado College in Colorado Springs. Home to America's largest numismatic group, this Museum hosts three major exhibition galleries. Traveling north to Denver on I-25, visitors will enjoy the Money

Museum at the Denver Branch of the Federal Reserve Bank of Kansas City and can watch coins being made at the United States Denver Mint. If contemplating a visit to California, the Federal Reserve Bank of San Francisco has exhibits at two locations. One is at its main San Francisco bank location; the other is at its Los Angeles branch where it hosts the "Fed Gallery: Your Central Bank in Focus" exhibit.

Colorado Springs, CO	• American Numismatic Association Edward C. Rochette Museum
Denver, CO	• Federal Reserve Bank of Kansas City, Denver Branch: The Money Museum
Los Angeles, CA	• Federal Reserve Bank of San Francisco, Los Angeles Branch – Fed Gallery: Your Central Bank in Focus
San Francisco, CA	• Federal Reserve Bank of San Francisco

American Numismatic Association
Edward C. Rochette Money Museum
Colorado Springs, Colorado

The American Numismatic Association Edward C. Rochette Money Museum, named in honor of former Executive Director and ANA Past President, Edward C. Rochette, is America's largest numismatic museum. Located on the campus of Colorado College, the Museum includes exhibits in three main galleries where visitors can find spectacular rarities and learn about the history of America and the world as seen through money. Through the discovery of money, numismatics brings culture to life. The Museum explores art, history, science and much more to promote the diverse nature of money and related items.

The ANA Money Museum building on the campus of Colorado College.

The Museum's collection consists of about 275,000 objects encompassing the history of money before coins were invented in the Lydian Empire to modern day issues—including paper money, coins, tokens, and medals from throughout the world. Several separate exhibit areas feature both permanent and rotating exhibits.

The Harry W. Bass Jr. Collection

This is a spectacular, comprehensive collection of American gold coins, experimental pattern coins, and paper money. Although Bass died in 1998, much of his impressive collection lives on. The core collection of over 500 coins, now on long-term loan to the ANA, features several extraordinary rarities, including a 1907 ultra-high-relief Saint Gaudens double eagle, and an 1804 (plain-4) Eagle. An 1870-S $3-gold piece is from a set of $3-gold coins containing not only a coin from every year and mint, but one from each year produced in astonishing gem proof condition.

The multimedia Bass Gallery housing the Harry W. Bass Collection.

History of Money

In the Maynard Sundman-Littleton Gallery, the History of Money exhibit contains an overview of money in all its forms—from beads and cowrie shells to ancient coins and polymer notes. On display is the oldest surviving example of paper money—a Chinese one-kuan note from the 14th century, as well as ultra-high denomination notes from Germany's hyperinflation era. Segments of the exhibit are changed out periodically to highlight the celebration of historically important events. The exhibit also features a working "mini-mint," which allows Museum staff to demonstrate how coinage was made on a screw press used to mint coins from the 1500s to the early 1800s.

Rare and Valuable Money

Many numismatic rarities are on display. Among these are: an 1804 dollar (15 known), a 1792 half disme, two of five known 1913 Liberty Head nickels, error notes and "No Motto" dollars, along with the first steam press from the Philadelphia Mint which dates from 1836.

The Whitman Publishing Gallery on the Museum's lower level features new exhibits every year, illuminating aspects of numismatics and collecting which is designed to appeal to both collectors and the general public.

Periodic Exhibits

In addition to its comprehensive permanent exhibits, the Museum periodically presents exhibits that capture world events that have numismatic tie-ins. Past themes include: A House Divided: Money of the Civil War; Colonial Money; Money of the Mexican Revolution; World War II; Money of the Ancient World; and Money of the World.

The Museum location is also the home of the Dwight N. Manley Numismatic Library, the world's largest numismatic lending library with 100,000 books, catalogs, and slide shows. Visitors can research their collections or read about money from any era or country.

The 1804-Idler/Bebee dollar, dubbed the "King of U.S. Coins."

Visitor's Checklist

American Numismatic Association Money Museum, 818 North Cascade Avenue, Colorado Springs, CO 80903 (on the campus of Colorado College)

- ❶ ℭ (719) 482-9834
- ○ Tuesday-Saturday: 10:30 a.m.-5 p.m.
- ● Sunday and Monday; January 1, Thanksgiving*, the Friday following Thanksgiving*, December 25. An asterisk (*) denotes a movable date.

✋ 🍴 ⑤ ⊗ 📷 🎧 🛒

Public Transportation

🚌 9 (N. Cascade Ave. and W. Cache La Poudre St.)

Internet

✉ museum@money.org

🌐 www.money.org/explore/money-museum

Federal Reserve Bank of Kansas City, Denver Branch

The Money Museum

Denver, Colorado

The Money Museum at the Federal Reserve Bank of Kansas City's Denver Branch, located in heart of downtown Denver on the 16th Street Mall, is a unique experience offering a free, up-close look of the nation's financial system in action. At the Money Museum, visitors can learn more about the Federal Reserve System as the nation's central bank through interactive exhibits that explore banking, how people pay for things, and how monetary policy decisions impact their family's bottom line.

The Denver Branch of the Federal Reserve Bank of Kansas City as seen from the corner of the 16th Street Mall and Curtis Street.

U.S Currency on Display

Visitors can travel back in time by viewing United States currency all the way back to 1775. This includes examples of different types of banknotes, such as state, demand, and National Currency. There is even a $100,000-bill, the highest denomination ever authorized by the Federal Reserve Bank, but one that is not allowed for public circulation.

The Role of the Federal Reserve System

Visitors can see the Federal Reserve Bank in action through interactive exhibits and videos that explain more about the nation's central bank, what it does to promote a healthy economy, and how it impacts citizens' daily lives. You can take a close-up peek at what $30,000,000 looks like, and see what happens to unfit currency after it is shredded.

Design Your Own Money

Although the look of the nation's currency has been changing over the last several years, visitors can give the nation's currency his or her personal own redesign by combining symbols and elements with an exhibit designed specifically for the Money Museum.

Interactive Exhibits

Several interactive exhibits are available. One allows visitors to test their skill at determining a real $20-bill from a counterfeit. Another shows a short film "The Fed and You," excerpted from the documentary, "10-J: The History of the Federal Reserve Bank of Kansas City."

Before leaving, visitors can grab a free bag of shredded money—though some assembly is required!

A view of part of the Money Museum Gallery.

Visitor's Checklist

Federal Reserve Bank of Kansas City, Denver Branch, 1020 16th Street, Denver, CO 80202. The main entrance is located on Curtis Street between 15th and 16th Streets.

ⓒ (303) 572-2429 or (800) 333-1020

○ Monday-Friday: 8:30 a.m.-4:30 p.m.; 1-hour tours at 9:30 a.m. and 1:30 p.m. (requires 15-day advanced registration).

● Saturday and Sunday; bank holidays.

✋ ⑥ ♿ (photo ID 18+; passports for international visitors)

📷 ☻ (bank vault, security officers) 🛒

Public Transportation
🚌 16th St Mall Shuttle (free); 15/15L (15th & Curtis)

Tram RTD light rail lines: D-Green F-Red H-Blue (16th & Stout Station)

Internet
✉ denvertours@kc.frb.org

🌐 kansascityfed.org/moneymuseum/denver.includes/index.cfm

🌐 kansascityfed.org/moneymuseum/denver/includes/tourReg.cfm (tour registration form)

A tour of U.S. currency dating back to 1775.

United States Denver Mint
Denver, Colorado

The United States Denver Mint was originally an assay office which the federal government decided to convert into a mint in 1904. After renovations and expansion, the Mint began operations on February 1, 1906, minting gold and silver coins. Production-coining of pennies began in 1911; nickels were produced beginning in 1912. Today, the facility still operates, producing coins for general circulation in addition to mint sets and commemorative coins with the capacity to produce more than 40 million coins per day. On February 1, 1972, the Mint was added to the National Register of Historic Places.

View of the United States Denver Mint along West Colfax Avenue.

The Historic Mint Building

The tours/exhibit area includes a walk through the historic Mint building which was constructed between 1898 and 1904 and housed the Denver Mint in its early days. Although it appears from the street to be two stories high, it actually has five floors, built in a Gothic Renaissance architecture modeled after the rusticated stone walls of the Riccardi Palace in Florence, Italy.

Tour Gallery

The Denver Mint tour gallery is on the mezzanine level, and includes glass walls where visitors can look down to see the activities on the production floor. The exhibit/ tour area is composed of five distinct sections with each area having exhibits highlighting the Mint's history. Among the displays are fifteen glass cases of an exhibit called, "Money, Trade, and Treasures," that portrays the curios and imaginative ways in which people respond to the economic life of their particular time in history.

A large balance beam scale.

The exhibit features coins, tools, ornaments, as well as precious gems and metals, all served as mediums of exchange going back to the barter system. Other displays include: an exhibit of foreign coins, large balance beam scales, and other machines used in the production of coins in the Denver Mint. The highlight of the exhibits is a display of three gold bars, with each bar weighing 400 troy ounces.

Visitor's Checklist

United States Denver Mint, 310 West Colfax Avenue, Denver, CO 80204. Tour Entrance is located on Cherokee Street between West Colfax & West 14th Avenues.

    ❶ ℂ (303) 405-4761 (recorded information); (303) 405-4759 (tour reservations for large organized groups)

○ Monday-Thursday: 8 a.m.-about 5 p.m.; tours start on the hour (8, 9, 10 and 11 a.m.; 1, 2, 3 and 4 p.m.) and advance registration is required at: www.usmint.gov/mint_tours/?action=Reservation

● Saturday and Sunday; all federal holidays.

The highlight of the exhibits is a display of three gold bars, each weighing 400 troy ounces.

Public Transportation

BUS RTD 16/16L (W. Colfax Ave. and Elati St., or W. Colfax Ave. and Bannock St.); 9/52 (Cherokee St. and W. 14th Ave.)

Internet

⊕ www.usmint.gov/mint_tours/?action=StartReservation (note the permitted and prohibited items, and security requirements)

The reverse of a 2001 American Buffalo Commemorative silver dollar showing the Denver (D) mint mark.

Federal Reserve Bank of San Francisco, Los Angeles Branch
Fed Gallery: Your Central Bank in Focus
Los Angeles, California

The lobby exhibition of the Los Angeles Branch of the Federal Reserve Bank of San Francisco, "Fed Gallery: Your Central Bank in Focus," opened November 2004. It uses interactive technology and vivid graphics highlighting the Federal Reserve's role in the American economy. Various displays focus on cash and check operations, bank supervision, and monetary policy.

The original Federal Reserve building, built in 1929 and located around the corner at 409 W. Olympic Blvd., is listed on the National Register of Historic Places.

The newer Los Angeles Branch building of the Federal Reserve Bank of San Francisco on S. Grand Avenue.

Currency Collection

Before entering the gallery, visitors can stop by to see some of the rare and valuable United States currency on display. Among the different type notes on display are the 1899 $5-note featuring Sioux Chief Running Antelope and the $500-, $1,000-, $5,000-, and $10,000-bills, which were discontinued printing in 1946 but are still legal tender.

Life of a Banknote

Visitors learn fun and fascinating facts about their money such as: did you know a $1-bill lasts an average of 22 months before it is taken out of circulation? Compare that to a $100-bill which lasts nine years. Worn notes are shredded at the Los Angeles Branch— about $45-million per day— and replaced with currency fit for circulation.

View of the currency collection display.

Every day billions of dollars in cash, checks, and wire transfers pass through the Federal Reserve. When visitors touch a glass-screen virtual waterfall, scrolling numbers open to reveal various facts about the payments system. For example, every month 47 million Americans receive social security deposits or checks through the Fed. Visitors will see the second largest cash vault in the U.S., and learn more about the Fed's role in distributing coins.

Dollar Detectives

Can you spot a fake? At the Los Angeles Branch, specially trained employees inspect banknotes to find potential fakes and take them out of circulation. Visitors can test their dollar savvy at this exhibit of their ability to identify security features on U.S. currency.

When customers walk into their bank, they need to know that their money is safe. Exhibits in this area focus about how the banks and the supervision and regulation duties of the Federal Reserve, help visitors (1) to understand the market forces that regulate banks and (2) how the Fed examines capital, asset quality, management, earnings, liquidity, and sensitivity to ensure that banks manage their risk. Visitors can test their skills as bank examiners using a pachinko-style game to determine the relative risk or safety and soundness of banks.

Monetary Policy

How does the Federal Reserve influence the nation's financial system to promote a healthy economy? Setting monetary policy is one of the Fed's most important and visible roles because its decisions affect the nation's economy. Touch screen computer games feature an interactive Fed Chairman game wherein visitors set the target federal funds rate and watch their decisions play out on the economy. In an adjacent room, a floor-mounted 10-foot screen plays a short video on the Federal Reserve.

Visitor's Checklist

Federal Reserve Bank of San Francisco, Los Angeles Branch, 950 S. Grand Avenue, Los Angeles, CA 90015

- 🛈 📞 (213) 683-2900 or (213) 683-2353
- ◯ Group tours are by appointment only, Monday-Thursday: 10:00 a.m., or 1:00 p.m.
- ⬤ All national holidays.
- ♿ 🅑 🚹 (photo ID/driver's license 18+ U.S. citizens; passports for international visitors) 📷 🚫

  Note: All electronics, cell phones, cameras, recording equipment, handbags, briefcases, all note-taking equipment, and other items deemed inappropriate by the security department will be placed in a secure locker during the tour.

The Fed Gallery lobby.

Public Transportation

Ⓜ Red/Purple (7th Street Metro Center Station)

🚌 10/14/37/28/70/71/76/78/79/96/378 (S. Grand Ave. and W. Olympic Blvd.); 28 (W. Olympic Blvd. and S. Hope St.)

Internet

✉ Use the online contact form for tours at: www.frbsf.org/federalreserve/visit/toursla/tour51a.cfm

🌐 www.frbsf.org/federalreserve/visit/toursla/toursla.html

Federal Reserve Bank of San Francisco
San Francisco, California

The Fed Center exhibition of the Federal Reserve Bank of San Francisco is conducted only by group tour made only by appointment. As the main branch of the Federal Reserve System's 12th District, the "Fed Center: Exploring our Nation's Central Bank," is a permanent installation designed to teach the public about the functions of the U.S. central bank through a series of guided hands-on and visually engaging experiences.

View of the Federal Reserve Bank of San Francisco building as seen from the corner of Spear and Market Streets.

Currency Theatre and Museum

Visitors enter here for an introductory presentation, and to view the most extensive public collection of rare and valuable antique currency in the United States. This collection includes engraved notes by Benjamin Franklin and Paul Revere, along with the celebrated "Grand Watermelon Note" of 1890, prized by collectors and is valued more than two million dollars in the collectors' market today.

Federal Reserve notes are the sole currency issued in the United States today. All U.S. currency issued since the first paper money was issued by the U.S. government in 1861 (except Military Payment Certificates) remains fully redeemable at face value. Federal Reserve notes were originally issued in denominations ranging from $5 to $10,000, although the primary purpose of the $500-, $1,000-, $5,000-, and

The American Currency Exhibit's Showcase of Banknotes.

$10,000-notes was to facilitate bank transfer payments. The largest bank transfer note printed is the $100,000-note, which features a portrait of President Woodrow Wilson, who signed the Federal Reserve Act in 1913. This note was never circulated among the general public and is on view.

The Central Bank

Here visitors learn how the Fed controls the supply of banks' reserves to affect the supply of money and credit in the economy as well as short-term interest rates. Visitors view an animated video about reserve supplies and check out smaller, more personal reserves. More than 200 antique and contemporary piggy banks from across the United States are displayed.

The Payments System

At the glass-screen virtual waterfall, visitors see an approximation of the high-speed transactions that keep the economy moving. When visitors touch the glass, the waterfall of scrolling numbers opens to reveal various facts about the payments system. Also, visitors learn about the creation and lifecycle of currency, test their skills at counterfeit detection, and follow the path of a check as it passes from the checkbook to the recipient of funds.

The U.S. Economy

How does the Federal Reserve influence the nation's financial system to promote a healthy economy? Setting monetary policy is one of the Fed's most important and visible roles because its decisions have the potential to affect the nation's economy. The goals of monetary policy are twofold: maximum sustainable employment and price stability. Visitors can affect the movement of the giant economy sphere to learn how the subtle influences of the Federal Reserve ensure that the economy runs smoothly. Nearby interactive computer games let visitors play the role of the FOMC Chairman by using interest rates to affect inflation.

A 1934 $100,000-gold certificate, or Bank Transfer Note – America's largest denomination banknote. Notes of this denomination only circulate within the Federal Reserve Bank system and are not legal to own.

Visitor's Checklist

Federal Reserve Bank of San Francisco, 101 Market Street, San Francisco, CA 94105

- ❶ ☎ (800) 227-4133 or (415) 974-2000
- ◯ Group tours are by appointment only, Monday-Thursday: 9:30 a.m. or 1:30 p.m.
- ● Friday; all national holidays.
- ✋ ♿ 🛗 (photo ID/driver's license 18+ U.S. citizens; passports for international visitors) 📷 🚫

   Note: All electronics, cell phones, cameras, recording equipment, handbags, briefcases, all note-taking equipment, and other items deemed inappropriate by the security department will be placed in a secure locker during the tour.

Public Transportation

- Ⓜ Embarcadero BART/MUNI Station
- 🚌 14/14L/14X/30X/41/80X/82X (Market and Main Streets); 2/6/9/9L/21/31 (Spear and Market Streets)
- 🚋 F/J/KT/L/M/N/S (Market and Main Streets-light rail); California (cable car)

Internet

- ✉ Use the on-line contact form for tours at: www.frbsf.org/tools/allmail. cfm?mail=625
- 🌐 www.frbsf.org/currency/index.html

North America

Canada

Canada's numismatic history somewhat parallels that of the United States. The early colonization by England and France brought their coins along with the traditional barter with the indigenous Indian tribes. Coins from other European nations and even the United States were accepted for goods purchased.

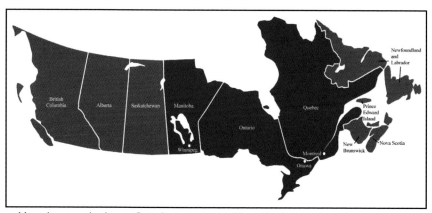

Map showing the lower Canadian provinces. Those having numismatic venues are shown in dark blue and their cities indicated by a white dot.

Starting with the Bank of Montreal in 1817 which issued its own banknotes, many other chartered banks in time followed in the upper and lower provinces. Eventually most of the chartered banks were consolidated by one or two major banks. In1934, The Bank of

Canada Act of 1934 no longer allowed the remaining chartered banks to issue their own banknotes—the privilege now rested with the new central bank.

A view of the Notre-Dame Basilica from the Place d'Armes in Montreal.

Although not as plentiful as its neighbor to the south, Canada nonetheless has several excellent numismatic venues. The nation's oldest bank, the Bank of Montreal, has a museum in its Montreal main branch, while the central bank, the Bank of Canada, has an excellent exhibition in its Currency Museum in the capital city of Ottawa. Also in Ottawa is one branch of the Royal Canadian Mint which in addition to minting the country's regular circulating coinage, also manufactures precious and base metal coins for collectors; bullion coins of gold, silver, palladium, and platinum; medals, medallions, and tokens. The other branch of the Royal Canadian Mint in Winnipeg, Manitoba produces the entire supply of circulation coins for over 75 countries.

Montreal, Quebec	• Bank of Montreal Museum
Ottawa, Ontario	• Currency Museum of the Bank of Canada
	• Royal Canadian Mint
Winnipeg, Manitoba	• Royal Canadian Mint

Bank of Montreal Museum
Musée de la Banque de Montréal
Montreal, Quebec

The Bank of Montreal's present Main Branch building with its dome was constructed in 1847 and remodeled in 1905. The Museum is located in the hallway between the Main Branch and its Head Office building, built in 1960 on the site of the original Montreal General Post Office. Today, the Bank is commonly known as BMO, or "BeeMo," and is Canada's fourth largest based on deposits.

The older section of the Bank of Montreal building on 129 Saint Jacques Street in the city's Old Montreal district which was built in 1847 and remodeled in 1905.

The Anteroom

All text in the Museum's exhibits is bilingual—French and English. In its anteroom, there are several wall-mounted displays. The first is titled "Early Currency," consisting of a selection of notes from several banks and railroads in the area. A second, titled "Early Bank of Montreal Currency," contains banknotes and tokens issued by the bank during the middle 19th century. There is also a recreation of its very first cashier's office.

The Main Gallery

Past the anteroom is the main gallery where, on the walls, are photos, paintings, and informational panels representing significant periods in the Bank's history. Also, there are eight floor-mounted cases housing the Museum's major banknote exhibits and other collectibles. In the first case are the original Articles of Association which formed the Montreal Bank on November 3, 1817.

View of the main gallery of the Bank of Montreal Museum with eight floor-mounted display cases. On the walls are photos, paintings, and informational panels representing significant periods in the Bank's history.

The successive cases take visitors on a brief tour of the paper money of both the Bank and the Bank of Canada, illustrating some of the highlights of the history of Canada's banknotes.

One display shows an 1817 $20-note of the Montreal Bank, its first year of operation and signed by both its president, John Gray and its cashier, Robert Griffin.

The time period then jumps quickly ahead: one case has a 1942 $5-note from the Bank's last issue, before The Bank of Canada Act of 1934 required chartered banks to give up their right to issue currency. In between the bank's first and last issues, there is an extremely rare 1844 $3-note issued by the Bank, one of two known.

Canada's Central Bank

The nation's central bank, the Bank of Canada, was created in 1934, and issued its first notes in 1935. On display is a $2-note bearing the portrait of Queen Mary. The unusual feature about this note is that this series was the only one to have two separate notes for each denomination; the French-language note is shown. The next series, issued in 1937, was the first bi-lingual issue, and is represented by a $2-note with the portrait of King George VI.

The third issue, following the death of King George VI in 1952, was released in 1954 with the portrait of a young Queen Elizabeth II on all denominations from $1 to $1,000.

As the $1-note ceased being issued in 1989, replaced with a $1-coin, the Bank of Canada in 1996 stopped issuing the $2-note and replaced it with a bi-metallic $2-coin, affectionately nicknamed the "Toonie."

The last case is devoted to illustrating the differences between genuine banknotes and confiscated counterfeits, generally defined by the poor quality of the paper, the imprint, and the engraved portraits.

Mechanical Savings Banks

The Museum also has on display several mechanical "piggy" savings banks. During the latter part of the 1800s, cast iron penny banks became a common sight in the home, and hundreds of different designs were made and sold.

An extremely rare 1844 $3-note issued by the Bank of Montreal, which is one of two such known surviving notes.

Visitor's Checklist

Bank of Montreal Museum, 129 Rue St-Jacques, Montréal, Québec, Canada, H2Y. (Located in the hallway between the Bank's Main Branch and Head Office buildings)

- ❶ ℂ (514) 877-6810
- ◯ Monday-Friday: 10 a.m.-4 p.m.; Sunday: 2 p.m.-5 p.m.
- ● Saturday and Sunday; holidays.
- ✋ ⑤ 📷

Public Transportation

Ⓜ Place-d'Armes

🚍 55-S/361-N/363-N (Place-d'Armes/Notre Dame); 129-S/365-S (Saint-Antoine/ Saint Urbain)

Internet

🌐 www.museumsquebec.ca/mtd/museumguide/datasheets/institution.php? ID=50-55-1233 (unofficial site)

Currency Museum of the Bank of Canada
Musée de la Monnaie de la Banque du Canada
Ottawa, Ontario

Canada's National Currency Collection, with over 100,000 artifacts, is the largest and most complete collection of Canadian banknotes, coins, and money-related artifacts in the world. The Currency Museum of the Bank of Canada, the nation's central bank, exhibits the National Currency Collection, and the collection supports the Museum's mission to preserve Canada's numismatic heritage.

Entrance to the Currency Museum on Sparks Street.

Is this Money?
Once inside, visitors begin exploring with bilingual text (French and English) the Museum's many areas, first with commodities once used as money. Some of the many strange items people used as money in different parts of the globe include: the huge Yap stone in the lobby, Liberian kissi pennies (flattened iron rods), Mexican cocoa beans, and Siberian tea blocks.

History of World Money
The evolution of monetary systems, supplemented with examples of coins and paper money, begins with the ancient Chinese who developed a system of coinage using cast

bronze spade and knife money. Round and punch-marked coins from China and India are shown that preceded the first Western coins from Lydia.

Specimens are then shown for the empires that followed: Persian, Greece, Republic and Imperial Rome, Byzantine, Sassasians, Islamic (Umayyads, Abbasids), the Carolingians, highlighted by Charlemagne's £.D.s system, and the Vikings.

Examples of coins from the many medieval European states, starting with the florin from Florence—the first important gold coin in 1252 to appear in Western Europe in centuries are displayed. This was followed by the Venetian ducat which was important for European trade up to the end of 14th century.

The Currency Museum's Coin Collector's Corner.

Informational Panels

Several panels are quite informative—three of which are about the dollar: "Origin of the Dollar," from the Joachimsthaler in Bohemia; "The Spanish-American Dollar," the silver 8 reales; and "The Beginnings of the Decimal Dollar."

Another panel is about inflation, showing the high denomination banknotes of Russia, Greece, Germany, and Hungary.

History of Canadian Money

Being Canada's premier collection, one should not miss this area detailing the evolution of Canada's money and banking. Before coins, examples of shells, wampum, woolen blankets from Hudson's Bay and other trading companies, and beaver pelts from the West Coast and Plains tribes used as money are exhibited.

Until the 1850s, the pre-Confederation provinces did not have their own coinage, and accepted a variety of foreign coins: U.S., French, British, and Spanish. One of the most famous was the Prince Edward Island silver "holey" dollar. In 1813 due to a shortage of money, Spanish dollars, i.e., silver 8-reales coins, were center-hole punched and made equal to 5 shillings. The center plug was made equal to 1 shilling.

A very comprehensive collection of Canadian banknotes is shown, which ranges from fractionals to the rarely seen $50,000 "bank legal" that were issued between 1918 and 1935.

The Collector's Corner

This area offers visitors a unique experience. It's like visiting a bank vault where there are specimens from the National Currency Collection arranged in four different sections: Canadian banknotes, foreign banknotes, Canadian coins and tokens, and foreign coins.

A 1913 $5-gold piece with the crown head of George IV.

Visitor's Checklist

Currency Museum Bank of Canada, 245 Sparks Street, Ottawa, Ontario Canada K1A 0G9. The Museum's entrance is between Bank and Kent Streets.

- ❶ ☏ (613) 782-8914
- ○ Tuesday-Saturday: 10:30 a.m.-5 p.m., Sunday: 1 p.m.-5 p.m. (October 1-April 30); Monday-Saturday: 10:30-5 p.m., Sunday: 1 p.m.-5 p.m. (May 1-September 30).
- ● Monday during October 1-April 30; December 25 and January 1 holiday period. See web site for exact details.
- 📷 (see Museum policy at: www.currencymuseum.ca/visiting-the-museum/filming-and-photography-policy/) ✋ ♿ 🎧 🛒

Public Transportation

- 🚌 OC Transpo 1/2/4/7/9/12/221/231/232 (Queen and Bank Streets); 1/2/7 (Sparks and Bank Streets)

Internet

- ✉ museum-musee@bankofcanada.ca
- 🌐 www.currencymuseum.ca (also in French)

Royal Canadian Mint
Monnaie Royale Canadienne
Ottawa, Ontario, Canada
Winnipeg, Manitoba, Canada

All of Canada's coins for circulation are produced by the Royal Canadian Mint's two locations in Ottawa, Ontario and Winnipeg, Manitoba. The Mint also designs and manufactures precious and base metal coins for collectors; bullion coins of gold, silver, palladium, and platinum; medals, medallions, and tokens. It also provides commercial gold and silver refinery and assay services. In addition, it mints coins for a number of other countries.

Both locations offer visitors guided tours in either French or English of their minting operations.

The Royal Canadian Mint's Ottawa facility as seen from Sussex Drive.

The Ottawa Facility
As the Province of Canada, its coins were minted at London's Royal Mint. The current building then was named the Ottawa Mint and was established as a branch of the Royal Mint. This was authorized to be built in 1901, but it was not until 1908 that its first coins were minted for circulation. In 1931, the Ottawa Mint was renamed the Royal Canadian Mint, or in French, *Monnaie royale canadienne.*

The Ottawa facility offers guided tours seven days a week, showing the high-tech manufacturing process of its collector coins and medals. Visitors also will learn about the $1-million gold bullion coin that was produced by the Ottawa facility in 2007. This coin weighed 100 kg (3,215 troy oz.) of 0.99999 pure gold and was made as a unique showpiece to promote the Mint's new line of 0.99999 pure one ounce Gold Maple Leaf bullion coins. This was also certified by Guinness World Records to be the world's largest gold coin. When asked why the Royal Canadian Mint made the world's purest and largest gold bullion coin, "Because we can," was the answer.

Also in the Mint's Museum, visitors have the opportunity to hold a solid gold bar (with security guards watching) that is worth over $750,000.

The prominent, eye-catching triangular structure of the Royal Canadian Mint's Winnipeg facility.

The Winnipeg Facility

The Winnipeg facility, which was officially opened in 1976, allowed the Ottawa facility to concentrate solely on collector coins, while Winnipeg would produce the entire supply of circulation coins for over 75 countries.

Like the Ottawa facility, the Winnipeg facility also offers guided tours, but only Tuesday through Saturday. There is an exception of the peak Victoria Day to Labor Day tourist season when it is open from Sunday and Monday.

Visitors can see the high-tech manufacturing facilities that use massive strips of metal to meet 50-ton presses to produce over 1,000 coins per second, and tour areas featuring interactive coin displays. The Winnipeg facility allows the minting of one billion circulation coins each year.

A 1912 $10-gold piece with the crown head of George V, struck at the then Ottawa Mint, a branch of the British Royal Mint.

Visitor's Checklist - Ottawa

Royal Canadian Mint, 320 Sussex Drive, Ottawa, Ontario, ON K1N 5C7, Canada

ℹ ℭ (613) 993-8990 or (800) 276-7714 (toll-free) to book a 45-minute tour (recommended)

◯ Daily 9:30 a.m.-5 p.m.

✋ ⑤ 🖊 📷 🚫 🛒

Public Transportation - Ottawa

🚌 9 (Sussex Dr. and Bruyère St.)

A 1998 $50, 1-ounce gold Maple Leaf bullion coin (0.9999 pure) struck at the Ottawa facility.

Visitor's Checklist - Winnipeg

Royal Canadian Mint, 520 Lagimodiere Blvd., Winnipeg, Manitoba, MB R2J 4J3, Canada.

ℹ ☏ (204) 983-6429 or (877) WPG-MINT (toll-free) to book a 45-minute tour (recommended)

○ Tuesday-Saturday: 9 a.m.-4 p.m.

● Sunday and Monday with the exception of between Labor Day (1st Monday in September) and Victoria Day (3rd Monday in May).

✋ ⑤ ♿ 📷 🚫 🛒

Internet

🌐 www.mint.ca/store/mint/about-the-mint/visit-the-mint-1200026mint.ca (also in French)

Central America

and the Caribbean

Because of its location, the Caribbean has been a trading cross-road among the Americas. The early coins were primarily from explorers and traders from Spain, Portugal, The Netherlands, Denmark, Sweden, France, and Britain. Central America, on the other hand, served as the convenient land conduit between Spanish Mexico and its colonies in South America.

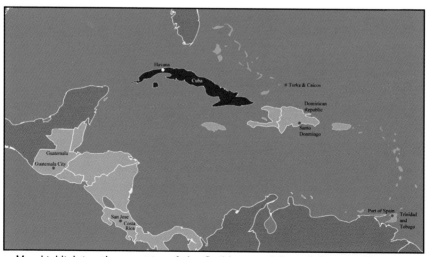

Map highlighting the countries of the Caribbean and Central America. The lone country (Cuba) having a numismatic venue with a detailed description in this chapter is shown in dark blue and Havana is indicated by a white dot. A red dot represents cities with limited information in those countries.

A photomontage of scenes of Havana, Cuba. From top to bottom, left to right: The Capitol building, front façade of the Museum of the Revolution, a panoramic view of the Havana cityscape, Great Theatre of Havana, the Morro Fortress Lighthouse, an Old Havana Square, and the Havana Cathedral.

The Caribbean hosts several museums that are noted in this section. The permanent collection of the Numismatic Museum in Havana, Cuba covers four phases of its history: Spanish colonization, American intervention, Cuban Republic, and the triumph of the Revolution up to the present. The Central Bank Numismatic and Philatelic Foreign Museum in Santo Domingo exhibits coins that once circulated in Hispaniola and a section on land and aquatic salvage. The Central Bank of Trinidad and Tobago Money Museum features an exhibition on the history of money in Trinidad and Tobago, beginning with the first inhabitants, the Amerindians, who used early forms of money, like the *obsidian*, a rock from cooled lava. On Grand Turk Island is the Turks & Caicos National Museum. The Museum has coins from the United States, Great Britain, Spain, Jamaica, Haiti, Bermuda, and the Danish West Indies. Many of these have at one time or another been legal tender in the Turks and Caicos Islands.

Central America has two venues of note. The Central Bank Museums of Costa Rica in San José features its permanent exhibition of the evolution of the real to the colón as the means of exchange from 1502 to the present. The Guatemalan Numismatic Museum presents a monetary history from the pre-Hispanic era to the present.

Havana, Cuba • Numismatic Museum

Additional institutions with limited information:

Caribbean

Santo Domingo, Dominican Republic	• Central Bank Numismatic and Philatelic Museum
Port of Spain, Trinidad	• Central Bank of Trinidad and Tobago Money Museum
Grand Turk, Turks & Caicos Islands	• Turks & Caicos National Museum

Central America

San José, Costa Rica	• Central Bank Museums of Costa Rica
Guatemala City, Guatemala	• Guatemalan Numismatic Museum

Numismatic Museum
Museo Numismatico
Havana, Cuba

The Numismatic Museum reopened in a 1915 building that was the previous head-quarters of the Banco Mendoza in Old Havana. The Museum was created in December 1975 as a cultural institution after a resolution of the National Bank of Cuba.

The front entrance of Havana's Museo Numismatico
on Calle Obispo.

The Permanent Exhibition

The Museum has a permanent exhibition of approximately 1,500 coins, which is the largest collection of Cuban coins. It is divided into historical sections of Cuba's history, representing the Spanish colonization (1511-1898), American intervention (1898-1902), Cuban Republic (1902-1959), and the triumph of the 1959 Revolution up to the present. In addition, visitors can also view decorations, medals, bonds, lottery tickets, numismatic documents and forgeries confiscated in the country. In short, the Museum provides a complete look at Cuba's numismatics history.

One of the many displays of coins and banknotes honoring the 1959 revolution.

Cuban Republic's First Currency

On display are examples from the first Cuban Republic's currency system, with its first gold and silver issues of 1915 and 1916, the silver certificates (*certificados de plata*) as the first banknotes of the Republic of Cuba starting in 1934, the creation of the National Bank (Banco Nacional de Cuba, 1948) and its first issue (1949), and the issues after the triumph of the 1959 Revolution. Also on display are medals, awards, and cards that were given in sugar mills as a money substitute. The Museum also features a collection of bills signed in 1869 by Carlos Manuel de Cespedes, an early revolutionary, which was the first attempt of the then-created republic in arms to have its own currency.

The face of an 1896 5-pesos banknote of the Bank of Spain of the Island of Cuba.

Coins Donated by Fidel Castro

In 2004, Cuban President Fidel Castro donated a thousand gold coins to the Museum, consisting of 920 $20 pieces minted in the United States between 1869 and 1928, and 80 Mexican 50-pesos coins struck between 1925 and 1945. The coins themselves were a 1985 gift to Castro from a Swiss biologist living in Canada and are on display in the Museum.

Besides coins that illustrate Cuban history, there are coins from the ancient world from between the 7th and the 1st centuries BC, in addition to coins from Latin American countries, Spain, and other cultures.

In addition to its numismatic exhibition, the Museum also has a specialized library and offers services for professional assessment of numismatic items.

1916 Republic of Cuba gold 1-peso with Cuban national hero José Julián Martí Pérez on the obverse.

Visitor's Checklist

Numismatic Museum (Museo Numismatico), Calle Obispo No. 305, Ciudad de La Habana, Cuba. The Museum is in Old Havana on Calle Obispo between Aguiar and Habana.

- ❶ ℂ +53 (0)7 861 5811
- ○ Tuesday-Saturday: 9:15 a.m.-4:45 p.m.; Sunday: 9:15 a.m.-12:45 p.m. (A few sources indicate Museum hours as Tuesday-Saturday: 1-8 p.m. and Sunday: 9 a.m.-1 p.m.).
- ● Monday
- ✴ ☕ 📷

Internet

✉ numismatica@bp.patrimonio.ohc.cu

Additional Institutions, Central America and Caribbean

The following institutions in the Caribbean and Central America are known to have numismatic exhibitions of varying degrees that are open to the public. These are listed here, either because sufficient information could not (1) be obtained about the museum, (2) be verified from other sources, (3) the museum did not respond to repeated requests for information, (4) the exhibition is closed due to long-term renovation of the building or other reasons, (5) or I learned about this venue just before the manuscript was to go to the publisher and complete information could not be included.

Caribbean

Dominican Republic
Central Bank Numismatic and Philatelic Museum
Museo Numismático y Filatélico del Banco Central
Avenida Pedro Henriquez Ureña, Former Central Bank Building, 3rd Floor, Santo Domingo
ⓘ ☎ (809) 221 9111, ext 3662 and 3712
✉ museo@bancentral.gov.do
⊕ www.bancentral.gov.do/english/museum.asp (also in Spanish)

Trinidad and Tobago
Central Bank of Trinidad and Tobago Money Museum
Eric Williams Plaza, Independence Square, Port of Spain, Trinidad
ⓘ ☎ (868) 625-4835, -4921, -2601, -5028
✉ info@central-bank.org.tt
⊕ www.central-bank.org.tt/content/museum

Turks & Caicos Islands
Turks & Caicos National Museum
Guinep House, Front Street, Grand Turk
ⓘ ☎ (01 649) 946-2160; from the U.S. (505) 216-1795
✉ info@tcmuseum.org
⊕ tcmuseum.org/collections/coins

Central America

Costa Rica
Central Bank Museums of Costa Rica
Museos del Banco Central de Costa Rica
Under the Plaza de la Cultura, Avenida Central and Calle 5, San José
- ℹ ℭ (506) 22 43 42 02
- ✉ www.museosdelbancocentral.org/eng/articles/contact-us-2.html
- 🌐 www.museosdelbancocentral.org/eng/general-information.html (also in Spanish)

Guatemala
Guatemalan Numismatic Museum
Museo Numismático de Guatemala
7a. Avenida 22-01, Zona 1, Guatemala City
- ℹ ℭ +502 2429 6000
- ✉ Use the on-line contact form at: www.banguat.gob.gt/inc/contacto.asp
- 🌐 www.banguat.gob.gt/en_museo/index.htm (also in Spanish)

South America

Map of the 13 countries of South America. The countries having numismatic venues with detailed descriptions are shown in dark blue and their cities indicated by a white dot. A red dot represents cities with limited information.

A photomontage of scenes of Brasilia, Brazil's capital city. From top to bottom, left to right: National Congress of Brazil, Juscelino Kubitschek Bridge, Esplanade of the Ministries, Palacio Alvorada – the official residence of the President of Brazil, and the Metropolitan Cathedral.

Much of South America's numismatic heritage stems from its colonial rulers. With the exceptions of Portugal, which colonized Brazil, The Netherlands which once ruled both Suriname and Guyana, then later by Great Britain, and French Guiana which is still an overseas French province, the remaining 10 South American countries were all ruled by Spain.

Because of the gold and silver deposits that were discovered, Spain set up numerous mints throughout the continent. Bartering was also the accepted practice by the indigenous native Indians inhabiting the countries prior to the arrival of the Europeans, and this continued to be a method of payment even after coins were introduced.

One of the most famous coins of the Western hemisphere struck by Spain was the silver peso de ocho (eight reales), also known as the Spanish dollar. It was frequently divided into eight parts, thus the name "pieces of eight." This coin became basis for the United States silver dollar and until 1857, was even legal tender in the U.S.

Spread across the continent, visitors will find numismatic exhibitions in museums, mints, and the central banks. In Buenos Aries, Argentina, there are two venues: the Mint of Argentina (Casa de Moneda de la República Argentina) and the Numismatic Museum of Buenos Aires. The Central Bank of Brazil's Museum of Money in the capital city of Brasília has exhibitions in four rooms covering

14,000 square feet (1,300 square meters). Exhibitions are found in the National Historical Museum in Santiago, Chile and the Museum of the Central Bank of Ecuador in Quito, the Numismatic Museum of the Central Bank of Uruguay in Montevideo, and the two-story Numismatic Collection of the Banco de la República in Bogota, Colombia, which is in a former mint. The small but interesting Numismatic Museum of the Central Bank of Suriname displays coins and banknotes from colonial Dutch Guiana and present-day Suriname.

Brasília, Brazil	• Central Bank of Brazil Museum of Money
Bogota, Colombia	• Numismatic Collection, Banco de la República
Paramaribo, Suriname	• Numismatic Museum of the Central Bank of Suriname

Additional institutions with limited information:

Buenos Aries, Argentina	• Mint of Argentina • Numismatic Museum of Buenos Aires
Santiago, Chile	• National Historical Museum
Quito, Ecuador	• Museum of the Central Bank of Ecuador
Montevideo, Uruguay	• Numismatic Museum of the Central Bank of Uruguay

Central Bank of Brazil Museum of Money
Banco Central do Brasil Museu de Valores
Brasília, Brazil

The Central Bank of Brazil's original Museum of Money was inaugurated in Rio de Janeiro on August 1972 as part of the 150th anniversary of Brazil's independence. When the country's federal capital was moved to Brasília, a new central bank building was constructed and the Museum was also transferred there, opening September 1981.

The Museum of Money's collection includes about 125,000 items of Brazilian and foreign origin, covering ancient to modern means of payment. This includes decorations, medals, historic documents, jetons and signet seals, and both private and government securities such as debentures, shares, bonds, checks, policies, and credit cards. In addition, the collection includes documents and objects related to the technological progress of minting, such as casts for banknotes, dice, color studies, monetary discs, and original drawings of banknotes and coins.

Four Exhibition Rooms

The exhibition covers about 14,000 square feet (1,300 square meters) in four rooms: Brazil Room, World Room, Gold Room, and the Brazilian Central Bank Issuance Room. The informational text is displayed in both

The building of the Central Bank of Brazil.

Portuguese and English, and printed publications are distributed free at the Museum in English, Spanish, and Portuguese.

The Brazil Room displays coins, banknotes and other printed valuables formerly circulating within the country. Part of the history of means of payment and investment are disposed in a course related to the Colonial and United Kingdom periods. One of the highlights is a gold 1822 6,400-reis coin with the laureate bust of Pedro I. There were only 64 pieces struck as the coronation piece, but 57 were melted down. The monetary systems of 55 countries are on display in the World Room, which is supplemented by photographs featuring widely known images of different regions of the world.

Entrance corridor to the Museum of Money.

The Gold Room

The Gold Room has eight displays of different forms of gold, foundry instruments, coin and investment gold, gold used in medals, signet seals, and gold delivery ingots that are traded on international gold exchanges. There are also several ingots and nuggets, among which is the largest nugget found in Brazil. This weighs about 132 lbs (60 kg) and was found in Serra Pelada, State of Pará, in 1983. It is considered, for its geological features, one of the rarest nuggets in the world.

The Central Bank Issuance Room was inaugurated on March 1997 and exhibits those Brazilian coins and banknotes issued since 1964, the date of the Central Bank was established, until the present. Also on display is a minting press donated by the Brazilian Mint to the Museum. This press, in operation from 1937 to 1973, features a minting capacity of up to 110 pieces a minute and is used for the distribution of medals as gifts to visitors.

A gold 1822, 6,400 reis with the laureate bust of Pedro I, Rio mint. Only 64 pieces were struck as the coronation piece for Pedro I and 57 were melted down.

Visitor's Checklist

Central Bank of Brazil Museum of Money (Banco Central de Valores), SBS Block 3 - Block B -1. Underground 70074-900, Brasília DF, Brazil. The Museum is located on the first underground floor of the Central Bank building.

- **ℹ** ☎ +(61) 3414-2093
- ○ Tuesday-Friday: 10 a.m.-5:30 p.m.; Saturday, Sunday and holidays (April 21, May 1, September 7, and November 15): 2-6 p.m.
- ● Monday
- ✋ ♿ 📷 (photo ID) 🎫 📷 🛒

Public Transportation

Ⓜ Laranja-Orange/Verde-Green (Galeria, 102 Sul)

Internet

✉ museudevalores@bcb.gov.br
Use the following on-line contact form: https://www3.bcb.gov.br/rdr/contact-us.paint?method=next

🌐 www.bcb.gov.br/?RED-MUSEUM (also in Portuguese)

Numismatic Collection, Banco de la República
Bogota, Colombia

The Numismatic Collection of the Banco de la República opened in December 1996 in the colonial cloister of the mint of Bogota. The Mint was originally established by Spain's Philip III and began operations in 1621. In the mid-18th century, the Spanish Crown ordered the extension of the building, and the second floor was added for the needs of the mechanized production of coins. José Solís y Folch de Cardona, Viceroy of New Grenada, reopened the Mint in 1756, as is noted on the stone frieze of the Museum's entrance. During the 19th and most of the 20th century, the Mint struck the national coins until 1985, when the Banco de la República moved the work of coinage to a modern factory.

The Museum front entrance which leads to an inner patio.

The collection includes over 15,500 pieces including coins and medals minted during the colonial period; Independence and Republican tickets; the 19th and early 20th centuries; foreign debt bonds and domestic stocks and other securities; and machinery and tools used in the process of coinage and banknote production. The exhibition is spread over 10 rooms on two floors with the displays in both Spanish and English.

The exhibition begins on the ground floor to illustrate the processes of monetary exchange of the Aborigines in pre-Colombian times, who inhabited the present territory of Colombia, using precious metals such as gold and other items such as salt, gemstones, stone, and ceramics.

The exhibition continues with the presentation of the most relevant aspects of the history of the 16th, 17th, and 18th centuries when Colombia was ruled by Spain. On display are important numismatic rarities struck at Santafé during the 17th, and 18th centuries. These were the *macuquina de oro*, known as cobs—exhibited specimens on display which were the first gold coins minted in the Americas.

The exhibition also includes examples of coins having a milled edge, made with the new machines sent by Spain in the mid-18th century. Matrices for coin designs, minting machines, models that illustrate the architectural changes that were submitted to the Mint, and the history of major political and economic events that marked the era of Spanish domination are also on display.

A gallery on the ground floor about the 18th century coins which features a fly, or screw press.

In the last gallery on the ground floor, visitors will find a large engine room which explains the various steps in the production of coins and seven original machines on display, dating from the 19th and mid-20th centuries. One of the major attractions of the Museum is the live demonstration of the process of exchange, medals which are minted in the presence of the visitors and awarded as souvenirs for playing games.

On the second floor, silver coins are displayed that were minted during and after the period of independence from Spain. Shown are the most representative examples of the 19th-century coins, including many designs made by the Republican governments. On display are examples of the introduction of paper money, the creation of private banks, the economic and political events that led to the creation of a central bank, the development of industry in Colombia and finally, the history of the Banco de la República since its founding in 1923 to the present as regulator of monetary policy.

Moneda macuquina (cobs) de oro, two escudos of 1636, which were the first gold coins in the Americas.

Visitor's Checklist
Exposición Permanente de la Colección Numismática, Casa de Moneda, Calle 11 No. 4-93, Bogotá, Colombia. The Museum is at the corner of Calle 11 and Carrera 5.

  ❶ ℂ +57 (0)1 343 1208

  ◯ Monday, Wednesday-Saturdays: 9 a.m.-7 p.m.; Sunday and holidays: 10 a.m.-5 p.m.

  ● Tuesday

  ✋ ♿ 🕮 (Biblioteca Luis Angel Arango, across the Street) 🖼 🚫 🛒 🍴

Public Transportation
  🚌 J (Museo del Oro)

Internet
  🌐 www.banrepcultural.org/blaavirtual/num/monedas.htm##p (in Spanish only)

Numismatic Museum of the Central Bank of Suriname

Numismatisch Museum van de Centrale Bank van Suriname

Paramaribo, Suriname

The Central Bank of Suriname has a small and modest Numismatic Museum, which was opened in April 2002. With just one exhibit area of 645 square feet (60 square meters), the Museum manages a collection of coins and paper money dating from the beginning of the West India Company to the present. The main part of this collection is formed by the then-circulating coins and parrot the card money, but also other coins and paper money are included, which was then used as legal tender in Suriname. The exhibition is in Dutch only, although audio-guides provide commentary in English and Dutch.

The Numismatic Museum of the Central Bank of Suriname.

History of Money in Suriname

Visitors learn about the history of money in Suriname and even about the time before conventional money existed when payments were made with commodities such as sugar, tobacco, and coffee as barter. Besides bartering with commodities when there was a lack of sufficient official money in the Dutch colony, an alternative form of money was created in 1761 by using play-ing cards. These were signed and stamped by an authority and given a value. The first coins that were made in 1679 are called the *papagaaimunt* (parrot coin), so named because a parrot is sitting on a branch. The history also mentions the first bank being founded in Suriname, the de Particuliere West Indische Bank (the Private Bank of the West Indies). The De Surinaamche Bank acted as a circulation bank until the Central Bank of Suriname was founded on April 1, 1957.

Obverse of the uniface 1679 colonial Dutch Guiana copper 4-duit coin, aka the "Parrot Coin."

Coins

Most of the coins that circulated in Suriname are on display in the Museum. The oldest coin on display that circulated in the Dutch Guiana colony is the uniface 1679 4-duit, or "Parrot Coin." The Parrot Coin, was named for the parrot on the obverse which is seated on a branch with 1, 2 or 4 leaves. They were drawn with the number 1, 2 or 4, which indicated that they were valued at 1, 2 or 4 pounds of sugar worth one penny per pound. Another early coin on display is the 1764 Society of Suriname duit.

1961 Dutch Guiana 2½-guilders banknote showing a Surinamese woman wearing a koto and angisa headscarf

Paper money

The display of paper money includes banknotes from the colonial era issued by the De Surinaamsche Bank through independence, the change in 1957 by the Central

Bank of Suriname to issue the banknotes with its *muntbiljet* (literally, "mint notes"), and the redenomination of its currency in 2004 from the guilder to the Surinamese dollar. Many of the banknotes from the Central Bank of Suriname from 1980s to 2000 are known for their colorful pictures of birds.

Commemorative Coins and Medals

The collection of commemorative coins and commemorative covers the entire history of coins and medals for special occasions in Suriname with about 20 different types of commemorative coins and medals. A highlight is the commemorative coin for honoring Anthony Nesty of Suriname, winner of the gold medal in the 100-meter butterfly at the 1988 Olympics in Seoul.

Visitor's Checklist

Numismatic Museum of the Central Bank of Suriname, Mr. F.H.R. Lim A. Po Straat 7, Paramaribo, Suriname

🛈 📞 +597 520 016 or +597 473741 ext. 577

◯ Monday-Friday: 8 a.m.-2 p.m.

⬤ Saturday and Sunday.

✋ 🍽 📷 🎧 🛒

Internet

✉ numismatischmuseum@cbvs.sr

🌐 www.cbvs.sr/dutch/museum/numis-intro.htm?lang=en (in Dutch only)

Additional Institutions, South America

The following South American institutions are known to have numismatic exhibitions of varying degrees that are open to the public. These are listed here, either because sufficient information could not (1) be obtained about the museum, (2) be verified from other sources, (3) the museum did not respond to repeated requests for information, (4) the exhibition is closed due to long-term renovation of the building or other reasons, (5) or I learned about this venue just before the manuscript was to go to the publisher and complete information could not be included.

Argentina
Mint of Argentina
Casa de Moneda de la República Argentina
Avenida Antártida Argentina 2085, Buenos Aires
ℹ ℂ +54 11 577 63545
✉ museomoneda@camoar.gov.ar
🌐 www.camoar.gov.ar/museo.html (in Spanish only)

Numismatic Museum of Buenos Aires
Museos Numismáticos de Buenos Aires
First floor, Bartolomé Mitre 326, Buenos Aires. Entrance is at 25 de Mayo and Reconquista.
ℹ ℂ +54 4347 6277
✉ tdelvillar@bna.com.ar
🌐 www.bcra.gov.ar/institucional/in040200_i.asp (also in Spanish)
    Click on Institutional/BCRA links

Chile
National Historical Museum
Museo Histórico Nacional
Plaza de Armas 951, Santiago
ℹ️ ☏ +44 (0)20-7323-8299
✉️ oirs@dibam.cl
🌐 www.museohistoriconacional.cl/Vistas_Publicas/publicContenido/contenidoPublic
    Detalle.aspx?folio=3684&idioma=0 (in Spanish only)

Ecuador
Museum of the Central Bank of Ecuador
Museo Nacional de Banco Central del Ecuador
Avenida Patria (between Avenida 6 de Diciembre and Avenida 12 de Octubre), Quito
ℹ️ ☏ +593 (0) 2 222 3258

Uruguay
Numismatic Museum of the Central Bank of Uruguay
Museo Numismático del Banco Central de Uruguay
Avda Fabini 777, Montevideo
ℹ️ ☏ +(598) 2 1967 int. 2452
✉️ museo@bcu.gub.uy
🌐 www.bcu.gub.uy/Billetes y Monedas/Museo/Paginas/Presentacion_Museo.aspx
    (in Spanish only)

Western Europe

Map highlighting the countries of Western Europe. The countries having numismatic venues with detailed descriptions are shown in dark blue and their cities indicated by a white dot. A red dot represents cities with limited information in those countries while a green dot indicates cities having venues with both detailed and limited information. Countries with a green background have their own individual maps in their respective sections.

Although the first coins did not originate in Europe, perhaps the world's greatest numismatic tradition can probably be found here. Throughout the various empires of Europe, the evolution of monetary systems paved the way for some of the denominations and monetary systems in use today. Virtually each country of Western Europe can claim some major numismatic contribution, whether by itself or as part of a larger empire it was once part of.

In this book, the European continent has been divided into Western and Eastern regions. In all, there are 16 countries having museums with extensive entries with pictures. Also, there are 13 countries that have museums whose entries have limited information.

A photomontage of iconic scenes of London – England's capital city. Top to bottom, left to right: City of London skyline from London City Hall; Tower Bridge; London Eye; Palace of Westminster – the Houses of Parliament and Big Ben, now renamed the Elizabeth Tower.

Naturally, the coins of Imperial Rome and the Roman Republic play a significant part of the evolution of the later monetary systems of Europe and even influenced many countries of the Middle East, giving the dinar. The many kingdoms throughout Germany that issued their own coinage before the 1871 unification provide a great diversity of type coinage, including other shapes besides round. The Holy Roman Empire, which included the Germanic states and some parts of Eastern Europe, most notably produced the silver thaler, a crown that is a shortened form of Joachimsthaler—the forerunner of the U.S. dollar. Italy gave us the florin (from Florence), the ducat and zecchino (from Venice). England, before the 1971 decimalization, had its pounds, shillings, pence, or LSD monetary system from the Roman librae, solidi, denarii coinage, although it had other coins in use in the Middle Ages like the noble, farthing, and groat.

Many of the museums in this section are among the world's best known and house some of the largest numismatic collections in the world, with only a small fraction of these collections on display. This list includes the British Museum with its newly renovated Citi Money Gallery, Berlin's Bode-Museum, the State Coin Collection at the Residenz in Munich, the Coin Cabinet of the State Art Collections in Dresden, the Royal Collection of Coins and Medals National Museum of Denmark in Copenhagen, and Stockholm's Royal Coin Cabinet.

Museums of five of some of Europe's smallest countries are represented: the Monaco Museum of Stamps and Coins, State Museum of San Marino, National Museum of History and Art Luxembourg, Vatican's Philatelic and Numismatic Museum, and the Bank of Valleta Museum on the island of Malta. Also included are exhibitions of university museums, such as Sweden's Uppsala University Coin Cabinet and the renowned United Kingdom museums: Heberden Coin Room of the Ashmolean Museum (University of Oxford), Fitzwilliam Museum (University of Cambridge), Manchester Museum (Manchester University), and the Hunterian Museum (University of Glasgow).

Some venues are a bit unusual. Two museums are for counterfeits—in Marcellaz Albanais, France and Saillon, Switzerland. One exhibit of archeological Roman coins is at the Roman Baths at Bath, England. Other interesting numismatic venues, although not museums, include a pair of flea markets held every Sunday in Madrid.

Brussels, Belgium	• Museum of the National Bank of Belgium
Copenhagen, Denmark	• National Bank of Denmark • National Museum of Denmark, Royal Collectionof Coins and Medals
Helsinki, Finland	• Bank of Finland Museum • National Museum of Finland
Berlin, Germany	• Altes Museum-The Ancient Coin: Work of Art, Money and Historical Testimony • Bode-Museum • German Historical Museum • German Technical Museum Berlin
Cologne	• Cologne Cathedral Treasury • Cologne Municipal Museum
Dresden	• State Art Collections Dresden Coin Cabinet
Frankfurt	• Deutsche Bundesbank Money Museum
Hamburg	• Hamburg History Museum
Munich	• State Coin Collection Munich and the Old Mint
Nuremberg	• Germanic National Museum Coin Cabinet
Dublin, Ireland	• National Museum of Ireland, Collins Barracks: Airgead– A Thousand Years of Irish Coins & Currency
Genoa, Italy	• Musei di Strada Nuova - Palazzo Doria Tursi Museum
Venice	• Correr Museum
Luxembourg, Luxembourg	• National Museum of History and Art Luxembourg
Monte Carlo, Monaco	• Monaco Museum of Stamps and Coins

Haarlem, The Netherlands	• Teylers Museum
San Marino, San Marino	• State Museum of San Marino
Madrid, Spain	• Madrid's Numismatic Flea Markets: Plaza Mayor and El Rastro
Stockholm, Sweden	• The Royal Coin Cabinet
Uppsala	• Uppsala University Coin Cabinet
Basel, Switzerland	• Basel Historical Museum
Bern	• Bernisches Historisches Museums
Lausanne	• Cantonal Money Museum, Cabinet of Medals
Zurich	• MoneyMuseum • Swiss National Museum in Zurich

United Kingdom

Bath, England	• Roman Baths at Bath
Cambridge	• Fitzwilliam Museum, University of Cambridge
London	• Bank of England Museum • British Museum • The Royal Mint at the Tower of London
Manchester	• Manchester Museum, University of Manchester
Oxford	• Heberden Coin Room, Ashmolean Museum, University of Oxford – Money: The Value of the Past
Edinburgh, Scotland	• Museum on the Mound
Glasgow	• Hunterian Museum, University of Glasgow
Cardiff, Wales	• National Museum Cardiff

Additional institutions with limited information:

Bruges, Belgium	• Gruuthuse Museum
Lyon, France	• Lyon Mint Cabinet
Marcellaz Albanais	• Museum of Counterfeit Money
Paris	• National Library of France
Gotha, Germany	• Friedenstein Castle
Cologne	• Historical Money Collection of the Cologne Savings Bank
	• Roman-Germanic Museum
Frankfurt am Main	• Historical Museum
Reykjavík, Iceland	• Central Bank of Iceland
Bologna, Italy	• Civic Archaeological Museum, Bologna
Milan	• Milan Civic Archaeological Museum
Rome	• National Museum of Rome, Balbi Crypt
	• National Museum of Rome, Palazzo Massimo alle Terme Rome
Valletta, Malta	• Bank of Valleta Museum
Lisbon, Portugal	• Museum of the Banco de Portugal
Madrid, Spain	• Cerralbo Museum
	• National Archaeological Museum of Spain
	• Spanish Royal Mint Museum

Additional institutions with limited information:

Chur, Switzerland	• Rätisches Museum, Münzkabinett
Geneva	• Art and History Museum of Geneva
Neuchâtel	• Museum of Art and History
Saillon	• Museum of Counterfeit Money
Winterthur	• Coin Cabinet and Collection of Antiquities of the City of Winterthur
Truro, England	• Royal Cornwall Museum
Edinburgh, Scotland	• National Museum of Scotland
Vatican City	• Philatelic and Numismatic Museum

Museum of the National Bank of Belgium
Musée de la Banque nationale de Belgique
Museum van de Nationale Bank van België
Brussels, Belgium

The Museum of the National Bank of Belgium is located on a small street across from the well-known Cathedral of Saints Michael and Gudula. It is the Museum of Belgium's central bank and the exhibits are distributed over 15 rooms, focusing on four main themes: the history of means of payment and the Bank's own background, its tasks and activities, the role of the currency in the economy and finally, money as a cultural phenomenon.

The majority of the displays are in French only, and to a lesser extent, a few are bilingual: French and Flemish. At the entrance to each room, the text is in French, Flemish, and English.

The first three rooms comprise the former office of the governor, the Board room, and the room in which the annual General meeting of shareholders used to be held. These offices were in use until 1953 and are now open to the public.

The front entrance to the Museum of the National Bank of Belgium.

Money in All Its Forms

In the largest of the exhibit rooms (Room 4), are displays of various forms of money used as means of exchange, as money did not always exist in its present form. Examples follow the evolution of money from its origins to the present day.

Pre-coinage commodities used for barter exchange such as teeth, ivory, and bracelets are on display, followed by the first known coins of Lydia and the Classical and Hellenistic periods of Greece. Other areas of coins on display include Celtic (150-50 BC), Roman Republic and Empire, 14th- and 15th-century Middle Ages, 17th- and 18th-centuries, Spanish coins in America, and Belgian coins from 1830 to 2001.

There are multiple displays of banknotes. Two have themes from World Wars I and II, with the latter including notes from Ravensbrück and Theresienstadt Nazi concentration camps, a Japanese East Indian occupation note, and a £20-Operation Bernhard forgery. Banknotes about wars and revolutions from the 16th-20th centuries feature a pair of U.S. 1864 Confederate notes, and high denomination inflation notes issued during the 18th-20th centuries. Also included are a series of Belgian notes from 1830 to 2002, notes from its previous Belgian Congo from 1885 and the independent country up to 1971, and one high-denomination note from each country prior to their entry in the euro area (i.e., euro zone).

A view of the center aisle of the "Money in All Its Forms" exhibit in Room 4.

Banknotes and Their Secrets

The various stages in the production of the banknote and the different security features incorporated into it is the theme of Room 6. All the euro banknotes are produced by 14 printing processes, under the control of the National Bank of Belgium. In order to fulfill its role properly, the banknote must be easily identifiable by the user, resistant to handling and safe against forgery attempts.

The Role of the Central Bank

Several rooms explain the National Bank of Belgium's role as the nation's central bank. Be it the guardian of the currency to keep prices stable, it also controls monetary policy by adjusting the interest rate on very short-term loans. Exhibits explain how the central bank influences the rates charged by the commercial banks and how it will raise or lower its rates in response to the threats of inflation or deflation.

Obverse of a 1619 gold double sovereign of Archdukes Albert and Isabella of the Spanish Netherlands.

Visitor's Checklist
Museum of the National Bank of Belgium, rue du Bois sauvage 10 (Wildewoudstraat 10), 1000 Brussels, Belgium

ⓘ ☎ +32 (0)2 221 22 06, +32 (0)2 221 36 21

○ Tuesday-Sunday: 10 a.m.-6 p.m.

● Monday; May 1, November 1 (All Saints' Day), November 11 (Armistice Day), December 25-January 1.

A rare 1834 Belgian gold 40-franc coin minted during the reign of Leopold I.

Public Transportation
Ⓜ 1-Gare de l'Ouest, 5-Erasme (Gare Centrale)

🅱🆄🆂 29/38/63/66/71 (Assaut); 29/63/65/66/71 (Gare Centrale); 29/63/65/66 (Parc); 29/63/65/66 (Treurenberg)

Tram 92/94 (Parc)

Internet
✉ museum@nbb.be

🌐 www.nbbmuseum.be/en/ (also in Flemish/Dutch, French, German)

National Bank of Denmark
Danmarks Nationalbank
Copenhagen, Denmark

Denmark's central bank, The National Bank of Denmark, opened its numismatic exhibition in August 2012 in the main lobby of its headquarters. Once two separate collections, the coin collection of the Royal Danish Mint and the banknote collection of the National Bank of Denmark are now combined into a single gallery with all explanatory text in Danish only.

The National Bank of Denmark along the Inderhavnen (Inner Harbor) Canal with its combination stone and glass façade.

Coins

The coins on display, numbering about 200, include coins minted after the establishment of Danmarks Nationalbank in 1818, even though Denmark's first coin goes back to that minted by Sweyn Forkbeard (c. 995). This is a display of two coins of each type, displaying the obverse and reverse sides for all monarchs from Frederik VI (1808-1839) to the present with one exception: the 20-krone coins in gold of Christian X (1912-1947).

Other rare and valuable coins also on display include the Christian d'Or and Frederik d'Or before the introduction of the krone in 1875 and the 1819 speciedaler, which is particularly interesting, as it is the last Danish coin to include the Norwegian lion. Denmark had surrendered Norway to Sweden at the Congress of Vienna in 1814, and in 1819 King Frederik VI promised to remove the Norwegian lion from the Danish coat of arms.

Furthermore, the exhibit includes the complete collection of 2-kroner silver commemorative coins, first minted in 1888, marking the 25-year reign of Christian IX up to the 1958 final issue, the occasion of the 18th birthday of then-princess Margrethe (Queen since 1972).

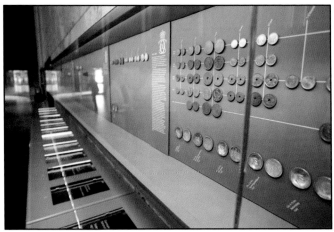

A view of the National Bank Denmark's wall of coins.

Banknotes

The exhibition of banknotes shows all those issued by Danmarks Nationalbank since 1818, ending with the current series, approximately 100 in all. This includes examples of the first Danish banknotes issued by various authorities in the 18th century. Following the 1813 Danish State bankruptcy, the Rigsbank was set up to issue banknotes, and some of its banknotes are also on display. Due to a lack of confidence in the Rigsbank, it was replaced by Nationalbanken i Kjøbenhavn in 1818, whose notes were just like the Rigsbank's, except that the name of the issuer had been changed.

Special Banknotes

A few special banknotes on display are: a 1-krone banknote issued at the time of World War I and a 2-krone banknote which was never put into circulation. There is a banknote shown used by the German Occupation forces in the early days of World War II, as well as a 1-krone banknote prepared by Danmarks Nationalbank in case there would be a shortage of coins but it never became necessary to put it into circulation. Finally, the special banknotes used by the British forces in Denmark after the Liberation are shown. There is also a display of Faroese banknotes. The first of these was issued in 1940, when the war separated the Faroe Islands from Denmark proper. After the war it was decided that the Faroe Islands would retain their own banknotes, but of the same sizes and denominations as the Danish banknotes.

The Royal Collection of Coins and Medals at the National Museum of Denmark (Nationalmuseet) is about 0.4 miles (700 m) away at Ny Vestergade 10, and a visit there is highly recommended.

The face of a 1970 Danish 100-kroner banknote with the portrait of
the physicist Hans Christian Ørsted.

Visitor's Checklist

Danmarks Nationalbank, Havnegade 5, 1093 Copenhagen K, Denmark

❶ ☏ +45 33 63 63 63

◯ Monday-Friday: 9 a.m.-4 p.m.

● Saturday and Sunday; Maundy Thursday*, Good Friday*, Easter Monday*, General Prayer Day (Store Bededag, 4th Friday after Easter)*, Ascension Day*, Bank holiday (Friday after Ascenion Day)*, Whit Monday (Monday after Pentecost)*, June 5 (Constitution Day), December 24 and 25.

✋ ♿ 📷

Public Transportation

Ⓜ M1/M2 (Kongens Nytorv Station)

🚌 1A/15/26 (Holmens Kirke), 2A/40/66 (Børsen), 11A (Tordenskjoldsgade)

Internet

✉ kommunikation@nationalbanken.dk

🌐 www.nationalbanken.dk/DNUK/NotesAndCoins.nsf/side/Coin_and_banknote_ exhibition!OpenDocument (also in Danish)

National Museum of Denmark, Royal Collection of Coins and Medals Nationalmuseet
Copenhagen, Denmark

The National Museum is located beside Christiansborg Palace in a classic 18th-century mansion called the Prince's Palace, which was the residence of Crown Prince Frederik (V), Crown Princess Louise, and other members of the royal family.

The Museum's Royal Collection of Coins and Medals comprise over half a million specimens, and the nation's leading collection of payment, medals, and other items related to payment instruments from around the world. The collection of Danish payment is considered the world's most extensive. Danish coins from Viking times to the present and coins from ancient Rome and Greece, and examples of the coinage and currencies of other cultures are also exhibited.

Front entrance to the National Museum of Denmark.

The Permanent Exhibit Gallery

The permanent exhibit gallery is spread over seven rooms with both floor and wall-mounted displays. The text is bilingual: Danish and English.

The first room (#141) shows Danish and foreign medals from the 1400s to the present. Special emphasis is on medals illustrating the history of Denmark. The oldest medals are cast, while current medals use both molded and embossed techniques.

The next two rooms (#142 and 143) exhibit the first coins from Lydia of the 7th century BC which were composed of the natural electrum alloy. The development of coinage is supported by examples from ancient Greece, Rome, Byzantium, Merovingian and Carolingian dynasties, early Arabic dynastic coins, and those from the Viking age.

A view of several interconnecting rooms of the coin gallery.

Danish Coinage and Paper Money

The next two rooms (#144 and 145) deal almost solely with Danish coinage and paper money. Here is a chronological exhibition of Danish coins from those ancient Viking coins minted in Hedeby in 800, inspired by Carolingian types. On display is the first Danish coin minted by Sweyn Forkbeard (c. 995), who was the first to put the name of the country, his image, and his name as the Danish king on a coin. It was not until Canute's reign (1018-1035) that organized Danish coinage was introduced according to the Anglo-Saxon pattern.

The coins of Christian IV (1588-1648) are noteworthy in that many include the four Hebrew letters, or *tetragrammaton*, that spell the Hebrew name of God on coins of the last four years of his reign. Some think the letters brought him good luck in helping him defeat Sweden in the 1613 Kalmar War. Since the 1700s, the Royal Collection received copies of all coins and medals that were struck at the Danish Royal Mint so that the National Museum now has a complete collection of Danish coins from this period.

There are examples of Danish coins from the former Danish possessions of Greenland, Faroe Islands, Danish West Indies, and Tranquebar. In the middle of the room is a chronological display of Danish banknotes from 1713 to the present.

World Coins

In the last rooms (#146 and 147) are world coins in pyramid-shaped display cases, giving visitors the opportunity to explore such diverse cultures as Japan, Byzantium, and Mexico and to compare countries' coins across time and space. Furthermore, there are different themes, for example: biblical coins, Crusader coins, and coins used as amulets. Also, there are examples of highly unusual coins like the Swedish copper plate coins and so-called primitive coins, including a wheel-shaped stone coin from the island of Yap in Micronesia.

The National Bank of Denmark (Danmarks Nationalbank) is about 0.4 miles (700 m) away at Havnegade 5, and a visit there is highly recommended.

The obverse of Denmark's first coin, ordered struck about 995 AD by Sweyn Forkbeard. This was the first to bear the name of the country and the name of the Danish king.

Visitor's Checklist

National Museum of Denmark, Ny Vestergade 10, 1471 Copenhagen, Denmark. The Royal Collection of Coins and Medals is on the 1st floor, Rooms 141-147.

❶ ℂ +45 (0)3313 4411

○ Tuesday-Sunday: 10 a.m.-5 p.m.

● Monday; December 24, 25, and 31.

✋ ♿ 📷 🎧 🛒 🍴

Public Transportation

Ⓜ M1/M2 (Nørreport Sation, Kongens Nytorv Station)

🚌 11A (Nationalmuseet Hovedindgang)

Internet

✉ nationalmuseet@natmus.dk

🌐 www.natmus.dk/sw33853.asp (also in Danish, German)

Bank of Finland Museum
Suomen Pankin Rahamuseo
Helsinki, Finland

As the Museum of the country's central bank, the Bank of Finland Museum is a place where the main focus is on the operation of the Bank of Finland, the European System of Central Banks, and monetary policy. Visitors learn about the history of money in Finland and abroad, and can also try their hand as a central banker by either playing the monetary policy game or seeing how the prices of everyday goods have changed from the 1860s to the present. It is the only museum in Finland specializing in the history and modern times of monetary policy.

The Museum is located in a building previously used to accommodate a post office. Its location in the center of Helsinki is ideal—one block away from the head office of the Bank of Finland. It is easy to find as it around the corner from the Helsinki Cathedral and Senate Square, two popular tourist venues.

The Bank of Finland Museum, in a former post office, is one block from the head office of the Bank of Finland.

Multiple Galleries
The exhibition has been divided into three sections:

• Monetary Policy
The heart of the Museum is the open area in the center of the exhibition, where central bank operations and monetary policy are illustrated with display windows and

145

multimedia shows. This part of the Museum lives to the heartbeat of the central bank and demonstrates abstract concepts in a clear and understandable way, making it a particularly helpful section for students of economics and finance. Among the concepts illustrated are: monetary theory, payment systems, stability of the banking system, monetary supply, exchange rate policy as well as operations of the Bank of Finland and of the European Central Bank.

- **History of the Bank of Finland and of the Finnish Money Market**
The history section presents the development of money and monetary policy in Finland and elsewhere, starting from the first coins issued in Lydia in approximately 650 BC. History comes alive through authentic objects, unique documents, and interesting photographs on display. The history of the Bank of Finland is particularly interesting, as it is the world's fourth oldest central bank, established on March 1, 1812 by Czar Alexander I of Russia.

One of several displays of numismatic exhibits of banknotes.

- **Banknotes and Banknote Art**
The banknote section provides a comprehensive overview of the payment instruments used in Finland throughout history. The display begins from the first markka coins minted in 1860 and ends with the introduction of the euro. The artists behind many banknote designs are also featured prominently. The exhibition presents the most influential artists and sheds light on their banknote art in relation to their other work. The displays also include enlarged photographs of money, enabling visitors to see how the graphic art involved in banknote design has evolved from the 1860s to the present day.

Seasonal Exhibitions
The Museum also includes a gallery set aside for seasonal exhibitions that change approximately once a year. These are constructed around themes of historical and

cultural interest dealing with money, banking, and economic phenomena, such as "The Last Finnish Markkaa." The inauguration of a new seasonal exhibition is announced on both the Bank of Finland's and the Museum's websites.

The printing plate used to print the face of the 1878 500-markkaa banknote.

Visitor's Checklist
Bank of Finland Museum, Snellmaninkatu 2, 00170 Helsinki, Finland

- ❶ ℂ +358 10 831 2981
- ○ Tuesday-Friday: 11 a.m.-5 p.m.; Saturday and Sunday: 11 a.m.-4 p.m.
- ● Monday; January 1, 6 (Epiphany), Good Friday*, Easter Monday*, May 1, Ascension Day*, Midsummer Holiday* (Friday-Sunday on/or following June 21), November 1 (All Saints' Day), December 6 (Independence Day), and December 24-26. An asterisk (*) denotes a movable holiday date.

✋ ⑤ 📷 🛒 🍴

Public Transportation
 1/1A/7A/7B (Hallituskatu Regeringsgatan)

Internet
✉ rahamuseo@bof.fi

🌐 www.rahamuseo.fi/en (also in Finnish, Swedish)

National Museum of Finland
Suomen Kansallismuseo
Helsinki, Finland

The building that houses Finland's National Museum was opened to the public in 1916. Its numismatic exhibition of coins, medals, banknotes, orders, and decorations of more than 20 display cases is located in the "Treasure Trove" section of the Museum's lower level. With few exceptions, all text is trilingual: Finnish, Swedish, and English.

Visitors are first guided through a small anteroom that has a few cases for new numismatic acquisitions. There is also a bust of Dr. H.F. Antell (1847-1893), a Finnish physician who collected coins, antiquities, and art, much of which is now found in both the National Museum of Finland and Finnish National Gallery.

The front entrance of the National Museum of Finland, a building originally completed in 1910 and renovated in 2000.

The Main Gallery

In the main gallery are more than 15 displays covering a wide range of numismatic material illustrating a small portion of the Museum's 210,000 coins, medals and other objects, including 58,000 items from the University of Helsinki Collection.

Starting with the "What is Money" case, visitors can view examples of various types of currency, such as postage stamp money and banknotes. "The Origins of Coinage" case begins the evolution of coins from Lydia, made from a naturally occurring electrum silver-gold alloy from around 650 BC. Eventually the Greeks made their coins using silver, gold, and copper. Other examples are those of Chinese money shaped like knives and spades cast in bronze.

One of the more than 20 display cases of the Museum's permanent exhibit.

History of Money in Finland

Six cases cover the history of money in Finland, it being ruled at various times by Sweden for six centuries and Russia from 1809 until its independence in 1917. Roman coins are displayed in the archeological exhibition of the Museum.

When part of Sweden, the monetary system was based on the mark, equal to 192 pennies. In the late 15th century, the örtug was equal to 8 pennies. Later denominations are shown, such as the öre, daler, and riksdaler, which were part of 16th-century monetary reforms. It was not until 1624 that copper coins were introduced. Between 1644 and 1776, the familiar rectangular Swedish copper plate money was produced. Outside of Sweden, this Museum probably has one of the best collections of plate money with over 25 specimens on display. Not all copper plate money is from Sweden; on display is a rare Russian 1726 10-kopeck plate.

Shown are several hoards, such as the Viensuu Hoard from Pielisjärvi, consisting of 585 Russian kopecks of the "wire money" type from the reign of Ivan the Terrible to 1610.

There is a significant grouping of 450 medals: Finnish (12 exhibits), Russian (1801-1917, in 3 exhibits), and Swedish (1560-1809, in 4 exhibits), and four exhibits of medallic art.

The only part of the exhibition that is solely in the Finnish language is the complete collection of Finnish banknotes from 1811 through the final series before changing to the euro.

Orders and Decorations

An adjacent room displays 150 of Sweden's orders & decorations in two floor-mounted and four wall-mounted displays. The most interesting of these is the Order of the White Rose of Finland Grand Cross with Collar, one of three official orders of Finland. The original collar's design, dating from 1919, had nine pairs of swastikas and white roses. Even though the swastika has long been a symbol associated with ancient civilizations of the Indus valley rather than the Nazis, it was replaced in 1963 by fir crosses on the collar.

Obverse of a silver 1867 2-markkaa coin, one of Finland's rarest.

Visitor's Checklist

National Museum of Finland, Mannerheimintie 34, 00100 Helsinki, Finland. The Coin Cabinet - Coins, Medals, Orders and Decorations are in Rooms 001-005 (Lower Level)

- ℹ ℂ +358 (0)40 128 6469, +358 (0)9 4050 9544 (ticket office)
- ○ Tuesday-Sunday: 11 a.m.-6 p.m.
- ● Monday; January 1, Good Friday*, May 1, June 20 (Midsummer Eve), June 21 (Midsummer Day), December 6 (Independence Day), and 25. An asterisk (*) denotes a movable holiday date.
- 🖐 ♿ 📷 🛒 🍴

Public Transportation

M Mellunmäki/Vuosaari (Rautatientori/Railway Station)
Tram 7A/7B/4/4T/10 (Kansallismuseo/National Museum)

Internet

- ✉ kansallismuseo@nba.fi
- 🌐 www.nba.fi/en/nationalmuseum/exhibitions/permanent (also in Finnish, Swedish)
  www.nba.fi/en/information_services/the_coin_cabinet (also in Finnish, Swedish)

Germany

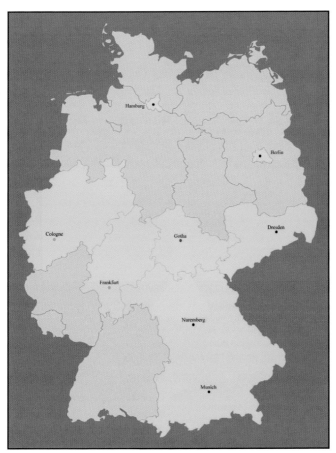

Map showing the 13 states (*Länder*) and 3 city states (*Stadt-staaten*) of Germany. The states with cities having numismatic venues with detailed descriptions are shown in light green and their cities are indicated by a black dot. A red dot represents cities with limited information while a green dot indicates cities having venues with both detailed and limited information.

Berlin, Germany	• Altes Museum-The Ancient Coin: Work of Art, Money and Historical Testimony
	• Bode-Museum
	• German Historical Museum
	• German Technical Museum Berlin
Cologne	• Cologne Cathedral Treasury
	• Cologne Municipal Museum
Dresden	• State Art Collections Dresden Coin Cabinet
Frankfurt	• Deutsche Bundesbank Money Museum
Hamburg	• Hamburg History Museum
Munich	• State Coin Collection Munich and the Old Mint
Nuremberg	• Germanic National Museum Coin Cabinet

Additional institutions with limited information:

Gotha, Germany	• Friedenstein Castle
Cologne	• Historical Money Collection of the Cologne Savings Bank
	• Roman-Germanic Museum
Frankfurt am Main	• Historical Museum

Altes Museum
The Ancient Coin: Work of Art, Money and Historical Testimony
Berlin, Germany

On the northern edge of the Museum Island's Lustgarten stands the Altes (Old) Museum, which until 1845, was called the Königliches (Royal) Museum. This numismatic exhibition of ancient Greek and Roman coins, with some changes, was previously displayed in the nearby Pergamon Museum. The Museum Island complex was designated a UNESCO World Heritage Site in 1999.

View of the front of the Altes Museum from the Lustgarten.

A Temporary Exhibit
The exhibition contains 15 displays holding nearly 1,100 coins. The explanatory text of each panel is in both German and English, but the descriptions of the subcategories and of the individual coins are in German only. There is a lone temporary exhibit, usually of a single coin of special interest, such as the tridrachm of Delphi (480-470 BC), and is changed at irregular intervals. The coin may be chosen for its unusual iconography or its importance in current research. A touch-controlled video screen nearby allows for searching the Museum's collection.

The Permanent Panels
The permanent 14-case exhibition encompasses the following themes:
- Early Coinage (7th-6th centuries BC)—coins of Asia Minor, starting with the Lydian stater where the first coins were made from electrum.

Some of the gallery's approximate 1,100 coins on display.

- Coins of the Classical Period (5th-4th centuries BC): Greece and the East—shows Athens developing a consistent set of coin imagery—that of the Athenian head and the owl.
- Coins of the Classical Period (5th-4th centuries BC): Sicily and Southern Italy—the dominance of Syracuse coinage with its four-horse chariot/head of nymph motif.
- Early Bronze Coinage (5th-4th centuries BC)—illustrating the introduction of bronze coins due to a shortage of silver from Athens.
- Hellenistic Period (4th-1st centuries BC): Ruler's Coinage—the period started by Alexander the Great are noteworthy as he adopted Attic weights as the standard for his gold and silver coins because his soldiers throughout the empire had to have their pay accepted everywhere. In effect, Alexander's tetradrachm and decadrachm became the first world-wide coins.
- Hellenistic Period (4th-1st centuries BC): Cities, Alliances, and Roman Provinces in the East—coins include examples of coinage of the Greek city states, Cleopatra VII, and a shekel and tetradrachm of the Jewish revolts.
- Celtic Coins (3rd-1st centuries BC)—many with unknown tribal markings.
- Early Roman Coinage (3rd centuries BC)—the beginnings of Roman coinage with many aes grave, aes signatum, and aes rude specimens.
- Roman Republican Coinage (c. 214-31 BC)—up through those of Julius Caesar and Marc Anthony, highlighted by the silver denarius.
- The Coinage of Augustus (31 BC-14 AD)—this early period give a striking, and at times puzzling record of this time of transition of this ruler, first known as Octavian.
- Reverse Images on Roman Imperial Coins (1st-3rd centuries AD)—images, many of which have religious subjects matter or personification of abstract concepts like equality or harmony.
- Roman Empire Provincial Coinage (1st century BC-3rd century AD)—praising the self-image of Greek states.

Two final panels address special themes:
- Strong Women, Women, and Amazons on Ancient Coins—Roman and Greek bearing female portraits, and Amazon heads from Kyme.
- Spatial Representation on Greek Coins—motifs on Greek coins represented the polis that issued them.

Visits to the nearby numismatic exhibitions at both the Bode-Museum and German Historical Museum are highly recommended.

The obverse of a gold octadrachm showing the portrait heads of Ptolemy II and Arsinoe II, minted in Alexandria, 260-240 BC.

Visitor's Checklist

Altes Museum, Am Lustgarten, 10178 Berlin, Germany. The Ancient Coin: Work of Art, Money and Historical Testimony is in Room 4 on the main floor

ℹ ℂ +49 (0)30-266 42 42 42

○ Tuesday-Sunday: 10 a.m.-6 p.m.; extended hours Thursday until 10 p.m.

● Monday; January 1, December 24-26.

⚒ ♿ 📷 🚫 🎧 🛒 🍴

Public Transportation

Ⓤ U6 (Friedrichstraße)

Ⓢ S1/S2/S25 (Friedrichstraße); S5/S7/S9/S75 (Hackescher Markt)

🚍 TXL (Staatsoper); 100/200 (Lustgarten); 147 (Friedrichstraße)

Ⓣ M1/12 (Am Kupfergraben); M4/M5/M6 (Hackescher Markt)

Internet

🌐 www.smb.museum/smb/standorte/index.php?lang=en&objID=24&p=2 (also in German)

Bode-Museum
Berlin, Germany

A prominent Berlin landmark, the Bode-Museum is located at the northern tip of the city's Museum Island, bounded by the Spree River on the east and the narrow Kupfergrabenkanal on the west. The Museum Island complex was designated a UNESCO World Heritage Site in 1999.

The dome-covered rounded corner of the Bode-Museum that provides the landmark at the northern tip of Berlin's Museum Island.

Once the Kaiser Friedrich Museum

When first opened, the Museum was originally known as the Kaiser Friedrich Museum, but its name was changed to that of the Bode-Museum in 1956 in honor of Wilhelm von Bode, an art historian and former director general of the Museum.

The Museum is composed of four areas: numismatic library, study room, Münzkabinett (coin collection vault), and exhibits. The numismatic library, which houses approximately 20,000 volumes, the study room, and the Münzkabinett all are located in the building's lower level. The library and study room are open to the public. Entrance to the study room and library is gained from the outside to the far right of the Museum visitor's entrance. Visitors must ring the bell and pull the door open when the buzzer sounds. The Münzkabinett contains 15,000 trays holding approximately 500,000 coins, medals, and banknotes in an environmentally-controlled vault maintained between 18 to 20 degrees centigrade (64 to 68 degrees Fahrenheit) with a relative humidity between 40 to 60 percent.

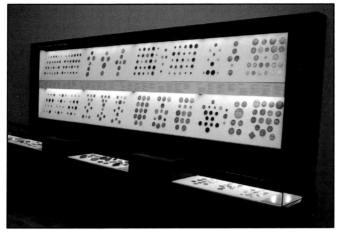

A view of one of the four major galleries.

One of the World's Largest Collections

Accredited scholars, researchers and collectors are afforded access to examine the coin and medallion specimens with advance appointments, but are permitted to examine only one tray at a time. For security reasons, only Museum personnel are allowed inside the vault.

From the Museum's vast collection, only approximately 4,000 items are on display in the permanent exhibit. The Museum's collection is one of the world's largest, containing specimens dating from the beginning of coinage in Asia Minor in the 7th century BC to the present. The holdings include more than 102,000 ancient Greek coins, 50,000 coins from ancient Rome, 35,000 Oriental-Islamic coins, and 160,000 European coins spanning the Middle Ages to the present period. The Museum's collection also includes paper money, historical seals dating from the Middle Ages, and examples of different forms of money used by primitive peoples. In addition, there are more than 15,000 minting tools, including over 10,000 dies with which coins were struck in Berlin from the 17th century onwards, as well as a large collection of casts.

The Museum's permanent numismatic exhibit is located on the second level, reached via either one of two majestic staircases. Visitors go through the café area where they are met by security personnel who scan the bar code on their ticket, allowing the door to open to the exhibit area. The permanent exhibit occupies four sequential rooms and has approximately 72 floor- and wall-mounted displays. Virtually all text is in German, although the titles of the displays include the corresponding English-language legends.

A fifth room houses a temporary exhibit. Also included is an interactive computer catalog of the Museum's Münzkabinett with descriptive information available, such as the year the specimen was acquired, tray number, geographical region, mint, and historical period. The user can select the text to be displayed either in German or English.

Visits to the nearby numismatic exhibitions at both the Altes Museum and German Historical Museum are highly recommended.

An assembly of 20th-century forgeries.

Visitor's Checklist

Bode-Museum, Am Kupfergraben 1, 10178 Berlin, Germany. The exhibition is on the 2nd level, Galleries 241-246.

❶ ☾ +49(0)30-2090-5577

○ Daily: 10 a.m.-6 p.m.; Thursday: until 10 p.m.

☙ Tuesday-Friday: 10 a.m.-12:30 p.m., 1 p.m.-4:30 p.m. (Lower level).

✋ ⓑ 📷 🛒 🍴

Public Transportation

Ⓤ U6 (Friedrichstraße)

Ⓢ S1/S2/S25 (Friedrichstraße); S5/S7/S9/S75 (Hackescher Markt)

🚌 TXL (Staatsoper); 100/200 (Lustgarten); 147 (Friedrichstraße)

Ⓣ M1/12 (Am Kupfergraben); M4/M5/M6 (Hackescher Markt)

Internet

✉ mk@smb.spk-berlin.de

🌐 www.smb.museum/smb/sammlungen/details.php?lang=en&objID=9 (also in German)

🌐 www.smb.museum/ikmk (Münzkabinett online catalogue)

German Historical Museum
Deutsches Historisches Museum
Berlin, Germany

The German Historical Museum, or its German acronym DHM (*Deutsches Historisches Museum*), is located at the far eastern end of the well-known Under den Linden boulevard, and is almost next to the prestigious Humboldt University. The Baroque-style building is also known as the *Zeughaus* (arsenal) as it was completed in 1730 as an arsenal by the Elector Friedrich III of Brandenburg (later King Friedrich I) for the Prussian army.

Selected items from the Museum's numismatic holdings are integrated with the permanent exhibition that covers the history of Germany, divided into 27 time periods from 100 BC to 1994.

The German Historical Museum from the Unter den Linden Boulevard.

Time Periods Marked by a Pillar with Coins

Each time period is marked by a square pillar, which as part of its design, usually includes one or more coins or medals from DHM's 80,000-item numismatic collection representative of that period. In some instances, additional numismatic specimens are integrated nearby with historical artifacts for that period. Most of the text is in both German and English.

Some of the numismatic contents in the DHM's permanent exhibition on display are:
- 100 BC–500 AD: Celts, Germans, and Romans. A silver denarius of Augustus, 2 BC; a bronze sesterce of Nero, 54/68 AD; a bronze sesterce of Hadrian, 132/134 AD; and a bronze follis of Constantine I, 328 AD.
- 500-900: Charlemagne and the Kingdom of the Franks. An 814/840 silver denier of Emperor Louis the Pious illustrates the long enduring symbolism of the cross and church on coinage.
- 800-1500: Medieval Ways of Life. A 1338 gold écu d'or of Emperor Ludwig IV of Bavaria was the first coin with the double eagle shield.
- 900-1500: Emperor and Empire. The Golden Bull of 1356 confirmed the elector's right of coinage. Mainz, Cologne, Trier, the Palatinate, and territories bordering the Rhine formed a coinage union. Unearthed gold guldens and silver groschens are shown.
- 1600-1650: Crises and War in Germany. A 1648 silver medal by Engelbert Ketteler on the Peace of Westphalia, ending the Thirty Year's War; a 1634 silver medal by Sebastian Dadler on the burial of Gustav II Adolf of Sweden, who lead his army on the side of the Protestants in the Thirty Year's War. Nearby are coins from the Kornöd Hoard of 259 coins, hidden in 1640 during the Thirty Year's War and found in 1956.
- 1789-1815: From the French Revolution to the Congress of Vienna. Shown are examples of various assignats of the French Revolution.
- 1815-1848: The Congress of Vienna and the Era of Metternich. An 1814 medal by Leopold Heuberger of the Congress of Vienna showing the profiles of the Holy Alliance monarchs: Emperor Franz I of Austria, Czar Alexander I of Russia, and King Friedrich Wilhelm III of Prussia. Also on display nearby is Napoleon Bonaparte's bicorn, or cocked hat, sword, and spurs taken from him at his 1815 defeat at Waterloo.

Mark and Pfennig replaces the Thaler and Guilder
- 1850-1871: On the Way to National Statehood. Type sets of both coins and banknotes of 1871 of the newly unified German Empire, based on the gold standard, are shown. The longstanding thaler and guilder have now been replaced by the mark and pfennig.
- 1918-1925: The Difficult Beginnings of the Republic. Shown are examples of banknotes of the period of inflation, such as a 1-mark note equaling one trillion marks in 1923 prior to the 1924 reforms.

Visits to the nearby numismatic exhibitions on Museum Island at both the Altes Museum and Bode-Museum are highly recommended.

An 814/840 silver denier of Emperor Louis the Pious shows the long enduring symbolism of the cross and church on coinage.

Visitor's Checklist

German Historical Museum, Zeughaus, Unter den Linden 2, 10117 Berlin, Germany

ℹ ☏ +49 30/20304-444

○ Daily: 10 a.m.-6 p.m.

● December 24 and 25.

A 1338 gold écu d'or of Emperor Ludwig IV of Bavaria was the first coin with the double eagle shield.

Public Transportation

Ⓜ U6 (Friedrichstraße/Französische Straße)

🚌 100 (Staatoper)

Internet

✉ info@dhm.de

🌐 www.dhm.de/sammlungen/kunst2/numismatik/ (also in German)

🌐 www.dhm.de/international/ (general information in Arabic, Chinese, Czech, Finnish, English, French, German, Hebrew, Italian, Japanese, Polish, Portuguese, Russian, Spanish, Swedish, Turkish)

German Technical Museum Berlin
Deutsches Technikmuseum Berlin
Berlin, Germany

The Deutsches Technikmuseum Berlin, or German Technical Museum Berlin (DTMB), is easily recognized by the twin propeller Douglas C-47 Skytrain, aka the "Dakota," sitting atop its roof. The DTMB was first established in 1982 on the site of a former trade hall housing more than 100 smaller, specialized collections.

The building of the German Technical Museum Berlin. On top of the building is a Douglas C-47 Skytrain, aka the "Dakota."

A Banknote Collection about Science

Among the displays of railway cars and engines, airplanes, ships, steam engines, automobiles, and even a brewery, are two walnut cabinets with 46 vertical slide-out panels holding a collection of banknotes. Most of the notes consist of modern (post-1960) international issues arranged by categories, such as physics or shipping. Each panel contains banknotes representing a particular topic and each banknote shows the vignette of a famous person, technical device, industry, or commodity. For each banknote, information is provided in German only with the country, date of issue, denomination, and a brief description of the banknote's face and back.

The cases may be hard to find as its location apparently changes. One year its location was just before entering the Railway Engine Shed Number 1; two years later, it was elsewhere. Nothing is special about them, set atop grey metal tables with a tarnished brass plaque with a German inscription. The banknotes were from the private collection of Dr. Anthony R. Michaelis, acquired in 1996 with the help from Bankgesellshaft Berlin AG and Urenco, Ltd. of England. On display are nearly 300 of the reported 1,300 banknotes Michaelis gave to the DTMB.

The DTMB's collection of paper money featuring vignettes of persons of science or technical subjects housed in 46 vertical drawers.

It All Started with the Ming Dynasty

The first panel contains only a single banknote, labeled as "The World's Oldest Advanced Printed Banknote." It is from the reign of Emperor Hung-Wu (1328-1398), the founder of the Ming dynasty. Technically, Sweden lays claim to the first "banknote," but this was the first form of paper money.

The next nine panels contain notes honoring Christopher Columbus and those persons of science. Generally, each panel displays six banknotes, so the banknotes for a particular topic are not an exhaustive grouping.

Panel 3 shows six notes with portraits of mathematicians. The 1980 Iraqi 10,000-dinar banknote has the image of Abu Ali al-Hasan ibn al-Hasan ibn al-Haytham, aka Alhazen, who is generally regarded as the father of optics.

Famous Physicists

Panel 7 shows six notes representing physicists. One banknote is a 1968 Israel 5-lirot banknote picturing Albert Einstein. Although Einstein is probably best known for his theory of relativity, his 1921 Nobel Prize for Physics was for the photoelectric effect. *Time* magazine named Einstein "Person of the Century" in 1999.

Other Topics

Not all banknotes are from the modern era, nor do they only picture people. The remaining 36 topics are divided among various industries and commodity products.

Three panels are dedicated to the railroads. In one of the two panels showing railroad vignettes before the year 1920, two banknotes are from the United States. One of these is an 1859 $10 Bank of Chattanooga, Tennessee banknote featuring an "express train" with three passenger cars.

An Israeli 1968 5-lirot banknote featuring the image of Albert Einstein, named *Time* magazine's "Person of the Century" in 1999.

Polymer Notes with Holograms

The last panel (number 46) concludes the collection with polymer banknotes having an optically variable device, or hologram—one of the latest advances in the printing of banknotes. Australia became the first to issue polymer banknotes as currency in 1988, shown by the 1988 Australian $10-banknote with Captain James Cook's ship on the front with a hologram of Cook's head.

Visitor's Checklist

German Technical Museum Berlin, Trebbiner Strasse 9, 10963 Berlin, Germany

🛈 ☎ +49 30 90254-0

◯ Tuesday-Friday: 9 a.m.-5:30 p.m.; Saturday and Sunday: 10 a.m.-6 p.m.; on certain holidays such as German Unification Day (October 3), December 26: 10 a.m.-6 p.m.

● Monday; December 25.

♨ ⑤ 📷 🛒 🍴

Public Transportation

🇺 U1/U2 (Gleisdreieck)

Internet

✉ Use the on-line contact form at: www.sdtb.de/Kontakt.132.0.html

🌐 www.sdtb.de/Englisch.55.0.html (also in German)

Cologne Cathedral Treasury
Domschatzkammer
Cologne, Germany

The celebrated *Kölner Dom* (Cologne Cathedral), a UNESCO World Heritage Site designated in 1996, is the city's most prized landmark. It is easily recognized by its twin spires which reach 515 feet (157 m) and is the world's tallest Roman Catholic cathedral. Inside the cathedral's *Schatzkammer* (treasury) houses a small, but excellent collection of gold coins that represents a significant part of its historic past.

Although building started in 1248, the Cathedral, whose official name is the Cathedral of St. Peter and St. Mary, was finally completed more than 600 years later in 1880, reigning as the world's largest gothic Catholic cathedral building. Entrance to the treasury is either from inside the Cathedral through its north transept, or from an outside entrance at the Cathedral's north side facing the railway station.

A bright gold sign with the word "Schatzkammer" marks the outside entrance to the Cologne Cathedral's treasury adjacent to the cathedral's northern transept.

Located Two Floors Below Ground

Once inside, the treasury's many exhibits are located on one of two floors below ground level as well as a ground level gallery. The display of coins is located on the 2nd level below ground on the wall near the steps or the elevator before the entrance to the Parament Room containing ornamental ecclesiastical vestments. With a total of 1 silver and 28 gold coins (generally ducats), the coins represent those minted during the tenure of 16 of Cologne's 48 Archbishops from Pilgrim (1021-1036) to Maximilian Friedrich (1761-1784). The coins are displayed in chronological order in three rows with a lighted lens that magnifies simultaneously one coin each of all three rows.

The wall-mounted display of the 29 coins of 16 of Cologne's Arch-bishops with a sliding lighted magnifier lens.

The coins shown were not the only ones minted for these 16 Archbishops, as there were often silver coins of lower denominations struck. The only silver coin of the 29 displayed is the non-dated denier of Pilgrim, showing the obverse. Except for the title in German and English, the text for each coin is in German only.

Gulden of Cologne's First Prince-Elector

The pair of guldens shown were minted in 1357 during the reign of Wilhelm von Gennep (1349-1362)—the obverse shows the image of St. John, while the reverse with lilies. It was Archbishop von Gennep who, under the terms of the Golden Bull of 1356, was made Cologne's first *Kurfürsten*, or prince-elector. All of Cologne's future Archbishops, along with six other prince-electors, formed the council that elected the Holy Roman Emperor.

There are five gold guldens that were minted in Bonn with different dates from 1420 to 1444 of Dietrich II von Mors—Cologne's Archbishop from 1414 to 1463. Another coin in the exhibit includes a 1695 gulden of Joseph Clemens von Bayern (1688-1723). Joseph Clemens was the brother of Maximilian II Emanuel, Elector of Bavaria, and he was subsequently banned by the Holy Roman Empire for his siding with France in the War of the Spanish Succession (1701-1714).

Other Religious Artifacts

Besides these coins, the treasury houses a number of priceless religious artifacts representing Cologne's Catholic history, some of which have been only been publicly displayed since 1867. These include reliquaries, Gospel books, signet rings, jewel-encrusted gold chalices, monstrances, crosiers, processional and pectoral crosses, miters, and vestments used by many of Cologne's Archbishops that date from as far back as the 10th century.

A 1526 gold gulden showing the coat of arms of the Cologne Archbishop Hermann V von Wied (1515-1546) on the reverse.

Visitor's Checklist
Cologne Cathedral Treasury, Roncalliplatz 2, 50667 Cologne, Germany. The coins are at 2nd level below ground; entrance is from either outside the north front (facing the train station) or inside the Cathedral through the north transept.

- ❶ ☏ +49 (0)221 179 40 300; ticket office +49 (0)221 179 40 530
- ○ Daily: 10 a.m.-6 p.m.
- ♨ ⓑ ◙ 🛒

Public Transportation
- Ⓤ U5/16/18 (Dom/Hbf)
- Ⓢ S6/11/12/13 (Dom/Hbf)
- 🚌132 (Dom/Hbf)

Internet
- ✉ info@domschatzkammer-koeln.de
- ⊕ www.dombau-koeln.de/index.php?id=11&ssl=0 (also in German)

Cologne Municipal Museum
Kölnisches Stadtmuseum
Cologne, Germany

The Kölnisches Stadtmuseum (Cologne Municipal Museum) was originally called the *Zeughaus*, or armory, which was built around 1600 by the Imperial Town of Cologne as a weapons arsenal in the Dutch Renaissance style. Today it serves as the Municipal Museum, providing an insight into the everyday life of the city and its citizens from the Middle Ages to the present. Exhibits are in German but free audio-guides are available that provide English explanations.

Cologne's Municipal Museum in a former weapons arsenal built around 1600.

Cologne Notgeld on Display

Germany is well-known for issuing notgeld, or emergency money vouchers, particularly by municipalities after World War I to about 1923. There are quite a number of such examples of these vouchers issued by the city of Cologne on display, some as small as 50 pfennig, and as one example, a note with the astronomical value of 250 billion marks that was issued on October 29, 1923 during Germany's hyperinflation period. With the currency reform of August 30, 1924, one gold mark replaced one billion paper marks.

Roman and Medieval Coin Hoards

Coins from the Roman and medieval periods found during many archaeological digs are also exhibited. One such hoard uncovered in 1953 consists of 38 gold coins, a mix of ecu d'ors of Ludwig of Bavaria (1326-1347), a mixture of guilders from Florence, Bohemia, Hungary, and Austria, plus 242 various silver coins. Because of the dates of the coins, one theory is that the owner, possibly Jewish, hid these coins because of the pogroms against Cologne's Jews in retaliation for the 1349 Black Death plague epidemic.

Another hoard on display is from a 1939 discovery when a gravedigger was digging at the Dünnwald Cemetery in northeastern Cologne. More than 1,400 coins, dating from the 13th century, were excavated. Most of the coins in this find were from the lower Rhine and the Netherlands with others from Westphalia and England minted during the reign of Henry III (1216-1272).

A hoard of 38 gold guilders and 242 silver grosch coins that were hidden in 1349, probably by someone in the city's Jewish community during the pogrom against the Jews for causing the Black Death.

Coins from Archaeological Digs

One nice exhibit shows coins found from the various archaeological digs in Cologne, with the coins separated by where they were minted. Included in this exhibit is a large map of Europe, with Cologne as one of Europe's most important trading centers and a member of the Hanseatic League as the focal point. From Cologne, there are arrows pointing to the cities where these coins were minted, such as Novgorod, Breslau, Genoa, London, Bergen, Stockholm, Tallinn, Riga, Paris, Basel, Zurich, Milan, and Vienna.

A 50-pfennig notgeld, dated January 12, 1922 from the city of Cologne.

Visitor's Checklist

Cologne Municipal Museum, Zeughausstraße 1-3, 50667 Cologne, Germany

ℹ️ ☏ +49(0)221 221 25789

◯ Tuesday-Sunday: 10 a.m.-5 p.m.; holidays: 10 a.m.-5 p.m.; extended hours: Tuesday until 8 p.m., Cologne Day (1st Thursday of every month) until 10 p.m.

⬤ Monday

♿ ⛑ 📷 🎧

Public Transportation

Ⓤ U3/U4/U5/U16/U18/U18* (Appellhofplatz)

🚌 Appellhofplatz

Internet

✉️ ksm@museenkoeln.de

🌐 www.museenkoeln.de/koelnisches-stadtmuseum/ (also in German)

State Art Collections Dresden Coin Cabinet
Staatliche Kunstsammlungen Dresden Münzkabinett
Dresden, Germany

The *Münzkabinett* (coin cabinet) is one of Dresden's oldest museums, having been founded around 1530. It contains one of the largest collections in Europe and is located in the Dresdner Residenzschloss (Dresden Castle). Its broad field ranges from coins of classical antiquity. The collection also includes orders and insignia, banknotes, historic bonds, models, seals, minting dies for coins and medals, as well as minting machines and equipment.

Multiple Locations

Since its founding, the collection and its library have seen several locations as its home. Until 1743, it remained in the Dresden Castle after which it was transferred nearby to the luxury Taschenbergpalais—a grand baroque hotel (now the Hotel Taschenbergpalais Kempinski). Then in 1786, Elector Friedrich August III moved the collection to the Japanese Palace (used primarily to store Japanese porcelain), and in 1877, the Münzkabinett was returned to the Dresden Castle.

Following World War II, the collection and the library material was seized by the Red Army and shipped to the Soviet Union. In 1958 the coins were returned to Dresden. Finally, the Münzkabinett returned to the Dresden Castle's Georgenbau (a building named for Duke George the Bearded, 1471-1539), its place of origin.

The Hausmannturm, completed in 1676, is the oldest still-existing portion of the Dresden Castle and is one of the city's most popular lookout settings.

Today, the Münzkabinett with its nearly 300,000 pieces is one of the three largest numismatic collections in Germany, after that of Berlin's Bode-Museum, and is estimated to contain about the same number of objects as the State Coin Collection in Munich. The collection has the status of a *Landesmünzkabinett*, or State Coin Collection, belonging to the Free State of Saxony, and is responsible for any coin hoards that may be found anywhere in the state. Currently, the Münzkabinett has approximately 30,000 coins and medals that represent different periods in Saxony's history.

View of the *Kleiner Schlosshof* (small castle courtyard) of the Dresden Castle where the entrance to the Hausmannturm is at the far wall.

Hausmannsturm Exhibitions

Until the permanent exhibition is put into place in the Dresden Castle, the Staatliche Kunstsammlungen Dresden holds a series of short-term exhibitions in the *Hausmannsturm* (Hausmann Tower). These exhibitions each encompass approximately 300 specimens that represent a cross-section of the various parts of the collection. The objects on display have been selected on the basis of their artistic quality, material value, significance in terms of cultural history, or by virtue of their documentation of restoration work.

The Münzkabinett is also a center of scholarly research and has a library of approximately 30,000 volumes located in the Georgenbau. It is open to the public on Wednesdays, or by appointment.

Visitor's Checklist

Staatliche Kunstsammlungen Dresden, Residenzschloss, Taschenberg 2, D-01067 Dresden, Germany. The library is at Residenzschloss, Georgenbau, Schlossstraße 25.

- 🛈 ℂ +49 (0)3 51 49 14 2000
- ◯ Monday, Wednesday-Sunday: 10 a.m.-6 p.m. (April to October).
- ● Tuesday; January 1, Day of Repentance (Buss- und Bettag, last Wednesday before November 23)*, December 24, 25, 26, and 31. An asterisk (*) denotes a movable holiday date.
- ⮑ Wednesday: 10 a.m.-5:30 p.m. or by appointment 🛈 ℂ +49 (0)3 51 49 14 3231

The obverse of a silver bracteate, struck in Meissen by the Margrave Konrad (1127-1156)

Public Transportation

 1/2/4 (Altmarkt), 1/2/4/8/9/11/12 (Postplatz), 4/8/9 (Theaterplatz)

The obverse of the 1544 silver Trinity medal, aka the *Moritzpfennig*, by Hans Reinhart the Elder, minted in Leipzig, which was intended to celebrate a point of unity between the Catholic and Protestant churches.

Internet

✉ besucherservice@skd.museum

🌐 http://www.skd.museum/en/museums-institutions/residenzschloss/muenzkabinett/index.html (also in German)

Deutsche Bundesbank Money Museum
Geldmuseum der Deutschen Bundesbank
Frankfurt am Main, Germany

The Deutsche Bundesbank's *Geldmuseum*, or Money Museum, has been open since 1999 in the quiet Ginnheim district of Frankfurt am Main. It's not hard finding it, as the 1,100-foot Europaturm TV tower, nicknamed the "Ginnheimer Asparagus," is behind the Museum.

The main entrance to the Deutsche Bundesbank's Geldmuseum in Frankfurt's Ginnheim district.

Money: What Different Types Are There and How Is It Produced?

Exhibits are divided into six theme "islands," each having a large column with in-depth information in both German and English. For the numismatic visitor, the first stage, "Money: What Different Types Are There and How Is It Produced?" will probably be the most interesting. Here on display are a small fraction of the approximately 90,000 coins and 254,000 paper money specimens from the Bundesbank's collection, inherited from and expanded upon that of the former Deutsche Reichbank.

The exhibition begins with a vast array of money substitutes from around the world like a Yap stone almost 20 inches (50 cm) in diameter. Less cumbersome commodities include: cowrie shells from the Maldives, salt bars used in Ethiopia in the late 19th century, and tea from Tibet and Mongolia that are pressed into bricks.

Next, the emphasis is on gold. A gold nugget from Papua, New Guinea and a 12.5-kg

(27.6 lbs) standard gold bar used by central bankers are shown.

Coins are arranged both chronologically and by region, beginning with the first coins of electrum minted in the early 7th century BC in Lydia, Asia Minor. Gold, silver, and copper coins up to the 1st century BC from the Hellenistic world feature the rare silver decadrachm with its characteristic Athenian owl on the reverse.

The era of Roman and Byzantine coinage introduces changes in the monetary system that would eventually be the basis of the future British LSD system. One extreme rarity on display is the gold aureus ordered struck by Brutus in 42 BC to commemorate the assassination of Julius Caesar on March 15, 44 BC. Brutus had both gold aurei and silver denarii minted, but only two aurei and 60 denarii are currently known.

A completely preserved 16th-century coin find of 468 silver coins in an earthenware jug, discovered in 1971, in the East Friesland village of Walle in Lower Saxony.

The Era of Migration and the Middle Ages

Coins of the era of migration and the Middle Ages from the 5th to the 11th century show the monetary reforms of the Carolingians with Christian symbols, and eventually the introduction of the Cologne Mark, a unit of weight, which remained in force in Germany until 1857. Coins from other countries from the 13th through 15th centuries were adapted to create new types such as the gulden from the Venetian florin and ducat. Coat of arms and portraits were also introduced as standard designs on coins of the various German rulers.

Origin of the U.S. Dollar

One of Germany's greatest numismatic contributions in the 16th century was the thaler. The U.S. dollar owes its origin to an example of a 1520 Joachmsthaler on display, struck at the Schlick mint and the silver was mined from the Saxony town of Joachimsthal, which is now in present-day Czech Republic as Jáchymov. The thaler remained the primary German coin until the introduction of the mark of the German Empire in 1871.

The Role of the Bundesbank
The remaining five stages are dedicated to the fundamentals of the role of the Bundesbank as Germany's central bank, and seek to answer the following questions:
- Money: What makes it valuable?
- Stable money: Why does it pay off?
- The central bank: What is its structure and what does it do?
- Monetary policy: How does it work?
- Foreign exchange policy: What is its impact?

There are two numismatic related libraries open to the public behind the Museum in the Deutsche Bundesbank building. In both libraries, checking out of materials is not permitted but workstations are available for visitors.

The 1520 Joachmsthaler from which eventually evolved the U.S. dollar.

Visitor's Checklist
Money Museum of the Deutsche Bundesbank, Wilhelm-Epstein-Strasse 14, 60431 Frankfurt am Main, Germany
- ❶ ℂ +49 (0) 69 9566 3073
- ○ Sunday-Friday, and public holidays: 10 a.m.-5 p.m.; extended hours: Wednesday 9 p.m.
- ● Saturday; January 1, Easter Sunday*, May 1, December 24, 25, 31. An asterisk (*) denotes a movable holiday date.
- ⊜ Monday-Friday: 10 a.m.-5 p.m.; both libraries.
- ✋ ⓖ 📷 🛒

Public Transportation
- 🇺 U1/U2/U3/U8 (Dornbusch)
- 🚌 34 (Deutsche Bundesbank)

Internet
- ✉ presse-information@bundesbank.de
- ⊕ www.geldmuseum.de/index.en.php (also in German)

Hamburg History Museum
Museum für Hamburgische Geschichte
Hamburg, Germany

Established in its current location in 1922, the Hamburg History Museum has been simply called the *hamburgmuseum*, or simply the letters *hm* since 2006. As a history museum that chronicles the birth of Hamburg to the present, highlighting its role in shipping and the Hanseatic League, the Reformation, the great Fire of 1842, and its Jewish community, there is also room to display its numismatic history.

The Museum's major numismatic exhibition is on the first floor (2nd level) in the *Das Jahrhundert der Reformation* (The Century of the Reformation) Wing which leads to the *Hamburg in der frühen Neuzeit* (Hamburg in the Early Modern Period) area. Entering the room, visitors see a costumed mannequin of a money changer seated at a table in the far corner with the tools of his trade. Next to him is a large floor chest, the forerunner of the modern safe.

The Hamburg History Museum, built between 1914 and 1923.

First Coin Finds

From various archaeological digs, on display are examples of Roman, Byzantine, Frisian, Merovingian, and Carolingian coins unearthed in Hamburg. Another panel shows silver coins of Count Adolf III of Holstein (1164-1225), using the bracteate minting technique, and stamped with three towers, the precursor of the Hamburg coat of arms.

Additional panels explain, in both German and English, changes in Hamburg's coinage. One of these is the adoption around 1365 of the witten, a white silver coin equal

177

to four pfennigs and was the basis for the Wendish Coinage Association for Northern Germany and the Baltic, and a later monetary policy for the Hanseatic League.

Other changes in coin denominations introduced the mark equal to 16 schillings or 192 pfennigs, and later the thaler. In addition to coins associated with Hamburg, there are many coins from other parts of medieval Europe and German states.

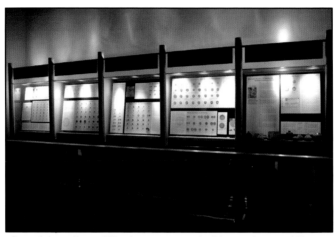

Part of the gallery of Hamburg coins on the Museum's second floor.

Executioner's Penny

A Hamburg specialty on display is the *Scharfrichterpfennig*, or executioner's penny. As the conclusion of his term of office, the executioner received a symbolic executioner's penny—a medal having no monetary value. On display are those from 1541 to 1607 and these have been issued up to 1810. Both sides of these pennies show the Hamburg coat of arms and the inscription of the name of senior justice of the court in question.

Cityscapes in Gold and Silver

Medals were the most precious medium used to represent the cityscape of Hamburg. The so-called portugaleser, named after a Portuguese gold coin equal to 10 ducats, was the start of a long series of gold medals, weighing 10 ducats, from 1653 to 1863 started by the Bank-Portugaleser. Popular motifs were ships and the bank building. On display are gold and silver medals by the noted medalists Sebastian Dadler and Johann Reteke the Elder from the 17th century; and Daniel Haesling, Christian Wermuth, and G.W. Vestner from the 18th century.

20th-Century Numismatics

In the basement, a second, but much smaller exhibit of coins and banknotes is in the first part of an exhibition titled, "Hamburg in the 20th Century." Here are various Nazi era coins and medals followed by a type set of the Allied Military currency of 1944 from ½ to 100 marks. Also shown are examples of West Germany's first banknotes from 1948, by Bank Deutsche Lander from ½ to 20 marks accompanied by a type set of early issued West German coins.

Scales were required for merchants to detect counterfeit and clipped gold coins. This set consists of a beam and a set of standard weights.

Visitor's Checklist
Hamburg History Museum, Holstenwall 24, D 20355 Hamburg, Germany

- ❶ ℂ +49 (0)40 428132 2380
- ◯ Tuesday-Saturday: 10 a.m.-5 p.m.; Sunday: 10 a.m.- 6 p.m.; on Christmas Day, Easter, Ascension Day, Pentecost, October 3 (German Unification Day):10 a.m.- 6 p.m.
- ● Monday; January 1, May 1, December 24, and 31.

💒 ♿ 📷 🛒 🍴

Public Transportation
- 🆄 U3-Yellow (St. Pauli)
- 🚌112 (Hamburgmuseum)

Internet
- ✉ info@hamburgmuseum.de
- 🌐 www.hamburgmuseum.de/index_e.html (also in German)

State Coin Collection and the Old Mint
Staatlichen Münzsammlung München
und Münzhof
Munich, Germany

The State Coin Collection in Munich is one of the oldest of its kind in Europe. Its origins go back to the second half of the 16th century when, in the Renaissance, members of royalty began collecting all sorts of rare and precious things. The collection currently consists of approximately 300,000 coins, medals, banknotes, securities and cut stones from as far back as the 3rd millennium BC, with its strongest areas being medals in addition to ancient and Bavarian coinage.

The permanent exhibition is divided among three exhibition rooms while a fourth room is used for special exhibitions. The text for all information is in German only.

The *Kapellenhof* (chapel courtyard) path that leads from the street entrance of the Residenz at the corner of Viscardigasse and Residenzstrasse to the entrance of the Museum under the archway in the background.

Room 1 – Special Exhibitions, Coin Cabinets, and Banknotes
This room is primarily used for special exhibitions, whose theme changes periodically. Similarly on display are a collection of coin cabinets, including lacquered Japanese cabinets and others made of rich inlaid wood.

In one corner of the room is a display of world banknotes, mostly from the 18th and 19th centuries, arranged in a large, heavy Plexiglass display. Of particular interest to American visitors are the following U.S. banknotes: Continental Currency 1776 one-third dollar, 1896 $1-Silver Certificate (Educational Series), and an 1864 $500 Confederate States of America banknote.

Room 2 – Medals and Plaques

Here are examples of European medals from the 15th to the 19th century: Switzerland, Austria, Italy, Poland, England, The Netherlands, Spain, and Portugal. Also, the display is strong in Germanic themes such as German religious and pilgrimage medals, event medals, featuring private individuals (17th-19th centuries), German electors (17th-19th centuries), and 16th-century medals of Nuremberg, Saxony, and Silesia.

Room 3 – Ancient Coins

This room's exhibit begins with the earliest evidence of coins, as stamped lumps of electrum around 630 BC from Lydia and the Greek cities on the West Coast of Asia Minor. Coins are displayed from other parts of the Greek empire including Attica, Thrace, Macedonia, Illyria, Thessaly, Sicily, Peloponnese, Crete, Aegean Islands, Etruria (Tyrrhenia), and lower Italy.

With the rise of Rome, coinage from both Republic and Imperial Rome and those illustrating city and provincial markings of the Roman Empire are shown. Additional specimens include Byzantine, East and West Celtic coins, as well as those of the Avars and Teutons of the 7th-8th centuries.

View of one corner of Room 4, the room holding medieval and modern coins.

Room 4 – Medieval Coins and Modern

This final room contains coins from approximately the mid-10th century to the present for much of Europe, Scandinavia, and both the Islamic and Christian periods of the Iberian Peninsula. The exhibit area is quite strong with representative coinage of Bavaria, such as the dukes and electors from the 11th century to 1918, Bavarian imperial cities (*Reichsstädte*) of Augsburg, Nuremberg, Regensburg, and the region of Swabia.

Nearby is the Old Mint (*Münzhof*) on Hofgraben 4, which was set up in 1809. This was previously the royal stables from 1563-1567 built in the Italian Renaissance style for Duke Albert V.

The courtyard of the Old Mint.

Visitor's Checklist: Residenz
State Coin Collection Munich, Residenzstraße 1, D-80333 Munich, Germany Street entrance is via Residenzstraße (where it meets Viscardigasse) and the Museum entrance made through the Kapellenhof.

- ❶ ☏ +49 (0)89 22 72 21
- ○ Tuesday-Sunday: 10 a.m.-5 p.m.; extended hours Thursday & Friday until 8:30 p.m.
- ● Monday
- ✋ ⑤ 📷 🛒
- 🐟 Monday-Thursday: 9 a.m.-4 p.m.; Friday: 9 a.m.-2 p.m.

Public Transportation: Residenz
- Ⓤ U3/U4/U5/U6 (Odeonsplatz); U3/U6 (Marienplatz)
- Ⓢ S1/S2/S4/S5/S6/S7/S8 Marienplatz)
- 🅱 100 (Odeonsplatz)
- Tram 19 (Nationaltheater)

Internet: Residenz
- ✉ info@staatliche-muenzsammlung.de
- 🌐 www.staatliche-muenzsammlung.de (in German only)

Visitor's Checklist: The Old Mint

The Old Mint (Münzhof), Hofgraben 4, 80539 Munich, Germany (At the corner of Hofgraben and Pfisterstrasse)

○ Monday-Thursday: 8 a.m.-4:15 p.m.; Friday: 8: a.m.-2 p.m.
● Saturday and Sunday.

✋ ⓖ 📷

Public Transportation: The Old Mint

Ⓤ U3/U6 (Marienplatz)
Ⓢ S1/S2/S4/S5/S6/S7/S8 (Marienplatz)
🅱🆄🆂 100 (Odeonsplatz)
Ⓣⓡⓐⓜ 19 (Nationaltheater)

Obverse of a 1593 6-thaler klippe of Wolf Dietrich von Raitenau, the Prince Bishop of Salzburg.

Germanic National Museum Coin Cabinet
Germanisches Nationalmuseum Münzkabinett
Nuremberg, Germany

The Germanic National Museum is the largest museum of cultural history in Germany. Its Department of Coins and Medals (*Münzkabinett*) comprises approximately 150,000 items made up of 100,000 coins, 15,000 notes and emergency notes, 20,000 medals, tokens and 5,000 characters, more than 6,000 seals and embossing dies as well as brands, counters, medals, order and decorations, and antique gems. A small fraction of these are exhibited in different rooms of the Museum, where they find themselves embedded in broader historical contexts with texts in both German and English. Other objects of the collection can be viewed in the Study Room by appointment.

Unlike most major numismatic collections, the Museum's coin collection was not built on an old royal collection, but was first created with the establishment of the Museum in 1852. The focus of the collection lies in the German-speaking world and includes the time of the Carolingians (8th and 9th centuries) until the present.

Front entrance of the Germanic National Museum on the narrow *Kartäusergasse*, or Carthusian's Alley.

Carolingian Art and Culture

Charlemagne, king of Franks since 768, introduced the denar as the standard coin for the whole empire. These coins bear his name and the city where they were minted. Examples on display in Room 4 are the silver denars of Charlemagne with multiple dates and mints (Milan, Bourges, and Paris), Louis the Pious (Paris, 814-840), Lothar I (Pavia, 840-855), Pippin I or II (Melle, 814-838 or 839-852), and Charles the Simple (Strasbourg, 898-923).

Coins of the Roman Iron Age

Roman coins minted since 216 BC include the silver denarius, bronze sestercius, and the copper as. While the denarius was initially based on pure silver, debasement lead to rampant inflation by 260 AD. Reforms by Diocletian (284-305) and Constantine (307-337) introduced a more stable gold standard.

In Room 8 is a display of 62 coins from the Roman Empire, beginning with the aureus of Augustus (27 BC-14 AD) and ending with the silver ½ siliqua of Severus III (461-465). Even though there were other emperors of the Western Empire that followed, no coins are given as examples. Coins are not provided for 31 of the Roman emperors cited that ruled between Augustus and Romulus Augustus (475-476).

A display of coins of 62 rulers of the Roman Empire.

Medallic Art and Badges

The Museum's first level (2nd floor, American) has several rooms (104, 106, 107 115, 118, and 121) showcasing medallic art from as early as the 16th century. Albrecht Dürer portraits greatly influenced contemporary makers of medals and medallions, particularly those in Nuremberg. Room 118 has a selection of funerary portrait medals by artists such as Sebastian Dadler, Matthes Gebel, and Christoph Ritter.

After the introduction of the Reformation in many locations, the poor could no longer be supported by monasteries. Beggars had to sew a badge on their clothing and received tokens for which they exchanged for bread. Examples of this badge and tokens are in Room 107.

A 1634 silver medal, "Death of Gustav II Adolph" by Sebastian Dadler, struck in Dresden.

Visitor's Checklist

Germanic National Museum, Kartäusergasse 1, 90402 Nürnberg, Germany. Numismatic exhibits can be found in Rooms 4 and 8 (ground floor) and in various rooms on the first floor.

- ❶ ☎ +49 (0)911-1331-0
- ○ Tuesday-Sunday: 10 a.m.-6 p.m.; extended hours: Wednesday until 9 p.m.
- ● Monday; Shrove Tuesday (Faschingsdienstag)*, December 25. Look at website for other special opening times (Sonderöffnung) and closures, as the dates will vary depending on the calendar. An asterisk (*) denotes a movable holiday date.

♨ ♿ ◻ 🎧 🛒 🍴

🍽 Monday-Friday: 9:30 a.m.-6 p.m.; extended hours Wednesday until 8 p.m.

Public Transportation
- **U** U1 (Lorenzkirche); U2/3 (Opernhaus)
- **Tram** 5/8/9 (Hauptbahnhof)

Internet
- ✉ Use the on-line contact form at: www.gnm.de/index.php?id=32
- ⊕ www.gnm.de/index.php?id=101 (in German only)

National Museum of Ireland, Collins Barracks
Airgead – A Thousand Years of Irish Coins & Currency
Ard Mhúsaem na hÉireann
Dublin, Ireland

The National Museum of Ireland in Dublin has an exhibition of coins and banknotes covering 1,000 years of Irish history. It is located at the Collins Barracks, which houses the Museum of Decorative Arts & History.

"Airgead (Gaelic for "money")—A Thousand Years of Irish Coins & Currency," tells the story of coins and money in Ireland from the 10th century to the present day. In four galleries, the exhibition includes specimens ranging from medieval coins and coin hoards, modern banknotes, tokens, and medals.

Courtyard and main entrance of the Museum of Decorative Arts & History at the Collins Barracks branch of the National Museum of Ireland.

Hammered and Milled Coins
Visitors first see a display titled, "Coins are Made to Move," explaining that coins are produced in large numbers; made to circulate widely; and allow people to buy and sell, passing from person to person with each transaction. Also, visitors are told that originally the amount of metal, usually silver, defined the coin's value. Like banknotes, they have no real value; only the face value assigned to them by the government. Also in this area is the 1926 Nobel Prize gold medal for literature awarded to countryman George Bernard Shaw.

In the next room are Anglo-Saxon and Norman coins from the 9th century. One case shows that medieval traders counted their coins using a board marked in squares called a "casting board," a simple device that was a form of calculator like an abacus, whereby merchants could perform complex arithmetic calculations. Other displays illustrate hammered coins, milled coins and medals. A theater shows the movie, "A Thousand Years of Irish Coinage."

The next room with eight wall displays covers the Irish period from 1450 to 1800. The common denominations during this period are shown with suitable specimens: crown, half crown, shilling, sixpence, groat, penny, and halfpenny. Despite repeated wars and rebellions, Ireland became more firmly tied to England. The coins people used reflected this political change and Irish coins gave way to standard English ones.

A five shilling "Inchiquin" money specimen, which was typically melted down from silver plate.

The Irish Halfpenny

"The Irish Halfpenny"display explains that throughout the 18th century, the distinctive Irish coin was the ubiquitous copper halfpenny as all the higher denomination silver and gold coins in circulation were standard British issues.

On display are specimens representing "gun money," town pence, varieties of tokens, and Dublin money, also known as "Inchiquin" money. These were melted down from silver plate and denominated in shillings, pence, or its weight in pennyweights.

Rare Irish Gold Coins

A floor display allows visitors a rare sight of examples of the only Irish gold coins ever minted in Ireland. During the chaos of the Civil War, the Irish Parliament in 1646 authorized two denominations: pistole and double pistole—a denomination taken from a standard Spanish gold coin of the period.

The last room ends with displays depicting Ireland's words and images on the nation's currency reflecting its history and aspirations from 1800 to 2002—the introduction of the euro.

The coins and banknotes circulating in Ireland mirror the country's political and social circumstances. There is even a display of how credit and debit cards have largely replaced physical money for substantial transactions while coins are increasingly used to buy goods and services from machines.

Symbolic Images on Banknotes

From its beginning, Irish banknotes used strong symbolic images drawn from many sources: history, mythology, landscape, architecture, and literature to assert the nation's pride in its heritage. Included are the "A" series (1927-1977), the "Ploughman" notes of the 1930s and 40s, which were the last issued by individual Irish banks; the "B" series (1976-1993); and the final "C" series (1992-2001) before the introduction of the euro.

Gun money small shilling of May 1690 with the portrait of James II (1685-1688).

Visitor's Checklist

National Museum of Ireland, Collins Barracks, Benburb Street, Dublin 7 Ireland. The Museum is directly across the River Liffey from the Guinness Storehouse. The exhibition is located in the South Block on the Museum's "first" floor (i.e., the second level).

- ❶ ☾ +353 (0)1-6777444
- ◯ Tuesday-Saturday: 10 a.m.-5 p.m.; Sunday: 2-5 p.m.
- ● Monday; bank holidays, Good Friday*, and December 25. An asterisk (*) denotes a movable holiday date.

✋ ⓖ ▣ ⊗ 🛒 🍴

Public Transportation

🚌 90 (Aston Quay); 25/25A/66/67 (Wellington Quay)

Ⓣram Museum (LUAS Red line)

Internet

✉ bookings@museum.ie

🌐 www.museum.ie/en/exhibition/list/exhibition-details-airgead.aspx (also in Gaelic)

Genoa, Italy • Musei di Strada Nuova - Palazzo Doria
Tursi Museum
Venice • Correr Museum
Additional institutions with limited information:
Bologna, Italy • Civic Archaeological Museum, Bologna
Milan • Milan Civic Archaeological Museum
Rome • National Museum of Rome, Balbi Crypt
• National Museum of Rome, Palazzo
Massimo alle Terme Rome

Italy

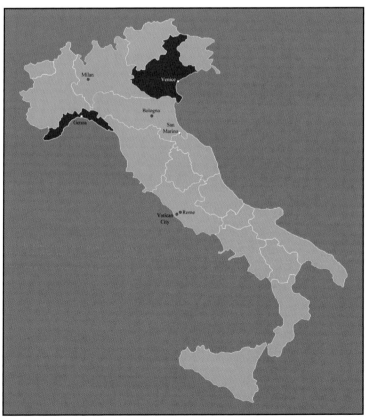

Map of 19 of the 20 regions (*regioni*) of Italy including the Republic of San Marino and the Vatican City. The regions having cities with numismatic venues with detailed descriptions are shown in dark blue and the cities indicated by a white dot. A red dot represents cities with limited information.

Musei di Strada Nuova -
Palazzo Doria Tursi Museum
Genoa, Italy

Genoa's most impressive museums are collectively located on a single street, Via Garibaldi, and are called the *Musei di Strada Nuova* (Museums of the New Street). The Strada Nuova are a UNESCO World Heritage Site. One of these is the Museo Palazzo Doria-Tursi, a museum devoted to a famous Genoa musician Niccolò Paganini, where among the relics is Paganini's violin, the "Canone," that is played once a year. Besides serving as the city hall and office of the mayor, the Museo Palazzo Doria-Tursi houses the city's coin collection.

The front entrance to the Museum on the Via Garibaldi.

The coin collection of the Municipality of Genoa was formed as a result of important legacies that date from the nineteenth century, when they were housed at the University Library.

The most significant pieces of the collection, including ancient coins, Genoese and Ligurian coins, medals, are presented in displays that allow for the viewing of both the obverse and reverse of the coin and magnification via a sliding lens. The introductory text of each historical section is in both Italian and English, but individual numismatic items are only labeled in Italian.

Greek and Roman Coins

The exhibition's coins begin with a gold daric of Darius I of Persia (521-486 BC). In the same group are approximately 30 Greek and Roman coins to include: a silver quinarius, Sicily mint, 211-210 BC; silver victoriatus, Luceria mint, 211-208 BC; gold aureus of Faustina I, Rome mint, 141 AD; gold aureus of Thracian, Rome mint, 111 AD; silver sestertius of Antoninus Pius, Rome mint, 140-144 AD; and a concluding gold solidus of Justinian, 527-565 AD.

Medieval Genoese Coins

Genoa began to mint coins in 1139 when the German king, Conrad III, made a concession to the Genoese to mint coins in his name such as a silver aquilino anti-government Ghibelline, 1330 AD.

Genoa, like Venice, was ruled by doges, or dukes, who were theoretically chosen from the general populace, but were effectively chosen from a few wealthy families. Originally, doges were elected for life. Simone Boccanegra was the first elected doge and the first to produce gold coins like his gold Genovino, 1339-1344 on display. There are coins of the succeeding perennial doges on display like the grossos of the doges Giovanni Valente (1350-1353) and Antoniotto Adorno (1378-1378), or the gold genovino of Nicolò Guarco (1378-1383).

A view of the gallery housing the Museum's numismatic collection.

The Biennial Doges (1528-1797)

Although originally elected for life, Andrea Doria in 1528 enacted the reform restricting the doges to rule for only two years. From then on, the rulers in Genoa were known as the biennial doges. The coins minted during this period are mostly distinguished by the magistrate's initials.

A number of examples on display are silver 1 scudo and doppia with various dates showing the city gate or tower on the obverse and a floreate cross on the reverse. Of particular note is a 1758 gold 25-lire coin.

Medals

Medals document the city's history and hand down the effigies of renowned Ligurians such as Christopher Columbus, Andrea Doria, and Niccolò Paganini. Of particular note is a specimen depicting the portrait of Odone of Savoy by Edoardo Chiossone and engraved by Guiseppe Collareta. There are also numerous medals from the Napoleonic era done by authoritative engravers such as Gerolamo Vassallo.

Obverse of a gold genovino of Simone Boccanegra (1339-1344) – Genoa's first doge.

Reverse of a 1758 gold 25 lire from the Genoese Republic.

Visitor's Checklist

Museo Palazzo Doria-Tursi, Via Garibaldi 9, 16124 Genoa, Italy
The numismatic exhibit of coins and medals, weights and measures is on the 3rd floor (Piano 3), Rooms 40-42 (Sale 40-42)

❶ ☏ +39 010 247 6351
◯ Tuesday-Friday: 9 a.m.-7 p.m.; Saturday and Sunday: 10 a.m.-7 p.m.
⬤ Monday
✋ ♿ 📷 🎧 🛒 🍴 (at Via Garibaldi 12)

Public Transportation

🚌 20/30/34/35/36 (Fontane Marose); 18/20/30/34/35/36/39/40 (Portello)

Internet

✉ museidistradanuova@comune.genova.it
🌐 www.museidigenova.it/spip.php?article63 (in Italian only)

Correr Museum
Museo Correr
Venice, Italy

The Piazza San Marco, or St. Mark's Square is the focal point for Venice's tourists with its many famous points of interest. In the center is St. Mark's campanile tower standing almost 100 meters high. At the east end is the doge's palace and St. Mark's Basilica. At the south entrance are two columns: a statue of St. Theodore atop the western column; a lion of St. Mark on the eastern one. The Correr Museum is one of three arcaded buildings at the Napoleonic Wing of the west end of the square.

The Correr Museum, as part of arcaded buildings, is located in the west end of the famed St. Mark's Square, and is also home for the ever present pigeons.

Spanning Almost a Millennium
The Museum's numismatic collection is contained in a single room with information in Italian only. On display is an almost complete series of coins minted by the Venetian Republic that is arranged chronologically clockwise from its beginnings circa 820 AD, with the oldest pieces in the display cases along the wall to the left as one enters the room. The series concludes with the defeat almost a millennium later by Napoleon in 1797.

New Coins and Denominations
The coins themselves mark out the development of the city's history in which trade

and Venice's strategic position were important. Also, the rulers were instrumental in the development of new coins and names for them.

The first coins to be minted in the name of a doge date from the reign of doge Vitale II Michiel (1156-1172), while the period of Enrico Dandolo (1192-1205) saw the introduction of a new, almost totally pure, but heavier silver coin—the ducato or grosso matapan, the latter term being of Muslim derivation and meaning "a seated figure."

In 1285 during the reign of doge Giovanni Dandolo, Venice then minted its own gold coin, the ducato d'oro, an exact duplicate of the gold florin of Florence. Eventually challenging the florin, the ducat—which in the time of doge Francesco Donato (1545-1553) took on the name of the zecchino, from the Italian *zecca* (mint), a coin whose very appearance remained unchanged for 250 years.

Ending with the coins minted under the last doge, Ludovico Manin in 1797, the coins are followed by two display cases dedicated to *oselle*, ("ducks" in the Venetian dialect), a sort of silver coin or medal. Since the second half of the 12th century there had been a tradition for the doge to present the patricians of the city with a New Year's gift of five marshland game birds, or ducks (*osei*). Eventually this was replaced by an equivalent in money and, from 1521 onwards, a special coin was minted for the occasion, the osella. The tradition remained in practice up to 1797.

The Museum's coins are housed in a single 2nd-floor gallery.

Tokens for the Poor

The last display case is dedicated to *tessere*—minted tokens of various kinds produced from the 14th century onwards. Included here are: rationing tessere, which poor families could then use in purchasing oil and salt; tessere that simply served as tokens in the exchange of goods; and tessere that indicated membership of some particular guild or Venetian scuola, or school.

A display case in the center of the room contains tools and dies from the Venetian Mint.

The Venetian gold zecchino, is from the Italian, *zecca* (mint), which was originally called a ducat after the ruling doge of Venice. This one was issued by Francesco Morosini, 1688-1694.

Visitor's Checklist

Correr Museum, San Marco 52, 30124 Venice, Italy
Public entrance is in the Napoleonic Wing at the Monumental Staircase. The numismatic exhibit is on the 2nd floor, Room 11.

  ❶ ℂ +39 041 2405211

  ◯ November 1-March 31: Daily 9 a.m.-5 p.m.; April 1-October 31: Daily 9 a.m.-7 p.m. Ticket office closes one hour before the Museum closes.

  ● January 1, December 25.

  ✋ ♿ (limited) 🅾 🍴 🍽

Public Transportation

  🚌 Vaporetto 3/4 (St. Mark/San Marco)

Internet

  ✉ info@fmcvenezia.it

  🌐 correr.visitmuve.it (also in Italian)

National Museum of History and Art Luxembourg
Musée National d'Histoire et d'Art Luxembourg
Luxembourg City, Luxembourg

The Luxembourg Society of Natural Sciences in 1854 established a museum that became the nucleus of the Luxembourg State Museums. The collections in 1922 were moved to the Marché-aux-Poissons (Fish Market). In 1966 the Medals Cabinet (*Cabinet des Médailles*) as it was then called, became a full section in the Museum. In 1988 the State Museums were divided into the National Museum of History and Art, which remained at the Fish Market, and the National Museum of Natural History, which moved to Münster Street in 1996.

The National Museum History and Art Luxembourg in the Old City Fish Market.

City on the UNESCO World Heritage List
The city of Luxembourg itself was placed on the UNESCO World Heritage List in 1994 on account of the historical importance of its fortifications.

The MNHA (*Musée National d'Histoire et d'Art*) preserves a large and rich collection of artistic, archaeological and historical items, including a numismatic collection. Currently, there are three rooms dedicated to numismatics with texts primarily in French. As a specific section of the Museum, the Coin Cabinet of Luxembourg is involved in the preservation and the conservation of coins and medals. Some 150,000 items compose the collection, which increased strongly during the last two decades, primarily as a result of new acquisitions as a result of archaeological excavations.

Celtic, Roman, Medieval and Modern Money

The medals collection consists of coins, medals, tokens, balances and monetary weights, dies used for minting coins, notes, decorations, religious medals, pilgrim insignia and other seals. The numismatic exhibition is spread throughout the entire Museum and displays a representative sample of Celtic, Roman, medieval and modern money. A very special area houses a selection of Roman intaglios found in Luxembourg. The emphasis is placed on the production of money in Luxembourg from the 13th to the 17th centuries, as well as on the circulation of money in the region dating from the Celtic era. A number of exhibits originate from archaeological digs carried out in Luxembourg, in particular in Titelberg, the site of a large Celtic settlement in the extreme southwest of Luxembourg, and in Dalheim, the site of Luxembourg's most important Roman ruins. Furthermore, a group of medals recalling the conquests of Louis XIV in Luxembourg as well as decorations from the end of the 19th century give an overview of the other aspects of the collection.

A 1790 copper 1 sol of Leopold II, Gunzburg Mint.

Visitor's Checklist

Musée national d'histoire et d'art, Marché-aux-Poissons (The Fish Market), L- 2345 Luxembourg. The Museum's coin collection is in three rooms on the first floor although in small groups, coins and other numismatic items are located on other levels integrated with other historical artifacts.

- ❶ ℂ +352 47 93 30-316
- ○ Tuesday-Sunday: 10 a.m.-6 p.m.; December 26: 10 a.m.-6 p.m.
- ● Monday; January 1, November 1, 2, December 24, 25, and 31.
- ✴ ✴ (Thursday: 5 p.m-8 p.m.) ⓖ ⬨ ⊙ ⛑ 🛒 🍴

Public Transportation

🚌19/20 (Arrêt Kasinosgaass)

A 1643 silver ½ Patagon, struck in Luxembourg under Philip IV.

Internet
- ✉ musee@mnha.etat.lu
- ⊕ http://www.mnha.public.lu/collections/cabinet_medailles/index.html (in French only)

Monaco Museum of Stamps and Coins
Musée des Timbres et des Monnaies
Monte Carlo, Monaco

Although the tiny Principality of Monaco has been continually ruled since 1297 by the House of Grimaldi, the *Musée des Timbres et des Monnaies*—Museum of Stamps and Coins—is a rather new venue, established and open to the public only in 1996. The Museum's collection of both stamps and coins are from the private collection of the late Prince Rainier III, a consummate collector who died in 2005 after having ruled since 1949.

The Musée des Timbres et des Monnaies – Monaco's Museum of Stamps and Coins, which opened in 1996.

Both Stamps and Coins

The layout of the Museum is divided into two major areas. The larger area is devoted to Monégasque philatelic history from its first stamps of 1885 issued under Charles III (1856-1889) to the present. The display boasts a complete collection of Monégasque stamps, as well as rare historical proclamations, hand cancellation stamps, hallmark proofs, printing plates, and color tests. There is also a copperplate rotary press that was used for printing Monégasque stamps for more than 60 years.

Occupying the smaller area of eight floor-mounted display cases, the numismatist should enjoy the exhibit of the equally rich history of Monégasque coins. As with the exhibit of stamps, all legends are in French. The minting of coins begins with the reign of Honoré II in 1641 and includes a complete chronology to the present that also takes in the change in 2002 to the euro. Although Monaco is not a member of the European Union, Monaco did acquire the right to mint standard euro coins with Monégasque designs on the national reverse.

Some of the outstanding early specimens include the 1649 and 1650 silver écus of Honoré II, a 1665 demi (half) écu of Louis I, and a 1682 silver (or "white") scudo, an écu equal to 3 livres of Louis I.

A view of the gallery devoted to Monégasque coins that began in 1641 during the reign of Honoré II.

18th and 19th Century Coins

Notable examples from the 18th century of the reign of Honoré V include an 1837 5-franc uniface having a reeded edge, a rare 1837-M 5-franc essai, and a rare bronze 40-franc pattern, all of which were designed by Emile Rogat. There are also several dies used to strike coins and medals on display, including the obverse and reverse dies of the 1838 copper 1-decime coin. Examples of the first Monégasque gold coins—the 20- and 100-francs minted in Paris during the reign of Charles III in 1878 and 1882 respectively—are included.

Honoring Princess Grace

As with its stamps, Monaco's numismatic offerings were greatly expanded during the reign of Prince Rainier III with its many proof coins and commemorative issues. Unlike previous regular Monégasque issues, many of these commemorative issues show the image of Monaco's prince and princess, Rainier III and Princess Grace—the former movie star Grace Kelly. An unusual issue is the 1982 silver 10-franc coin showing the lone bust head of Princess Grace, in honor of her tragic death. This is the first time a Monégasque coin displayed the image of its princess by herself.

For the paper money collector, Monaco does not have much of a history of issuing its own banknotes, relying instead on using French notes prior to the euro. There is one exception and it is devoted to one display case.

A 1682 silver scudo, or écu equal to 3 livres of Louis I.

Visitor's Checklist
Musée des Timbres et des Monnaies, 11 Terrasse de Fontvieille, Monte Carlo, 98000 Monaco

❶ ℂ +377 98 98 41 50

○ Daily: 10 a.m.-5 p.m. (October 1-June 30); 10 a.m.-6 p.m. (July 1-September 30).

✋ ⓗ 📷 🛒

Internet
✉ mtm@gouv.mc

🌐 www.oetp-monaco.com/index.php?route=information/
information&information_id=10 (also in French)

The obverse die of a rare 1934 500-franc essais designed by Maubert.

Teylers Museum
Haarlem, The Netherlands

The Teylers Museum is the first and oldest museum in The Netherlands. It was built in 1784 during what was the "Age of Enlightenment" to house exhibits charged by Pieter Teyler van der Hulst (1702-1778), a wealthy banker and merchant.

A view of the entrance to Teylers Museum on the bank of one of Haarlem's many canals.

The Numismatic Cabinet

The Numismatic Cabinet manages one of the most important medals and coin collections in the Netherlands. The basis for this was established with the private collection of Pieter Teyler van der Hulst. Particularly noteworthy are the medal collection of Dutch art and the West Frisian and gelder coins. However, it was not until 1886 that a separate gallery was created to display the collection.

Originally the cabinets had drawers that visitors could open up to see the coins. Today, only the top showcases give an overview of the coins and tokens. The remaining objects from the trays are now safely stored in a vault.

The collection contains a very fine series of Dutch medals, with an emphasis on historical and genealogical medals. In addition, there are smaller numbers of counters, tokens and foreign medals. Two highly specialized collections are those of the West Frisian and guilder coins. Roman and Dutch coins from other regions are also part of the collection.

Of the 7,937 medals and 7,414 coins in the collection, 646 objects are on display in 35 display cases, with objects searchable on the Museum's web site. The text of the displays are in Dutch only.

The Museum's coin cabinet, established as a separate gallery in 1886.

Origin and Composition of the Collection

1,613 objects, mainly medals, are from the collection of Pieter Teyler van der Hulst. 2,295 coins of the county and duchy gulders are from the collection of Theodorus Roest, the first president of the Dutch Royal Numismatic Society and the first curator of Teylers' numismatic collection. This is the world's most complete collection of gulders coins.

558 Roman and Byzantine and 675 West Frisian coins are from the collection of Adriaan Enschedé, a collector and member of Teylers Second Society. Enschedé was the first to open the doors of the cabinets of the numismatic collection in the 1870s, almost 100 years after Teylers' death, and paved the way to appoint a numismatic curator. Together with Roest, he collected almost every medal described in the "Van Loon" books about Dutch medals. In total, they added over 9,000 objects to the collection. Finally, 1,485 coins from the county of Holland are from the collection of Wim Roodenburg, a loan from the Roodenburg-van Looy foundation.

The Museum has an audio tour, also in the numismatic cabinet, which is available in English, German, French and Dutch.

In December 2011, the Museum was nominated to be added to the list of UNESCO World Heritage Centers.

The obverse of an 1808 silver ducat from the Kingdom of Holland, Utrecht Mint.

Visitor's Checklist

Teylers Museum, Spaarne 16, 2011CH Haarlem, The Netherlands. The Coins and Medals Gallery is in Room 8 on the ground floor close to the Oval Room.

ⓘ ℂ +31 (0)23-5319010

◯ Tuesday-Saturday: 10 a.m.-5 p.m.; Sunday and public holidays: 12 noon-5 p.m.

● Monday; January 1, and December 25.

✋ ⓖ 🗓 📷 ⊗ 🎧 🛒

The obverse of a 1684 silver two guilders from Holland of the Dutch Republic.

Public Transportation

🚌 73 (Teylers Museum)

Internet

✉ info@teylersmuseum.nl

🌐 www.teylersmuseum.eu/index.php?item=68&lang=en&ci=1 (also in Dutch)

State Museum of San Marino
Museo di stato di San Marino
San Marino City, San Marino

At 24 square miles (61 square kilometers), San Marino is the third smallest state in Europe. Only the Vatican City and Monaco are smaller. Founded in 301 AD, it is the world's oldest surviving sovereign state and constitutional republic.

The State Museum of San Marino situated in the city's Piazetta del Titano.

Not a Member of the EU but Allowed to Use Euros

Although San Marino is not a member of the European Union, the Council of the European Union has allowed it to use the euro as its currency and also granted it the right to use its own designs on the reverse of the coins. Before the euro the Sammarinese lira was pegged to, and exchangeable with the Italian lira at par.

Opening of the Museum

The State Museum was inaugurated in 1899 in the Palazzo Valloni, seat of the State Library. After becoming an autonomous entity in 1982, it was relocated to the ancient Palazzo Pergami-Belluzzi, its alternate name, and was reopened to the public on March 18, 2001.

Numismatic exhibits can be found in two locations in the Museum. On the ground floor, coins are included among archaeological exhibits in rooms I and II where the text is in Italian. Room I concerns itself with the Neolithic to the Roman Republic and Imperial periods (5th century BC-4th century AD).

Room II features the Roman Period and the site in Domagnano, a San Marino castelli, or municipality. The cases display artifacts and coins found during the most recent archaeological excavations, in particular those from the site in Domagnano. Silver coins of King Berengar of Italy (888-915) were found along with those of from the Republican and Imperial Roman periods.

Gallery view of San Marino coins, tokens, and medals in the State Museum's lower level.

San Marino Coins and Medals

In room XVI on the lower level, this gallery exhibits some precious and ancient San Marino coins and medals issued between 1864 and 1939, as well as recently purchased medals, mainly papal and of the *Risorgimento* (resurgence)—the 19th-century movement for Italian unification that culminated in the establishment of the Kingdom of Italy in 1861.

After becoming king of Italy, Victor Emmanuel II in 1862 allowed the free circulation of San Marino coins in the Kingdom of Italy. With a subsequent convention concluded in 1939, San Marino stopped minting all but gold coins, and did not resume minting until 1972.

The oldest coin minted by San Marino is a 5-centime piece, dated 1864. On display is a rare and interesting 1867 silvered copper proof 5-lira "San Marino scudo" which was never minted. Only six examples of this coin are known, among which only the silver specimen was part of the collection of Victor Emmanuel III, king of Italy (1900-1946).

Among the medals minted by San Marino, the oldest one dates back to 1865, which celebrated the 600th anniversary of the birth of the Italian poet Dante Alighieri. Among the medals not minted by the Republic is the three-medal set celebrating the 100th Anniversary of the first convention signed with the Kingdom of Italy on April 11, 1862.

There is also an eight-sided glass pyramid case of Napoleonic, Garibaldi, and Risorgimento medals from 1797 to 1910.

A gold 1925 San Marino 10-lire coin, minted in Rome, with an image of St. Marinus on the obverse.

Visitor's Checklist

San Marino State Museum (Palazzo Pergami Belluzzi), Piazetta del Titano 1, San Marino City, San Marino. Numismatic exhibits are found on the ground floor: Rooms I, II; and 1st floor underground: Room XVI

  ❶ ☾ +378 (0)549 883835, +378 (0)549 882670

  ○ Daily: 9 a.m.-5 p.m. (January 2-June 7); 8 a.m.-8 p.m. (June 8-September 13); 9 a.m.-5 p.m. (September 14-December 31).

  ● January 1, November 2 (in the afternoon), and December 25.

  ✸ ⑤ 📷 🛒

Internet

  ✉ info@museidistato.sm

  ⊕ www.museidistato.sm/Museo_trad/mds/pianoprimosotto-sala-16.htm

Madrid's Numismatic Flea Markets:
Plaza Mayor and El Rastro
Madrid, Spain

Visitors to Spain's capital will be able to experience two distinctly different flea markets that are of interest to numismatists. The good thing is that both are held on Sunday. The bad thing is that because of large crowds, skilled pickpockets are a common hazard.

A panoramic view of the Plaza Mayor.

The Plaza Mayor Flea Market

One of Madrid's famous tourist attractions, the Plaza Mayor is an enclosed rectangular square with nine entrances that was originally built in 1619 and last reconstructed in 1790 after a series of fires. There are three stories with residential units having over 230 balconies facing the plaza above arcades that surrounds it. Besides its current name, the plaza had been known by many others, including Plaza del Arrabal, Plaza de la Constitución, Plaza Real, and Plaza de la República.

Over the centuries the plaza has been graced with the royal court, bullfights, and the Spanish Inquisition, where heretics were tried and executed.

Today, every Sunday morning, rain or shine, many of Madrid's coin and stamp buyers and sellers converge on the Plaza Mayor's arcades for the weekly flea market. This is nothing fancy. Some sellers operate using a simple card table and a few notebooks filed with coins; other have more elaborate setups. Most of the items are Spanish coins, banknotes, postcards, bottle caps, and stamps, but on any given day, some dealers will have non-Spanish items, even U.S. mint and proof sets. It gives a good idea what some Spaniards collect. Like most flea markets, some haggling is encouraged.

When tired or in need of a brief rest, there are several cafes in the Plaza's arcades in which to grab a snack. Also there are several numismatic and philatelic shops in the arcades and on the side streets within one or two blocks of the Plaza. One is Filatelia Arias at Plaza Mayor 28, and its sister store, El Clavileño, is around the corner at Calle Felipe III nº 1.

Eager buyers look over the offerings of one seller's table at the Plaza Mayor flea market.

Visitor's Checklist: Plaza Mayor
Plaza Mayor, Madrid, Spain
○ Sunday and holidays: about 9 a.m.-3 p.m.

Public Transportation: Plaza Mayor
BUS 1-Blue/2-Red/3-Yellow/commuter lines C-3, C-4 (Puerta del Sol)
Ⓜ EMT 17/18/23/31/35 (Plaza Mayor)

El Rastro de Madrid Flea Market

Every Sunday morning and on public holidays, tens of thousands of bargain hunters converge on one of Europe's biggest flea markets at the Plaza de Cascorro. The el Rastro del Madrid market, which goes back to the Middles Ages, has up to 3,500 different stalls and runs along the Ribera de Curtidores (Riverside of Tanners) between Calle Embajadores and the Ronda de Toledo.

The name *el Rastro*, meaning "the trail" or "line," probably owes its origin to the trail of blood that was left on the street when slaughtered cattle were transported from the slaughterhouse to the tannery at the Ribera de Curtidores.

Unlike the Plaza Mayor market held under the protection of the arcades, this is an "open air" affair with many things, new and used, besides coins for sale. On any given market day, visitors may have to really look hard to find anyone selling coins at el Rastro, but then, some people can't resist hunting the flea market for a good bargain or a souvenir. Remember, haggling is expected. As a suggestion, start at about 30 percent below the asking price.

The el Rastro flea Market, one of Europe's largest.

Visitor's Checklist: El Rastro

El Rastro Flea Market, Plaza de Cascorro, Madrid, Spain. The main street of the flea market is Ribera de Curtidores.

◯ Sunday and public holidays: about 9 a.m.-3 p.m.

Public Transportation: El Rastro

Ⓜ 1-Blue (Tirso de Molina), 3-Yellow (Embajadores, Lavapiés), 5-Green (La Latina, Puerta del Toledo); commuter lines C-5 (Embajadores)

Internet: El Rastro

⊕ www.elrastro.org

The Royal Coin Cabinet
Kungliga Myntkabinettet
Stockholm, Sweden

The Royal Coin Cabinet is the national museum of economy with a special interest in history of money, history of finance, economic and social history and the art of medals. It is one of Sweden's oldest museums with collections dating back to the 1570s. Commissioned by King John III (1568-1592), old coins were accumulated to justify Sweden's right to the three crowns in the national coat of arms. The oldest inventory was drawn up in 1630 when the collection contained only 57 coins and medals.

Although it was once located in the Royal Palace, and then in several other locations, the Museum moved to its current home on Castle Hill in Stockholm's Gamla Stan, or the Old Town section in 1996.

The collection consists of more than 600,000 objects from around the world from the first known coins to the present. The largest and most important part of the collection is comprised of coins, but there are also other means of payment, e.g., paper money, ethnographical money and share certifications. Another essential part are the medals.

The Royal Coin Cabinet on Stockholm's Castle Hill across from the Royal Palace.

Money of the World

In many places around the world the concept of money existed long before actual coins. But what is money? And who rules the flow of money? These issues are addressed in the exhibition.

213

Light is shed on different aspects of the monetary economy, such as the history of precious metals and their relevance to money. The displays exhibit the Greek tetradrachms, which served as trade coins during the 5th century BC in the eastern Mediterranean area and how Roman silver and gold coins helped shape an empire. There are trade coins from Florence and Venice dating back to the late Middle Ages.

One section of the gallery containing the largest colection of Swedish plate money and the world's largest coin.

Swedish coins

This exhibition displays the function of Swedish monetary economy, both in Sweden and the rest of the world. In a central section, every type of Swedish coin is shown, from the first Swedish coin, a silver penning of King Olof Skötkonung, aka Olaf Eiríksson (995-1022), to those of King Carl XVI Gustaf (1973-present).

Important events in the Swedish history of coins and banknotes are displayed in different cases: the bracteate coinage of the 12th century, the age of many denominations of King Gustav Vasa, coins of the Swedish possessions, and the emergency money of King Charles XII.

The Financial Realm

The Royal Coin Cabinet is the only European museum concentrating on financial history. We live in an economically complicated world with concepts such as options, GNP, inflation and currency markets confronting us daily. This exhibit attempts to explain and put these ideas into perspective.

Important financiers are introduced from the 17th century to the present, explaining trade with foreign countries and presenting Sweden's first banks—Stockholm Banco and Rikets Ständers Bank, and the National Bank of Sweden, which is the world's oldest central bank (from 1668). Also, the banknote is a Swedish innovation from 1661, and was first issued by the Stockholm Banco. An impressive collection of copper plate money from 1611-1751 is exhibited, the largest weighing 19.7 kg (43.4 lbs).

The Art of Medals

The medal, probably the oldest form of mass-produced art, is prominently repre-sented. The works of numerous Swedish artists such as Erik Lindberg, Carl Eldh, Carl Milles, and Bror Hjorth, are displayed. Being the country of the Nobel Prize, many Nobel Prize medals are also shown.

The obverse of Sweden's first gold coin, the 1568 ungyersk gyllen with the laureate face of Eric XIV.

Visitor's Checklist

The Royal Coin Cabinet, Slottsbacken 6, 111 30 Stockholm, Sweden

❶ ℂ +46 (0)8 519 553 00

○ Daily: 10 a.m.-4 p.m.

● January 1, Good Friday*, Holy Saturday (the day after Good Friday)*, Easter*, May 1, Midsummer's Day (the Saturday during the period from June 20-26)*, December 24, 25. An asterisk (*) denotes a movable holiday date.

✋ ✋ (Monday) ♿ 📷 ✑ (by appointment) 🎧 🛒 🍴

Public Transportation

Ⓜ T-bana 13/14/17/18/19 (Gamla Stan)

🚌 2/43/55/71/76/96/191/192/194/195 (Slottsbacken)

Internet

✉ info@myntkabinettet.se

⊕ www.myntkabinettet.se/web/English.aspx (also in Swedish, French)

Uppsala University Coin Cabinet
Uppsala Universitets Myntkabinett
Uppsala, Sweden

As Sweden's fourth largest city, Uppsala is home to the oldest university in Scandinavia. Founded in 1477, Uppsala University has a coin cabinet with one of Sweden's greatest coin and medal collections.

The University Main Building, home of the Uppsala University Coin Cabinet.

The Coin Cabinet

The Coin Cabinet's history goes back with its first object, the Augsburg Art Cabinet, or *Kunstschränke* (cabinet of curiosities), which was given to King Gustav II Adolf in 1632 during the 30 Years War. This was later donated to Uppsala University in 1694 by Karl XI.

The collections have grown and now include coins and medals worldwide, and coins dating back to the inception of coinage about 2,600 years ago. In total, the collection now includes close to 40,000 objects. The collection is, above all, strong in rare and unusually well-preserved Swedish coins and medals.

Through its privileged position, the University has retained both royal medals and other medals, which have then been preserved, almost entirely untouched in the collections. A great many of the coins and medals are unique, both those which were minted in Sweden and those which were minted for Sweden during its "Era of Great Power" (1611-1718) in the Swedish possessions.

Two Numismatic Exhibitions

The University has two numismatic exhibitions. The primary exhibition of coins and medals from the Middle Ages up to the present day is at the University's Main Building. On display is a rich selection of Sweden's plate money with some weighing up to 20 kg (44 lbs), rare and unique coins testifying to Swedish history including those of the Carolingians, German Viking coins, Anglo-Saxon Viking coins, Islamic Viking coins, and coins from both the Swedish Viking Age and Middle Ages.

Swedish coins from the 1500s to today are also shown. As for paper money, on display is the world's first banknote, the world's first bill type, an 8-dalers copper plate of the type that prompted the bill, and a German inflation note of one billion marks.

Large Selection of Medals

There is a large selection from the Coin Cabinet's collection of medals on display, such as those depicting women who have distinguished themselves, from Greta Garbo to the singer/actor Alice Babs. Royal medals, many related to California or the University, the medals of Carl Linnaeus, art medals, reward medals, including the Nobel Prize medals of Allvar Gullstrand (1911, Medicine) and Theodor H. E. ("The") Svedberg (1926, Chemistry).

The text of the displays is only in Swedish and visitors are always guided by staff who are able to provide translations into either English or German.

The other exhibition comprises two showcases of ancient Greek and Roman coins in the Museum Gustavianum, the University's oldest preserved building built in 1625 and named after King Gustav II Adolf.

A view of the Uppsala University Coin Cabinet.

The 1926 Nobel Prize Medal for Chemistry awarded to Theodor H. E. ("The") Svedberg, who did his work at Uppsala University.

Visitor's Checklist

Uppsala University Coin Cabinet, Biskopsgatan 3, SE-753 10 Uppsala, Sweden. This is located in the University's Main Building, not the University Museum (Museum Gustavianum). Access is provided via the handicap entrance at the corner of Övre slottsgatan and St. Olofsgatan.

- ❶ ☎ +46 (0)18 471 75 71 (for both the Coin Cabinet and Museum Gustavianum)
- ○ Tuesday-Sunday: 11 a.m.-4 p.m.; for June-August, Tuesday-Sunday: 10 a.m.-4 p.m.
- ● Monday; closed during the winter season (November 1-March 31) but open by appointment.

🖐 ♿ 🐚 📷 🚭 🍴

Museum Gustavianum, Akademigatan 3, SE-753 10 Uppsala, Sweden. This Museum contains two showcases of ancient Greek and Roman coins.

- ○ Tuesday-Sunday: 11 a.m.-4 p.m.; for June-August, Tuesday-Sunday: 10 a.m.-4 p.m.
- ● Monday

🖐 ♿ 🐚 📷 🚭 🛒

Public Transportation

🚌 22/41 (Universitetet) for the Coin Cabinet in the Main Building
🚌 41 (St. Eriks Torg) for the Museum Gustavianum

Internet

✉ museum@gustavianum.uu.se
🌐 www.myntkabinettet.uu.se/en (also in Swedish)

Switzerland

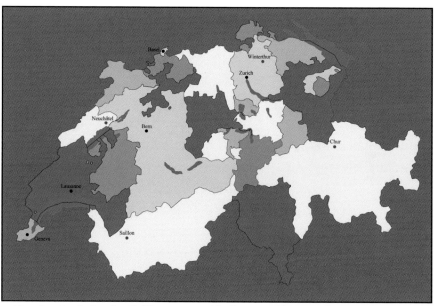

Map showing Switzerland's 23 cantons and half cantons. The cities having numismatic venues with detailed descriptions indicated by a black dot. A red dot represents cities with limited information.

Basel, Switzerland	• Basel Historical Museum
Bern	• Bernisches Historisches Museums
Lausanne	• Cantonal Money Museum, Cabinet of Medals
Zurich	• MoneyMuseum
	• Swiss National Museum in Zurich

Additional institutions with limited information:

Chur, Switzerland	• Rätisches Museum, Münzkabinett
Geneva	• Art and History Museum of Geneva
Neuchâtel	• Museum of Art and History
Saillon	• Museum of Counterfeit Money
Winterthur	• Coin Cabinet and Collection of Antiquities of the City of Winterthur

Basel Historical Museum
Historisches Museum Basel
Basel, Switzerland

Since 1894, the main building of the Basel Historical Museum has been located in a former church known as the *Barfüsserkirche*, or litertally translated, "barefoot church." The Museum stands on the site of an original church dedicated in 1256 and later, a Franciscan monastery. Its name is taken from the monastery of the Franciscan Order Barfüsserkirche before the great Basel earthquake in 1356.

Coins and medals in two rooms are represented as objects of historical and cultural interest. Under the title "The World's History in Your Hand," coins are presented as testimonies of the past, one of the main interests of collecting coins. In this sense a big variety of historical aspects of coins and money are displayed in an intuitive way with headlines, explanations and with many examples. Currently, it is thought to be one of the largest permanent exhibition of coins and medals in Switzerland, with more than 2,100 numismatic objects on display.

The Barfüsserkirche, home to the Basel Historical Museum.

In a similar way, medals are represented as art and propaganda, putting in evidence the main interests and intentions for their production, departing from Pisanello and the early Renaissance artists through 16th-century artists like Benvenuto Cellini and Hans Schwarz. Highlights include excellent classical coins like the Dionysos stater of Naxos and an Euainetos dekadrachm of Syracuse, a solidus of the Merovingian king Theudebert I to 17th-century siege money (*Belagerungsklippen*), as well as Swiss medieval and early modern rarities.

Coin cabinet section featuring women on medals and German portrait medals.

The medals include Erasmus' personal medal and gifts, the finest collection of struck Padovans of Giovanni da Cavino, an impressive series of Leone Leoni and northern Italian Manierism artists, top quality German portrait medals and baroque medals of the best German and Swiss medallists until the famous modern artist Hans Frei (Basel, 1868-1947). All objects are of fine quality, particularly the 16th-century medals, mainly from Amerbach's contemporary collection.

The majority of the coins and medals are located in two rooms close to the virtual cabinet of rarities and coins, while other forms of money are integrated. The objects are displayed in an impressive and modern way, with intuitive touchscreens throughout the exhibition, explaining each object in its historical context. Additionally there are also practical tools like audio points with historical scenes explaining technical and economic aspects, a display with touchable copies as well as a forgery display with a self-test function asking, "Which coin is a forgery?" There is even the possibility to strike a medieval Basel penny on special occasions.

Additional coins and medals are scattered throughout the other parts of the permanent exhibition, for example, in the context of the symbols used by the bishops and city of Basel or in the context of historical events like the Reformation.

Visitor's Checklist
Historisches Museum Basel, Barfüsserplatz, CH-4051 Basel, Switzerland
🛈 ☏ +41 (0)61 205 86 00
◯ Tuesday-Sunday: 10 a.m.-5 p.m.
⬤ Monday; Good Friday*, May 1, Ascension Day*, August 1 (Swiss National Day), December 24, 26, 31. An asterisk (*) denotes a movable holiday date.
✋ ⓖ ⋛ 📷 ⊘ 🛒 🍴

The 1685 official honorary gold medal of the city of Basel by Gabriel LeClerc.

Public Transportation
Tram 3/6/8/11/14/16 (Barfüsserplatz); 10 (Theater)

Internet
✉ historisches.museum@bs.ch
🌐 www.hmb.ch/en/sammlung/muenzen-und-medaillen.html
(also in French, German)

223

Bernisches Historisches Museums
Musée d'Histoire de Berne
Bern, Switzerland

The Bernisches Historisches Museums is considered to be the second largest historical museum in Switzerland. Built in 1894 in a neo-Gothic style, it looks like a fortified medieval castle. The Museum contains collections related to the history of Bern from the era of prehistory to the present and other permanent exhibitions from Asia, Oceania, Egypt, the Orient, and America.

The main entrance on the Helvetiaplatz to the Bernisches Historisches Museums.

It Started in the City Library

Its numismatic collection numbers approximately 80,000 specimens from civilization's first known coins dating around 7th century BC to the present. The collections were started by the City Library and came to the Historical Museum in 1898. They include the most important collection worldwide of Bernese coins and medals as well as coin and medal dies. It is also one of the most important collections of Swiss and ancient Greek and Roman coins in Switzerland. Moreover it comprises an internationally renowned and nationally unique assemblage of Oriental coins. The drawers of the numismatic collection cover the whole of history from ancient Greece to the European Monetary Union. The coin collection is an important source for researchers both in Switzerland and abroad.

224

The storage facility for the coins and medals covers an area of 16 square meters (172 square feet) with the individual pieces neatly stored in a total of 2,000 drawers. To ensure order in the collections, each object is placed in a separate compartment.

Coin hoard from Moosseedorf, hidden around 1661.

From the Stone Age to the Present

There are over 330 coins, medals, dies, and banknotes from the Museum's collection on display as follows: coins from the Stone Age, Celts, and Romans; coins from the Middle Ages to the Old Regime; captured treasure—court art in Bern; banknotes from Bern and the 20th-century coins as art from Asia and Oceania; and coin treasures from the tombs of ancient Egypt.

Among the Highlights of the exhibition are: the 1493 guldiner of the city of Bern from the exhibit, "From the Middle Ages to the Ancient Régime," and the coin treasure from Moosseedorf, a hoard that was hidden around 1661.

The obverse of a 1493 silver guldiner from Bern.

Visitor's Checklist

Bernisches Historisches Museums, Helvetiaplatz 5, CH-3005 Bern, Switzerland

ℹ️ ☎ +41 (0)31 350 77 11

○ Tuesday-Sunday: 10 a.m.-5 p.m., and on all national public holidays.

● Monday; for other closures, please check on www.bhm.ch/en.

♿ ♿ (questionable entrance access) 📷 (permanent exhibits OK)

📵 (not for temporary exhibits) 🛒 🍴

Public Transportation

🚌 19 (Helvetiaplatz)

Ⓣram 6/7/8 (Helvetiaplatz)

Internet

✉️ info@bhm.ch

🌐 www.bhm.ch/en/collections/numismatic-collection/ (also in French, German)

Cantonal Money Museum, Cabinet of Medals
Musée monétaire cantonal, Cabinet des médailles
Lausanne, Switzerland

Formerly the Cabinet des Médailles Cantonal (Cantonal Money Museum), the Money Museum of the Canton Vaud is part of a complex of museums of the Rumine Palace that was completed in 1904 at Riponne Square.

The Rumine Palace on Riponne Square.

The Money Museum's 21 centuries of history is evoked through its rich collections of coins, medals, tokens, seals, paper money, weights, balances, and ledgers. In addition, there is a numismatic library with more than 20,000 volumes. All of these factors give the Museum three distinctions: (1) it is one of the oldest museums in the canton; (2) its collection is one of the largest numismatic museums in Switzerland; and (3) its library is the largest numismatic library in Switzerland.

The Museum currently has four permanent exhibits: Barter and Monies; Money, of the Invention to Use; Monetary and Trade Workshops; and *Des Oberland* (the Bernese/ the upper country) in the Canton of Vaud. All of these serve to help answer many questions, such as: What is paleo-money? What is the earliest piece discovered in the Canton of Vaud? Do we find many treasures?

The permanent exhibitions, which draw on cantonal monetary collections, feature coins dating from antiquity to the present times. Its collections contain more than 80,000 monetary objects and approximately 1,200 new items are added each year. It is also the legal depositary for all coins found in Vaud canton. This currently represents more than 150 hoards and 10,000 scattered coins.

The Money Museum exhibition presents the first stages of the creation of money, that is, the commodities used to barter with the invention of coinage, manufacturing techniques, and the various functions of money. Following the course of history, the exhibition leads visitors to the first Greek coins around the seventh century BC up to the creation of the euro, with an emphasis on regional findings.

As part of the educational activities, children can make casts of antique coins, test their knowledge of Greek and Roman mythology, copy old coins, and create their own money on metalized paper.

In addition to the four permanent exhibitions, the Money Museum has a temporary exhibit in both French and English, which is changed periodically.

Entrance to the Money Museum.

A 1698 silver medal of the 42 bailiwicks of Berne showing the armorial escutcheons of Vaud.

Visitor's Checklist

Palais de Rumine, Place de la Riponne 6, CH - 1014 Lausanne, Suisse (Rumine Palace, Riponne Square 6, CH - 1014 Lausanne, Switzerland). The Currency Museum is on the 3rd level.

🛈 ℭ +41 (0)21 316 39 90

◯ Tuesday-Thursday: 11 a.m.-6 p.m.; Friday-Sunday: 11 a.m.-5 p.m.

⬤ Monday

♨ (1st Saturday every month) ♨ ♿ 📷 (on demand) 🛒 🍴

🍽 Tuesday-Thursday: 9 a.m.-12 noon; 2 p.m.-5 p.m.

Roman gold aureus representing the emperor Hadrian (117-138 AD) on horseback. This is from a hoard of 70 aurei discovered in 1936 at Lausanne-Vidy.

Public Transportation

Ⓜ M2 (Riponne-M. Béjart)

🚌 1/2 (Rue Neuve), 8 (Riponne-M. Béjart)

Internet

✉ musee.monetaire@vd.ch, or use the on-line contact form at: www.musees.vd.ch/fr/musee-monetaire/annexes/contacts/

🌐 www.musees.vd.ch/fr/musee-monetaire/accueil/ (in French only)

MoneyMuseum
Zurich, Switzerland

The MoneyMuseum is the Museum platform of the Sunflower Foundation, and was established by the historian and financial entrepreneur Dr. Jürg Conzett in 1999 as one of the first online museums on the history of money and currency. Since 2003 it has been at its current location near the foot of the Zürichberg (Zurich Mountain) overlooking Hadlaubstrasse in the Oberstrass neighborhood of Zurich.

Showcases and digital gallery of the exhibition on the ground floor.

The Museum is a visible expression of Conzett's desire to make his coin collection available to the general public. He did this from the realization that coins are expressive witnesses to their times. The coins tell us of power and powerlessness, stability and change, highlights and crises in the economic, political and social conditions of a country.

Contemporary witnesses to monetary affairs are also at the center of the changing exhibitions at the MoneyMuseum, their exhibits documenting the main areas of the western development of money from antiquity to modern times. The collection is constantly growing and in the meantime, also comprises pre-numismatic or traditional means of payment, which, among other things, allow us to gain an insight into parts of the Eastern, Arab and African history of money.

What is money? Where does it come from? What do we do with it? What does it do with us? These are the kinds of questions which the MoneyMuseum deals with. The MoneyMuseum has three rooms presenting exhibitions:

- The foyer on the ground floor has exhibits of traditional means of payment from Africa, Asia, and Oceania.
- The Treasure Chamber in the basement presents numismatic highlights from western history of money and currency. These include mintages from Greek and Roman antiquity, modern coins with their ancient examples and coins of which the motifs are influenced by Greek and Roman religion.
- The hall in the basement has exhibits of special exhibitions that change periodically.

Detail from the Treasure Chamber in the basement.

The exhibits of over 2,000 items on display are complemented by a range of multimedia equipment. This offers visitors extensive background information to include digital galleries with coin and picture tours about the exhibitions and, as a special highlight, screens on the showcases, where visitors can call up information about every exhibit and enlarge its obverse and reverse sides.

On display are: a manual coin press, a drop hammer, a screw press, and a rolling mill. Groups who book in advance can mint their own coins. In addition, there is also a coin vending machine with which a 20-rappen coin can be overstruck with the MoneyMuseum's own currency. These are some of the interactive activities at the MoneyMuseum which enable visitors to experience a lively visit.

Apps are also available for both the iPhone and iPad.

The obverse of a 1739 ½ thaler of the Republic of Zurich.

Visitor's Checklist

MoneyMuseum, Hadlaubstrasse 106, CH-8006 Zurich, Switzerland

ℹ️ ☎️ +41 (0)44 350 73 80, +41 (0)44 242 76 80 (for guided tours)

⭕ First Friday of each month: 10 a.m.-5 p.m.; Guided Tours Monday-Friday by appointment.

⚫ Monday; January 1, 2 (St. Berchtold's Day), Good Friday*, Easter Monday*, May 1, Ascension Day*, Whit Monday*, August 1 (Swiss National Day), December 25, and 26. An asterisk (*) denotes a movable holiday date.

The obverse of an 1800 gold 16 francs (duplone) from the Helvetic Republic, Berne mint.

Public Transportation

 33 (Seilbahn Rigiblick, Hadlaubstrasse)

 9/10 (Seilbahn Rigiblick, Hadlaubstrasse)

Internet

✉️ info@moneymuseum.com

🌐 www.moneymuseum.com/moneymuseum/?lang=en (also in German)

Swiss National Museum in Zurich
Schweizerisches Nationalmuseum-
Landesmuseum Zürich
Zurich, Switzerland

The Landesmuseum Zürich, the Swiss National Museum in Zurich, is one of the three museums united under the Swiss National Museum system. The castle-like building for the Zurich museum was completed in 1898 to commemorate the 50th anniversary of the first federal constitution. It is located between the main train station (*Hauptbahnhof*) and the Platzspitz Park.

Swiss National Museum in Zurich as seen from the Platzspitz Park.

The Coin and Medal Collection

The Museum's numismatic cabinet houses some 100,000 objects, including banknotes, securities, credit cards, and dies in addition to coins and medals. Its time-line runs from Celtic to current coins and banknotes. The Museum is the only institution that systematically collects coins from all across Switzerland. With roughly 30,000 pieces, its collection of Swiss coins is probably the largest of its kind in the world.

Specialties of the Collection

The core of the collection is the assortment of Swiss coins, comprising those that were struck or circulated in the territory now known as Switzerland. The collection focuses on coins struck at individual Swiss mints—in cities, dioceses, abbeys and cantons—as well as by the modern federal state. The collection also includes coinage of the Celts, who once resided in what is now Switzerland, as well as coins struck by the Merovingian and Frankish overlords in that area.

The collection of Swiss coins is enhanced by a representative universal collection kept on deposit for the Zurich Central Library. This collection boasts key series of coins of northern Italian, French and southern German provenance from the Early Modern period (16th-18th centuries).

The numismatic cabinet also contains the Roman coin collection of Rheinau Abbey, coins found in archaeological digs in the canton of Zurich, and various special collections. The special collection of the famed Swiss medal maker J.C. Hedlinger (1691-1771) and the important assortment of Swiss medals assembled by Rudolf Isenschmid and Gerold Meyer of Knonau, which were donated to the Museum in 1919. The objects in the collection are supplemented by what is likely the best numismatic specialist library in Switzerland.

Since end of July 2010, the redesigned coin cabinet of the Swiss National Museums has been reopened, but only a small part of the collection is on display. The artistic coins and medals can be studied in detail by the help of computer screens showing enlargements. All texts are in English, German, French, and Italian.

A view of the one-room numismatic gallery at the Swiss National Museum in Zurich.

The Seal Collection

The Museum owns Switzerland's leading collection of seals, one of the largest in Europe. The collection contains some 80,000 objects, comprising original seals, lacquer imprints and plaster casts, as well as around 800 stamps, or signets, made of a variety of materials.

The seals held by the Museum were used mainly in the territory now known as Switzerland, as well as in its immediate vicinity, and from the early Middle Ages until the 20th century.

The collection of seal imprints is arranged in three categories: secular, ecclesiastic, and official (i.e., state, cantonal, communal and corporate) from the 17th to the 19th centuries. The numerous objects from the short-lived Helvetic Republic (1798-1803) form a thematically complete and well-documented field.

Obverse of a thaler (c. 1500) of the League of God's House of Chur.

Visitor's Checklist

Swiss National Museum, Landesmuseum Zürich, Museumstrasse 2, 8021 Zurich, Switzerland

❶ ℂ +41 (0)44 218 65 11

◯ Tuesday-Sunday: 10 a.m.-5 p.m.; extended hours Thursday 7 p.m.; check website for other hours for December 24-January 2.

● Monday; Easter*. An asterisk (*) denotes a movable holiday date.

✋ ⑤ ☕ ☒ ⊗ 🎧 🛒 🍴

Public Transportation

🚌 46/E

Tram 4/11/13/14/17 (Bahnhofquai/HB); 4/13/17 (Sihlquai/HB)

Internet

✉ webcollection@slm.admin.ch

⊕ webcollection.nationalmuseum.ch/en/sammlungen/numismatik/ (also in French, German, Italian)

United Kingdom

Bath, England	• Roman Baths at Bath
Cambridge	• Fitzwilliam Museum, University of Cambridge
London	• Bank of England Museum • British Museum • The Royal Mint at the Tower of London
Manchester	• Manchester Museum, University of Manchester
Oxford	• Heberden Coin Room, Ashmolean Museum, University of Oxford – Money: The Value of the Past
Edinburgh, Scotland	• Museum on the Mound
Glasgow	• Hunterian Museum, University of Glasgow
Cardiff, Wales	• National Museum Cardiff

Additional institutions with limited information:

Truro, England	• Royal Cornwall Museum
Edinburgh, Scotland	• National Museum of Scotland

United Kingdom

Map showing the cities of the United Kingdom having numismatic venues with detailed descriptions with their cities indicated by a white dot. A red dot represents that city with limited information.

Roman Baths at Bath
Bath, England

The once ancient Roman city of Bath, a UNESCO World Heritage Site since 1987, is situated on the Avon River in Wessex. Because of its natural hot springs, the city has been a popular resort for almost two millennia.

When Romans occupied Britain in the 1st century AD, they built their own bath complex along with an ingenious under-the-floor heating system, or hypocaust. Because they also recognized the medicinal properties of the natural spring, the Romans combined the name of their goddess of war and medicine, Minerva, with the local Celtic goddess of healing, Sulis, as Sulis Minerva, and renamed the city in 43 AD as Aquae Sulis in her honor.

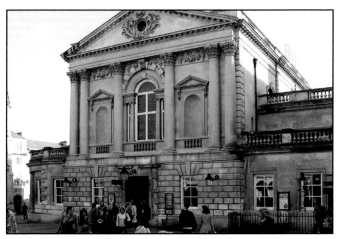
The entrance to the Roman Bath on the Abby Church Yard.

The Great Bath

Although the Romans built their bath complex almost 2,000 years ago, it fell into ruin and the open-air Great Bath, the heart of the city's spa complex, was not discovered until the 1870s. All of the surrounding building, terrace, and statues of Roman dignitaries are from the late 19th century. Once past the entrance hall, the Museum complex contains several baths which are below street level, a temple to Sulis Minerva, the Sacred Spring, and a museum exhibit.

The Great Bath is lined with 45 sheets of lead and is about five feet deep. It is supplied with water from the natural spring at a constant temperature of 46 degrees Celsius (115 degrees Fahrenheit).

The open-air Great Bath, a lead-lined pool lined supplied water from the natural spring at a constant temperature of 46 degrees Celsius (115 degrees Fahrenheit) that was not discovered until the 1870s.

Roman Coins Found

Near the end of the Museum complex, there is a small exhibit of some of the more than 12,000 coins recovered from the hot Sacred Spring, thrown by Romans wishing good luck from the gods. This is the largest votive collection in Britain. Although the quality of the 40 or so coins on display is nowhere near the level one would expect of those on display in say, the British Museum, these coins nonetheless do serve an educational purpose to those unfamiliar with ancient Roman coinage.

The exhibit explains that most Roman coins (gold, silver, and bronze) reached Britain via the army and civil service. Among those shown are: a silver antoninianus of Philip II (247–249 AD), a bronze centenionalis of Magnentius (350–353), and a gold solidus of Valens (364–378), with both obverse and reverse specimens.

Other coins in the exhibit help to explain that the obverse of Roman coins normally bore the image of the emperor with the legend giving his name and titles in abbreviated form, as illustrated by bronze coins of Tiberius, Claudius, Nero, Vespasian, Antonius Pius, Commodus, and Diocletian.

Coin Motives

Very often following the emperor's death, coins were struck, giving his newly divine status, such as the bronze coin of the Emperor Augustus (27 BC–14 AD). One commemorative coin shown is that of Faustina, the wife of Antionius Pius (138–161 AD), who chose to honor a member of the Imperial household with his wife's portrait rather than his own.

239

The exhibit also explains that the reverse designs of Roman coins were generally used as a means of conveying throughout the empire the military and political achievements of the emperor or events about his family. Popular gods, such as Neptune and Sol, and symbolic figures, like Liberty and Virtue, were portrayed, often standing with the emperor as head of the state religion. Animals, such as boars, elephants, and the she-wolf (with the mythical founders of Rome—Romulus and Remus), were also popular motifs. Coins found in the Sacred Spring also serve to pinpoint the dates during which the baths were in use.

Some of the coins excavated from the Sacred Spring that serve to illustrate portraits of Roman emperors. Clockwise from upper left: sestertius of Claudius (41-54 AD), tetradrachm of Diocletian (284-305 AD), and a dupondis of Tiberius (14-37 AD).

Visitor's Checklist
The Roman Baths, Abbey Church Yard, Bath, BA1 1LZ, England

ℹ ℭ +44 (0)1225 477785

○ January-February: 9:30 a.m.-4:30 p.m., exit 5:30 p.m.; March-June: 9 a.m.-5 p.m., exit 6 p.m.; July-August: 9 a.m.-9 p.m., exit 10 p.m.; September-October: 9 a.m.-5 p.m., exit 6 p.m.; November-December: 9:30 a.m.-4:30 p.m., exit 5:30 p.m.

● December 25 and 26.

✋ ⑤ 📷 🎧 🛒 🍴

Internet
✉ romanbaths_enquiries@bathnes.gov.uk

🌐 www.romanbaths.co.uk (also in Chinese)

Fitzwilliam Museum,
University of Cambridge
Cambridge, England

Because of academic and religious disputes, scholars broke away from Oxford University in 1209 and settled in Cambridge to form the second oldest university in the English-speaking world. University of Cambridge currently has 31 colleges, the newest being established in 1979.

The city of Cambridge is located on the River Cam in Britain's East Anglia region. The Museum is on Trumpington Street where it meets Fitzwilliam Street, two blocks up from the town's historic Hobson's Conduit monument at Lensfield Road.

The classic Greek stoa façade of the Fitzwilliam Museum's Founder's Building located on Trumpington Street.

Formation of the Museum

The initial groundwork for the Museum was the artworks, library, and money bequeathed to the University in 1816 by the seventh Viscount Fitzwilliam of Merrion. The classic Greek temple façade, called the "Founder's Building," was completed in 1848.

There is no one area or gallery specifically set aside exclusively for the display of coins and medals. Instead, coins are integrated into the displays throughout the Museum having a particular cultural or artistic context. For instance, several Italian coins and medals are part of a display of "Papal Rome in the Baroque Age" in the gallery set aside for Italian art of the 16th-18th centuries.

The coins and medals displayed are but a small fraction of the approximately 200,000 objects in the Fitzwilliam Museum's collection. The largest categories that dominate its holdings are: ancient Greek (35,000), continental Europe medieval (22,000), Roman (20,000), and modern post-1800 world coins (18,000). Also included among the holdings are those of paper money, jetons, tokens, coin weights and forgeries, medals, plaquettes, wax models, seals, gems and cameos. The medals are not military or civil awards and decorations, such as the Victoria Cross, but are historical, art, and school prize medals.

A display illustrating the coinage of medieval England. The replica wooden box holds coins from a hoard of 1,805 silver and nine gold coins discovered in 2000 in Cambridge which were thought to have been buried in the 1350s.

Denominations Used in Medieval England

Walking through the one of the galleries, there is an interesting display of coins minted during the reign of Edward III (1327–1377). This exhibit explains the money denominations used in medieval England. Until 1344 when gold coins were introduced, the silver penny was the principal coin in use. As examples, the exhibit displays coins from a hoard of 1,805 silver and nine gold coins discovered in 2000 at Cambridge, which were thought to have been buried in the 1350s shortly after the Black Plague. Shown from this hoard are: two silver pennies, a gold half noble (1351), and a gold noble (c.1355), which was then equal to one-third of a pound. Other coins in this display, but not from this Cambridge Hoard include: English and French brass jetons used for calculation of sums of money in trade (c.1310–1314), a silver halfpenny (1344–1351), a silver farthing (1344–1351), a silver halfgroat (c. 1354), a silver groat (1351), and a gold quarter noble (c.1355).

An additional item that should catch one's eye is a cast copy of a gold 200 mohur of Shah Jahan (1627–1658). At 136 mm (5.4 inches) in diameter, the original coin was minted at Shahjahanabad (now Delhi) in 1064 AH (1653 AD), but it subsequently disappeared. Fortunately, a cast was taken before its disappearance and is now held in the British Museum, from which this copy was undoubtedly made.

On-Line Catalog Available

On its website one can retrieve information on, and images of coins in its collections from its public online access catalog. Currently, retrieval information and images are available for approximately 28,500 coins, and there are a number of online exhibitions that cover varied topics of interest to numismatists.

A cast copy of a gold 200 mohur of Shah Jahan (1627–1658) at 136 mm in diameter. The original coin disappeared and its sulfur cast is in the British Museum.

Visitor's Checklist

Fitzwilliam Museum, University of Cambridge, Trumpington Street, Cambridge, England CB2 1RB (corner of Trumpington and Fitzwilliam Streets)

ⓘ ☏ +44 (0)1223 332900

○ Tuesday-Saturday: 10 a.m.-5 p.m.; Sunday: 12 noon-5 p.m.

● Monday, except for bank holidays; January 1, December 24-26.

☰ By appointment; ☏ +44 (0)1223 332918

✋ ⓖ ▣ ⊗ ◑ (English only) 🛒 🍴

Internet

✉ fitzmuseum-coins@lists.cam.ac.uk

⊕ www.fitzmuseum.cam.ac.uk/dept/coins

Bank of England Museum
London, England

The Bank of England is formally known as the Governor and Company of the Bank of England. In London's business district, it is often called the "Old Lady of Threadneedle Street," and its Museum around the corner proudly showcases its history of being both the country's central bank while printing its banknotes.

The "Old Lady of Threadneedle Street" – The Bank of England, the nation's central banker. The bank's Museum is around the corner on Bartholomew Lane to the right.

Beginning In 1694

The Bank of England was founded by Scottish merchant William Patterson. Displayed are Patterson's proposal, the July 27, 1694 Royal Charter granted by William III, and the ledger book recording the names of those who loaned the initial £1.2 million capital.

Also shown is an iron chest, which dates from around 1700, the precursor of modern safes. This is the oldest piece of furniture owned by the Bank and is known as "The Great Iron Chest in the Parlour."

Growth and Expansion: 1734-1797

On display from the early 19th century is an undated £1-million note. Although the highest denomination ever issued by the Bank was for £1,000, which ended in 1923, notes for £1 million have been used since the 18th century for internal accounting purposes only.

As gold was no longer available from the Bank from February 1797, silver was hoarded by the public, resulting in a serious shortage of coins. The Bank then used Spanish 8-reales coins, i.e. "pieces of eight," from their vaults, counter stamping them with the head of George III. Several examples are on display with the original oval and the later octagonal shaped marks.

Also shown is a £5-banknote, dated 15 April, 1793—the earliest known £5 Bank of England banknote. The £10-banknote, first issued in 1759 during the Seven-Year's War due to a shortage of coins, was the lowest denomination until the introduction of the £5-banknote.

The Rotunda

The Rotunda is the Museum's second major area. On a podium inside a protected clear case is a 13-kilogram (28.7 lbs) bar of pure gold on a pedestal under the surveillance of several security cameras and guards. A scale provides a digital readout of the actual value of the bar based on that day's London gold price. A small opening allows visitors to reach in to handle the bar, permitting the bar to be lifted up with some effort from its pedestal with only one hand. Also on display is a 12-troy ounce (373 g) ingot of 24 carat gold, known as the "Coronation Bar," given by Elizabeth II to Westminster Abbey during her 1953 coronation.

Banknote Gallery

On display in the nearby Banknote Gallery are a printing press and a 1905 geometric chuck lathe to generate the highly complex patterns used for anti-forgery methods in producing banknotes and other security

A display that describes England's 24-year Restriction Period (1797-1821) and shows the earliest known Bank of England £5-note, dated 15 April, 1793.

documents. It was not until 1928, however, that the Bank instituted this method for printing its banknotes.

The gallery also recounts the origin and evolution of its banknotes, and includes a shiny intaglio plate of the face of 28 £50-notes bearing the portrait of Queen Elizabeth II.

Other displays include captured original artwork, sketches, dies, and forgeries of £5, £10, £50, and £1,000 Operation Bernhard notes produced by Jewish prisoners from the Sachsenhausen concentration camp.

The Path to Decimalization

In another gallery, Britain's historic 1960s conversion to monetary decimalization is revisited. The centuries old pounds-shillings-pence monetary system from Anglo-Saxon times was replaced by a decimal currency with the pound now divided into 100 pence.

Before the bookshop in the main hall is a display of coins struck by the Royal Mint. This was started in 1932 with the aim of compiling a representative collection of British regal coins—those bearing the portrait of the reigning monarch that were issued since 1694, the year the Bank was founded.

The Banknote Gallery features a 1905 geometric chuck lathe and Operation Bernhard counterfeits.

Visitor's Checklist

Bank of England Museum, Threadneedle Street, London, EC2R 8AH

ℹ️ 🕐 +44 (0)20 7601 5545

⭕ Monday-Friday: 10 a.m.-5 p.m.; last entry 4:45 p.m.; December 23 and 30: 1 p.m.

⚫ Saturday and Sunday, public, and bank holidays.

✋ 👶 🚼 📷 🚫 🎧 🛒

ℹ️ Language guides: available in Chinese, English, French, German, Italian, Japanese, Russian, Spanish, Welsh

Public Transportation

🚇 Bank (Northern, Central, Waterloo, and City; Docklands Light Railway); Monument, Cannon Street or Mansion House (District and Circle)

🚇 8/11/21/23/25/26/43/76/133/141/242/388 (Bank Station)

Internet

✉️ museum@bankofengland.co.uk

🌐 ww.bankofengland.co.uk/education/museum/index.htm

British Museum
London, England

Founded in 1753, the British Museum is the oldest museum in the world and is home to an extensive collection of impressive artifacts from almost every region of the world spanning more than two million years of history. With all of its vast treasures, like the Rosetta Stone, the British Museum has not forgotten coin collectors. The Department of Coins and Medals has over 650,000 objects in its collection covering the time period from the 7th century BC to the present. The Department also maintains an extensive numismatic library for use by both scholars and the general public by appointment.

Main entrance to the British Museum on Great Russell Street.

Reopens as the Citi Money Gallery

After an almost 15-year run as the HSBC Money Gallery, Room 68 was closed for nearly six months for renovations. It reopened in June 2012, renamed as the Citi Money Gallery under the sponsorship of Citi Bank for the next six years. The transformed gallery has over eight wall-mounted displays and additional floor mounted displays holding over 1,000 objects as the Museum's major permanent exhibition.

The displays on one side of the gallery's wall deal with how money is used in finance, in addition to its cultural significances. Displays progress chronologically through the history of money starting with "The Beginnings of Money—Egypt and Mesopotamia (2500-100 BC)", along with how money has been made using different forms and metals.

The displays on the opposite wall of the gallery are concerned with the institutions that placed money into circulation and guaranteed its value.

Six floor mounted displays examine the manufacture of money, such as a 1960s geometric lathe from the USA, and cast money in clay molds from the Han dynasty (China, 206 BC-220 AD). The counting of money is illustrated using a 1800s counting board from Travancore, India. One example of several discovered hoards on display is the Corbridge Hoard of Northumberland (c. 160 AD) of 160 gold aurei in a bronze jug.

A view of the transformed Citi Money Gallery.

Several Interesting Displays

The curating staff has put together several interesting displays. One is a spiral of coins—one coin from each member state of the United Nations. In a floor mounted display in the center of the gallery, there are two outward spirals demonstrating forgeries: one is a hoard of 815 fake Roman copper coins (330-340 AD) found at Hockwold, Suffolk; the other is 100 £1-counterfeit coins removed from circulation in 2011.

A popular section of the gallery, especially with children, is the "Hands On" program. With the assistance of Museum volunteers, visitors are able to handle actual objects from the Museum's collection.

Additional Galleries

While the Museum's main numismatic attraction is the Citi Money Gallery, there still are additional numismatic items from other parts of the world located throughout the Museum that are incorporated among artifacts from that region, as follows:
- Level -1: Room 34, The Islamic World
- Level 1: Room 33, China, India, Asia and Southeast Asia
- Level 2: Room 67, Korea
- Level 3: Room 69, Greek and Roman Life
- Level 3: Room 69a, Exhibitions and Changing Displays

- Level 3: Room 70, Roman Empire
- Level 3: Room 71, Etruscan World
- Level 3: Room 73, Greeks in Italy

"Hands On," a popular gallery feature allowing visitors to handle genuine numismatic objects from the Museum's collection.

Visitor's Checklist

British Museum, Great Russell Street (Southern Main Entrance), London, WC1B 3DG; Montague Street (Northern Entrance). The Citi Money Gallery is on Level 3, Room 68.

🛈 ☏ +44 (0)20-7323-8299

◯ Daily: 10 a.m.-5:30 p.m.; extended hours Thursday and Friday: until 8:30 p.m.

⬤ January 1, December 24, 25, and 26.

✋ ♿ 🍽 📷 🛒 🍴

Public Transportation

🚇 Holborn (Piccadilly, Central); Russell Square (Piccadilly); Totenham Court Road (Central, Northern)

🚌 29/134 (Bloomsbury St.); 7/390 (Great Russell St.; 7 (Montague St.)

Internet

✉ coins@britishmuseum.org

🌐 www.britishmuseum.org/the_museum/departments/coins_and_medals.aspx

The Royal Mint
at the Tower of London
London, England

The Tower of London, a UNESCO World Heritage Site, is one of the city's most popular tourist venues, and was once the site of the Royal Mint on Mint Street as early as 1279 until about 1810, when operations were moved to East Smithfield. Even Sir Isaac Newton was once Warden of the Mint in 1696, and held the office of Master of the Royal Mint from 1699 until his death in 1727.

One of the 21 towers is the White Tower, completed by William the Conqueror in 1097. At the time it was the highest structure in London at 90 feet high. Although the Tower's original function was that of the "keep"—a power base of the castle complex, it is today a Museum highlighting medieval weapons and armory.

A view of the southeast side of the White Tower with the wooden entrance steps to the left.

Two-Part Exhibition on the Top Floor

Amid the implements of warfare, the British Royal Mint opened a new permanent exhibition in April 2011 on the top floor, or 3rd level. The Royal Mint's numismatic exhibition is in two parts, due to the partial dividing wall of the Tower's top floor. On one side is an exhibit showing a reproduction of a screw press used to strike coins in the Tower from the 1660s to 1810. Another display shows a nest of six troy weights, dating from 1588, arraigned in a large pile, or nest that were used to establish uniform standards throughout the kingdom. Also included is a selection of coins from the Tudor era: Henry VII sovereign, Henry VII testoon (shilling), Henry VII crown of the double rose, Henry VIII testoon, Edward VI crown, Edward VI sixpence, Philip and Mary shilling, Elizabeth I shilling, Elizabeth I angel, Elizabeth I pound, Elizabeth recoinage medal, two trial plates of 1560—one for 22 carat gold and the other for sterling silver.

On the other side of the wall the exhibition comprises 10 displays, some of which are the "hands on" type. The first gives a brief history of the Royal Mint, locating it between the Tower of London's inner and outer walls on Mint Street, which contained the workshops for melting gold and silver, hammering metals into sheets, and striking coins. From these beginnings, the Royal Mint, now located in Llantrisant, Wales makes coins for over 50 countries each year.

Visitors looking at the Royal Mint exhibit in the White Tower.

240 Silver Pennies and a Gold Sovereign

A display explains that the sovereign was introduced in 1489 by Henry VII, being the first time a coin was issued with a value of a pound. It shows a gold sovereign and 12 rows of 20 silver pennies, equal to 240 in all.

The Charles I silver crown is shown in a display containing a hoard of silver shillings found in Dersingham, Norfolk. During the Civil War, Charles lost control of the Tower and with it, the mint, but he set up alternate mints around England as indicated by an accompanied map. One of these mints was at Oxford, where he struck the well-known Oxford Crown. Other displays describe historical coins like the William I silver penny and the Edward III gold noble, the meaning of the term "sterling," and the tools and process used to make a medieval coin.

In the Tower's basement before the gift shop, visitors can make a Tower of London coin from one of four designs by pressing a supplied penny along with the payment of £1.

Visitor's Checklist
Tower of London, London EC3N 4AB, United Kingdom. The British Royal Mint exhibit is on the 3rd level of the White Tower inside the Tower of London complex. Note: this venue is not handicap accessible.

- ❶ ℂ Tel: +44 (0)20 3166 6000
- ○ March-October: Tuesday-Saturday 9 a.m.-5 p.m., Sunday and Monday 10 a.m.-5:30 p.m.; November-February: Tuesday-Saturday: 9 a.m.-4:30 p.m., Sunday and Monday 10 a.m.-4:30 p.m.
- ● January 1, December 24-26.
- ✋ 📷 🖼 (Jewel House only) 🛒 🍴

Public Transportation
- 🚇 Tower Hill (Circle, District, and City; Docklands Light Railway)
- 🚌 42/78/100/RV1 (Tower of London); 15 (Great Tower Street)

Internet
- ✉ VisitorServices_TOL@hrp.org.uk
- 🌐 www.hrp.org.uk/toweroflondon (also in French, German, Italian, Spanish)

A nest of six troy weights, dating from 1588, arraigned in a large pile, or nest to establish uniform standards.

Manchester Museum, University of Manchester

Manchester, England

The Manchester Museum's Money Gallery is a collaborative venture with the British Museum, under the United Kingdom Partnership Scheme. Despite its modest collection of approximately 850 objects, it aims to be universal in scope by looking at the different traditions of coinage in the West and East, as well as pre-monetary value systems.

The introductory panel looks at these early value systems, and their linguistic legacy in modern English and German. It also shows how, in certain parts of the world, traditional forms of currency continued to function until the end of the 19th century.

The Museum's front entrance on Oxford Road.

Starting with Early Cuneiform Tablets

The main body of the gallery runs along the side walls. The principal display cases proceed chronologically, within three broad periods: 2500 BC-600 AD, 600-1700, and 1700-present day. They begin with early cuneiform tablets of the 3rd millennium BC, which recorded transactions in weighed amounts of precious metal, move onto the invention of coinage in the West and East in the late 7th century BC, which heralded a rich and continuous 2,600-year heritage, and end with the 21st-century use of credit/debit cards to replace paper money that, in turn, had replaced much of the coinage. On the way, many important moments in history are highlighted, and visitors can trace the movements of people and ideas that have formed much of our modern world.

253

The displays of objects, artifacts as well as coins, are accompanied for each particular period, by a map, with trade being the linking factor. This overarching theme of the gallery is picked up and reflected in the frieze that runs continuously over the wall cases.

Manchester's rich social and economic history is illustrated in a choice display of medallions and tokens in the last of these cases, which provides subject matter for school projects as well as moments of nostalgia for older Mancunians.

A view of several displays of the gallery.

15th-Century Fishpool Hoard

The central cases have two themes: technology and treasure. The former illustrates the different processes used to make coins over the centuries, and features examples of molds for casting the earliest pieces and iron dies used to make the hammered coins of the medieval world and modern dies for striking the new £1-coin. This display brings the story of money up-to-date with a brief review of electronic banking. The latter theme will appeal to those who dream of finding buried treasure with coins from some of the important finds from the Manchester area, as well as spectacular examples of medieval gold pieces from the famous 15th-century Fishpool Hoard. This consisted of 1,237 coins, four rings, four pieces of jewelry, and two lengths of chain found in 1966 hidden around 1464 after the Battle of Hexham during the War of the Roses.

Gallery Highlights

Some highlights of the gallery are a Mesopotamian duck weight (3rd-2nd millennium BC), Roman medallions in gold and silver (4th century), silver pennies of Edward the Elder (c.900-924) showing an Anglo-Saxon tower and the *manus dei* (hand of God), a 13th-century gold double dinar of Genghis Khan (d. 1227), a huge coin of the Mongol Yuan dynasty (14th century), copper plate money from Sweden (18th century), and a 1699 Bank of England £200-banknote.

The obverse of a Gold noble of Edward III, 1327-1377.

Visitor's Checklist

Manchester Museum, The University of Manchester, Oxford Road, Manchester M13 9PL, England

   The Money Gallery is on the 2nd Floor (3rd level)

   ⓘ ℂ +44 (0)161 275 2634

   ◯ Tuesday-Saturday: 10 a.m.-5 p.m.; Sunday, Monday, and Bank holidays: 11 a.m.- 4 p.m.; December 27-31: 11 a.m.-4 p.m.

   ● January 1, December 24-26.

   ✋ ⑤ 📷 🎧 🛒 🍴

Public Transportation

   🚌 Chorlton upon Medlock, Booth St West/College of Music; Chorlton upon Medlock, Oxford Rd/University Shopping Center

Internet

   ✉ museum@manchester.ac.uk

   🌐 www.museum.manchester.ac.uk/collection/money

Heberden Coin Room, Ashmolean Museum, University of Oxford
Money: The Value of the Past
Oxford, England

The Ashmolean Museum reopened to the public on November 7, 2009 and included 38 new galleries. The numismatic collections of the Heberden Coin Room of the Museum are chiefly displayed in the new "Money" Gallery, and also in twenty five other galleries throughout the Museum where they complement other objects from the Ashmolean collection. Additionally, coins feature prominently in graphic elements that support displays in the entire Museum.

The "Money" gallery is composed of object displays and hands-on interactive components, supported by extensive graphic elements. Structurally, the gallery is divided into three main areas: the north and south walls, and a central aisle of free-standing cases. There is space for temporary exhibitions on the west wall.

The Museum's front entrance facing Beaumont Street.

Themes of the North and South Walls

The north and the south walls, both of which are long, carry two broad themes. The north wall showcases world cultures through the coinages they produced and also doubles to reflect the curatorial areas represented in the Heberden Coin Room. These displays are augmented by graphic elements such as enlarged pictures of coins and images of prints, architecture, icons and sculpture.

The south wall provides an overview of money through thematic displays that emphasize the physical, cultural and historical aspects of money—articulated through a selection of objects and graphic panels.

The Oxford Crown

The central aisle has three important focuses—displays concentrating on the

Greeks, the Romans in Britain, the Anglo-Saxons, the Tudors, and the Victorians. The Victorians are shown through a selection of medals, rather than coins, thus bringing a significant part of the Coin Room's non-monetary collection into the gallery's domain. There are three cases, which contain "vista objects." These are significant in their regional as well as collective historical importance, and are accentuated by large graphics that act as a visual magnet for visitors. These are the Oxford Crown of Charles I as the first English coin to depict a town when King Charles I moved his capital to Oxford, having been expelled from London by Parliament; the Crondall Hoard of the earliest Anglo-Saxon gold coins discovered in 1828, which marked the reintroduction of coinage into Britain two centuries after the abandonment of the province by the Romans; and the Chalgrove Hoard, discovered in 2003 near Oxford, in which was found the second known specimen of a radiate of Domitianus, a previously unknown, but short-lived Gallic usurper (271 AD). This last case is surrounded by other displays of local money, including the Didcot Hoard of Roman aurei. It also includes a section dedicated to the Portable Antiquities Scheme.

A view of the gallery of the Heberden Coin Room.

The obverse of the Oxford Crown, struck by Charles I in 1644 in the mint at Oxford.

Interactive Activities

The interactive elements offer educational and cultural information through tactile and visual activities such as "Design Your Own Coin" and "Magnify Me." There is also an enlarged model of the Oxford Crown and an electronic map that takes the viewer through time and space using coin-like counters.

The gallery also has graphic panels that supplement the temporary exhibition, the "Money" wall and the entrance to the gallery. At the entrance, a board titled, "What's it Worth?" gives an indication of prices through ages using objects on display and also doubles as a chronological guide to the gallery.

Coins in a clay pot from the Chalgrove Hoard, discovered in 2003 near Oxford.

Visitor's Checklist

Heberden Coin Room, Ashmolean Museum, Beaumont Street, Oxford OX1 2PH, England. The Heberden Coin Room is in Gallery 7 on Level -1. Coins can also be found in 25 other galleries throughout the Museum.

❶ ☾ +44 (0)1865 278058

◯ Tuesday-Sunday: 10 a.m.-6 p.m.; on Bank Holiday Monday: 10 a.m.-6 p.m.

● Monday; December 24-26.

📚 Sakler Library; entrance on St. John Street

♨ ☺ 📷 🎧 🛒

🍴 Café: Tuesday-Sunday: 10 a.m.-6 p.m.; Ashmolean Dining Room: Tuesday-Saturday: 10 a.m.-10 p.m.; Sunday: 10 a.m.-6 p.m.

Public Transportation

🚌 6/14/14A/300/500 (Magdalen Street-Stop C3); 17/17A/17C/25/25A/59/59A/ S2/S4/S5 (Magdalen Street-Stop C4)

Internet

✉ coin-room@ashmus.ox.ac.uk

🌐 www.ashmolean.org/departments/heberdencoinroom/

Museum on the Mound
Edinburgh, Scotland

The Museum on the Mound, which opened in 2006, is located on the ground floor of the iconic headquarters building of what was once the Bank of Scotland in the New Town area of Edinburgh. Prior to being part of the Lloyds Banking Group in 2009, the Museum was the HBOS Museum on the Mound.

The iconic building of the Museum on the Mound has served as the headquarters of the Bank of Scotland since 1806 and appears on every Bank of Scotland banknote in circulation today.

Multiple Galleries

The Museum has five main galleries:

- A Bank for Scotland. This gallery explores the origins of the Bank of Scotland from 1695 and the development of banking within Scotland. The Bank of Scotland was involved in several mergers and acquisitions with different banks, such as the British Linen Bank and in 2001 merged with the Halifax Bank to form HBOS. On January 19, 2009, the Bank formed a key part of the Lloyds Banking Group, following the acquisition of HBOS.

- The Bank on the Mound. This gallery details the history of the iconic building which houses the Museum. The Mound, aka Geordie Boyd's Mud Brig, is a man-made hill created from earth of the city's New Town foundation. The Bank's directors purchased the site in 1800 at a cost of £3,500.

Over a period of 200 years the building has been enlarged and adapted to meet the bank's growing business and changing need. The iconic building of the Museum on the Mound appears on every Bank of Scotland banknote in circulation today.

- Money Matters. All of these galleries feature coins and/or banknotes to help tell the Bank's stories, but the main coins and banknotes displays are in the central Money Matters gallery. There is a small selection of coins from Lydia, Greece, Persia and Rome, and Scottish and British coins showing every monarch's reign from David I (1123-1153) to Elizabeth II (1952-). There is also a display showing the manufacture of coins from early hammered, through mill and screw to the 2004 Forth Bridge £1-coin. This includes artist Edwina Ellis' original lino cut of the artwork for the Forth Bridge design, and a selection of dies courtesy of the Royal Mint.

One of the gallery displays showing an example of every type coin minted in Scotland from the 1136 silver penny of David I up to those of Elizabeth II.

Scottish Notes From 1716

There are displays relating to the design and manufacture of banknotes, a study case showing examples of Scottish banknotes from 1716 to the present and some fascinating forgery cases. The Museum has study guides available which provide detailed information on every coin and banknote on display throughout the galleries.

In the past, coins were made from precious metals and weighing them was an important measure, or test, of their value. However, today's coins have only a token value but are minted with such precision that their weight can be used to determine whether or not they are genuine. Knowing the exact weight of coins serves another purpose. When they need to be counted in large quantities, they can be weighed en masse.

- Buying Security. This gallery explains the origins of both Building and Life Assurance Societies.
- Making It Work. Here is a look at the changing world of work and leisure for the people employed by the bank over the years.

Throughout the year there are special and temporary exhibits. As an example, a 2008 exhibition titled, "Faking It," was devoted to banknote forgery. Drawing on material from the Bank's own collections, the exhibition looked at forgers and forgeries over three centuries.

Visitor's Checklist

Museum on the Mound, The Mound, Edinburgh EH1 1YZ, United Kingdom

🛈 🕐 +44 (0)131 243 5464

○ Tuesday-Friday: 10 a.m.-5 p.m., Saturday and Sunday: 1 p.m.-5 p.m.; Bank holiday Mondays: 1 p.m.-5 p.m.; extended hours during the Edinburgh Festival in August. Check Museum website for details.

● Monday

The reverse of a gold lion struck during the reign of Robert III (1390-c.1403) showing St. Andrew crucified on a saltire cross, the first gold coin to circulate in Scotland.

Public Transportation

🚌 Lothian 23/27/41/42/45/67 (The Mound, Market Street)

Internet

✉ info@museumonthemound.com

🌐 www.museumonthemound.com

The obverse of a 1540 gold ducat of James V, or "Bonnet Piece," the first dated coin of the British Isles.

Hunterian Museum, University of Glasgow
Glasgow, Scotland

Founded in 1807, the Hunterian Museum is Scotland's oldest public museum. It is named in honor of Dr. William Hunter, a Scottish obstetrician and antiquarian who was an ardent coin and book collector and owned one of the best private museums. This Museum should not be confused with the Hunterian Museum of the Royal College of Surgeons in London, based on items assembled by Hunter's younger brother, John Hunter.

The Museum's numismatic collection consists of approximately 70,000 coins, medals, tokens, and related objects. Of these, only about 250 specimens are on display among the Museum's historical artifacts. A select number of coins and medals are on display in the Huntarian Art Museum across the street.

Glasgow University's Hunterian Museum on University Avenue.

Victoria's First Coins

In a display case labeled "Coats Coins," are the first coins of Queen Victoria's reign. Assembled by Thomas Coats (1809-1883), this was one of the best private coin collections in Scotland of the late 19th century. The Coats family in 1921 donated the collection of some 7,000 ancient Greek, Roman, English, and British coins in gold, silver, and copper to the University.

The coins which show the portrait of Victoria with the "young" or "bun" head on the obverse were part of the design from 1839 to 1887. There is a complete type set consisting of the copper penny, half penny, farthing, threepence, fourpence, sixpence, shilling, florin, half crown, silver crown, half sovereign, and gold sovereign. Also included is the rare gold 1839 £5-proof "Una and the lion" pattern not struck for general circulation.

The Hunterian Museum's 4th-floor gallery.

The Profile of a Queen

One highlight of the coins on display among the Lady Shepenhor mummy (c. 600 BC) and other artifacts is an 80-drachma bronze coin minted in Alexandria, 51-30 BC. This is the best example in the world of a Cleopatra coin. Cleopatra VII is regarded as one of the world's most powerful women and she personally approved this portrait.

Imperial Rome and Greece

Another highlight in a display case contains a series of 88 gold coins of the Imperial Roman emperors that span 500 years, providing an extensive miniature portrait gallery of the Roman emperors. Among these was Antonius Pius, who was emperor when Romans marched in Scotland in the 2nd century AD and built the Antonine Wall. The series begins with a coin showing the portrait of Augustus, Rome's first emperor (27 BC-14 AD) through Zeno, when the empire ended with his death in 491 AD.

In the same display case are 169 Greek coins from Hunter's collection covering the Archaic, Classical, and Hellenistic periods of Greek coinage. The archaic coins shown are usually identified by a portrait or attribute of a patron god, goddess, or legendary hero with the earliest of these coins made from electrum. In the Classical period, the use of inscriptions on coins began and often included the name of the Greek "polis" (πολις)—the people of the city-state.

One of the many collections Hunter purchased was that of James Bruce, aka "Abyssinian Bruce," the explorer of the Nile. On display is his superb group of 3rd-2nd century BC Ptolemaic gold coins. It is unfortunate that none of Hunter's 88 Roman, 169 Greek, or Ptolemaic coins have any identifying or informational labels to assist visitors.

Visitor's Checklist

Hunterian Museum, University of Glasgow, University Avenue, Glasgow G12 8QQ, United Kingdom. The coins are located on the 4th floor Kelvin Gallery.

ℹ ℭ +44 (0) 141 330 4221

○ Tuesday-Saturday: 10 a.m.-5 p.m.; Sunday: 11 a.m.-4 p.m.

● Monday; January 1, December 25; check website for any additional information about closure for Christmas and New Year's holidays.

✋ ⑤ 📷 🛒

Reverse of a gold 1839 £5-proof Una and the lion pattern.

Public Transportation

🚌 7/11/17/17E/44 (University Library on University Avenue)

Internet

✉ hunterian-enquiries@glasgow.ac.uk

🌐 www.gla.ac.uk/hunterian/collections/collectionsummary/coinsandmedals/#d.en.199557

The best known example of a Cleopatra coin, the 80-drachma bronze coin minted in Alexandria, 51-30 BC.

National Museum Cardiff
Amgueddfa Genedlaethol Caerdydd
Cardiff, Wales

The National Museum Cardiff is part of the National Museum of Wales system currently of eight museums that was founded in 1907 when it inherited the collection of the Cardiff Museum. Although the current building at Cathays Park began in 1912, World War I delayed its construction and public opening until 1927.

Museum entrance from Cathays Park.

Coins & Medals Gallery
The National Museum Cardiff has over 1,200 of the finest specimens covering the full range of its numismatic collection displayed in the Coins and Medals gallery. The numismatic collection is wide-ranging, from ancient times to the present, with five main areas of strength: Celtic coins, Greek and Roman coins, coins of England and the British Isles, tokens, banknotes, and what may be termed "paranumismatica"—items that are primarily Welsh, and commemorative medals and awards relating to Wales and the exploits of Welsh people. Beside these items, there are also small comparative collections of European, British Colonial, and world coins.

Hoards
The collection includes numerous hoards, archaeological site finds, and single coin finds from the Roman period onwards. Coins found in or relating to Wales remain an

265

important element of contemporary collecting. Occasional Welsh finds of treasure, such as: the English Civil War Hoard from Tregwynt, Pembrokeshire, thought to have been buried around 1648 and rediscovered in 1996; the Bryn Maelgwyn Hoard of 204 silver pennies of Canute the Great (c. 985-1035) found near Deganwy Castle, Llandudno Conwy; and several from around Anglesey and Gwynedd provide spectacular individual acquisitions.

One of the many hoards of medieval coins found in Wales.

The collection's Roman and medieval coins are included in the "Origins: in search of early Wales" gallery and a display of medals in the Main Hall relates to the two world wars. The text in all the displays are in both English and Welsh (or Cymric).

A hoard of 199 silver pennies of English kings Edward the Confessor (1042-1066) and William the Conqueror (1066-1087) that were probably lost or buried around 1085 AD near Abergavenny, Monmouthshire, Wales.

Aureus showing the bust of Nero, 61-62 AD.

Visitor's Checklist
National Museum Cardiff, Cathays Park, Cardiff CF10 3NP, United Kingdom
- ❶ ⓒ +44 (0)29 2057 3321
- ○ Tuesday-Sunday: 10 a.m.-5 p.m.; open most bank holiday Mondays.
- ● January 1, December 24-26. Check website for exact dates for closings during Christmas and New Year's holidays.
- ✋ ⊛ 📷 ⊗ 🛒 🍴
- ⊜ ⓒ +44 (0)29 2057 3202 or ✉ library@museumwales.ac.uk

Public Transportation
- 🚌 27 (Cathays Park)

Internet
- ✉ Use the on-line contact form at: www.museumwales.ac.uk/en/enquiries/
- 🌐 www.museumwales.ac.uk/en/archaeology/numismatics (also in Welsh, or Cymric)

Additional Institutions, Western Europe

The following Western European institutions are known to have numismatic exhibitions of varying degrees that are open to the public. These are listed here, either because sufficient information could not (1) be obtained about the museum, (2) be verified from other sources, (3) the museum did not respond to repeated requests for information, (4) the exhibition is closed due to long-term renovation of the building or other reasons, (5) or I learned about this venue just before the manuscript was to go to the publisher and complete information could not be included.

Belgium
Gruuthuse Museum
Dijver 17, 8000 Bruges
ⓘ ☏ +32 (0)50 44 87 22
🌐 http://www.free-city-guides.com/bruges/gruuthuse (unofficial site)

France
National Library of France
Bibliothèque nationale de France
5, rue Vivienne, 75002 Paris (Richelieu Library)
ⓘ ☏ +33(0)1 53 79 59 59
🌐 www.bnf.fr/en/collections_and_services/numi_eng/s.coins.html?first_Art=oui
(also in French, Spanish)

Lyon Mint Cabinet
Musée des Beaux-Arts de Lyon, Cabinet des médailles de Lyon
20 place des Terreaux, F-69001 Lyon
ⓘ ☏ 33 (0)4 72 10 17 40
🌐 www.mba-lyon.fr/mba/sections/fr/collections-musee/medaillier4495/departement
7239 (in French only)

Museum of Counterfeit Money
Musée de la Fausse Monnaie
1355 route de Chapeiry Les Vorges, 74150 Marcellaz Albanais
✉ chrporcheron@yahoo.fr
🌐 www.fausse-monnaie.com/v2/index.php (in French only)

Germany
Friedenstein Castle
Schloss Friedenstein
Schlossmuseum, 99867 Gotha
ℹ ℭ +49 (0)3621 8234 0
🌐 www.stiftungfriedenstein.de/index.php?id=731&L=1 (in German only)

Historical Money Collection of the Cologne Savings Bank
Geldgeschichtliche Sammlung der Kreissparkasse Köln
Neumarkt 18-24, 50667 Cologne
ℹ ℭ +49 (0) 221 227 2370
✉ info@geldgeschichte.de
🌐 www.geldgeschichte.de (in German only)

Historical Museum Frankfurt
Historisches Museum Frankfurt
Fahrtor 2 (Römerberg), 60311 Frankfurt am Main
ℹ ℭ +49 (0)69 21235599
🌐 www.historisches-museum.frankfurt.de/index.php?article_id=89 (in German only)

Roman-Germanic Museum
Römisch-Germanisches Museum
Roncalliplatz 4, 50667 Cologne
ℹ ℭ +49 (0)221/221 ext. 24438, 24590
✉ roemisch-germanisches-museum@stadt-koeln.de
🌐 www.museenkoeln.de/homepage/default.asp?s=169
(also in German at: www.museenkoeln.de/roemisch-germanisches-museum)

Iceland
Central Bank of Iceland
Seðlabanki Íslands
Einholt 4, 105 Reykjavík
❶ ☏ +354 569 9962, +354 569 9964
✉ safnadeild@sedlabanki.is
🌐 www.cb.is/the-bank/libraries-and-collection (also in Icelandic)

Italy
Civic Archaeological Museum, Bologna
Museo Civico Archeologico di Bologna
2, Via dell'Archiginnasio, Bologna 40124
❶ ☏ +39 051 27 57 211
🌐 www.comune.bologna.it/museoarcheologico (in Italian only)

Milan Civic Archaeological Museum
Milano Civico Museo Archeologico
Corso Magenta 15, 20123 Milan
❶ ☏ +39 02 804 843

National Museum of Rome, Balbi Crypt
Museo Nazionale Romano, Crypta Balbi
Via delle Botteghe Oscure 31, 00186 Rome (corner of Via M. Caetani)
❶ ☏ +39 06 39967700

National Museum of Rome, Palazzo Massimo alle Terme
Largo di Villa Peretti 67, Rome. The numismatic items are in the basement.
❶ ☏ +39 06 39967700

Malta
Bank of Valleta Museum
St. John Square, Valletta
❶ ☏ +356 2131 2020
✉ customercare@bov.com
🌐 www.bov.com/page.asp?p=12877&l=1

Portugal
Museum of the Banco de Portugal
Museu do Banco de Portugal
Avenida Almirante Reis 71, Lisbon

✉ info@bportugal.pt

⊕ www.bportugal.pt/en-US/ServicosaoPublico/Museu/Pages/default.aspx
(also in Portuguese)

Spain
Cerralbo Museum
Museo Cerralbo
Calle de Ventura Rodríguez 17, 28008 Madrid

ℹ ☎ +34 (0)915 47 36 46/47

✉ museo.cerralbo@mcu.es

⊕ en.museocerralbo.mcu.es/coleccion/galeriaDelmagenes/monedas.html (also in
Spanish at: museocerralbo.mcu.es/coleccion/galeriaDelmagenes/monedas.html)

National Archaeological Museum of Spain
Museo Arqueológico Nacional de España
Calle de Serrano 13, 28001 Madrid

ℹ ☎ +34 (0)91 577 79 12

✉ sugerencias.man @mcu.es

⊕ man.mcu.es/coleccion/CatalogoTesoros_Numismamtica.html (in Spanish only)

Spanish Royal Mint Museum
Real Casa de la Moneda
Casa del Doctor Esquerdo 36, 28009 Madrid

ℹ ☎ +34 (0)91 566 65 44

✉ Use the on-line contact form at: www.fnmt.es/index.php?spec=faq&page=9
(in Spanish only)

⊕ www.museocasadelamoneda.org/museum

⊕ www.fnmt.es/index.php?cha=citizen&scha=22&page=106&spage=107
(both sites in Spanish only)

Switzerland
Art and History Museum of Geneva
Cabinet de médaille du Musée d'art et d'histoire
Rue Charles-Galland 2, CH-1206 Geneva, Switzerland.
ℹ️ ℂ +41 (0)22 418 26 00
✉️ mah@ville-ge.ch
🌐 www.ville-ge.ch/mah/index.php?content=1.2.1.3.3.7.&langue=eng (in French only)

Coin Cabinet and Collection of Antiquities of the City of Winterthur
Münzkabinett und Antiken Sammlung der Stadt Winterthur
Villa Bühler, Lindstrasse 8, 8402 Winterthur
ℹ️ ℂ +41 (0)52 267 51 46
🌐 www.muenzkabinett.winterthur.ch/default.asp?Sprache=D&Thema=0&Rubrik=0
&Gruppe=27&Seite=69 (in German only)

Museum of Art and History
Musée d'art et d'histoire, Cabinet de numismatique
Faubourg de l'Hôpital 4, CH-2000 Neuchâtel
ℹ️ ℂ +41 (0)32 717 79 18
🌐 www.mahn.ch/collections-numismatique (in French only)

Museum of Counterfeit Money
Musée de la Fausse Monnaie
13 Rue du Bourg, CH-1913 Saillon
ℹ️ ℂ +41 (0)27 744 40 03
✉️ musee@saillon.ch
🌐 www.saillon.ch/tourisme/culture/le-musée-de-la-fausse-monnaie.aspx (in French
only)

Rätisches Museum, Münzkabinett
Hofstrasse 1, CH-7000 Chur
ℹ️ ℂ +41 (0)81 257 48 40
🌐 www.rm.gr.ch (also in Romanch, Italian)

United Kingdom
England
Royal Cornwall Museum
25 River Street, Truro TR1 2SJ
ℹ ℂ +44 (0)1872 272205
✉ enquiries@royalcornwallmuseum.org.uk
🌐 www.royalcornwallmuseum.org.uk

Scotland
National Museum of Scotland
Chambers Street, Edinburgh EH1
ℹ ℂ +44 (0) 300 123 6789
✉ info@nms.ac.uk.
🌐 www.nms.ac.uk/our_museums/national_museum.aspx

Vatican City
Philatelic and Numismatic Museum
Il Museo Filatelico e Numismatico
ℹ ℂ +39 06 69883005
✉ expo.ufn@scv.va
🌐 www.vaticanstate.va/EN/News/The_new_Museum.htm

A montage of scenes from Sofia, Bulgaria. Top to bottom, left to right: Downtown skyline; Parliament Square; Sofia University rectorate; National Palace of Culture; Mall of Sofia; Ivan Vazov National Theater; Basilica; and Eagle's Bridge.

Eastern Europe

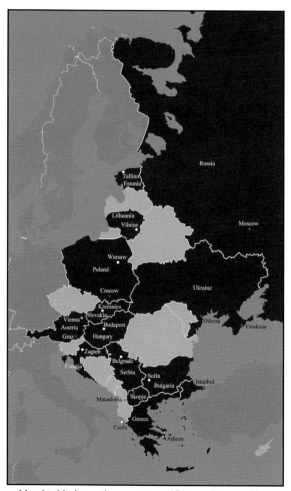

Map highlighting the countries of Eastern Europe. The countries having numismatic venues with detailed descriptions are shown in dark blue and their cities indicated by a white dot. A red dot represents cities with limited information in those countries while a green dot indicates cities having venues with both detailed and limited information.

The coins of ancient Greece established a template for the base metals and designs—images of buildings, deities, animals, plants, and their rulers that would appear on coins of other countries for many hundreds of years.

After the fall of Rome, coins of Byzantium as a continuation of Rome, dominated the region until the collapse of Constantinople. Like ancient Roman coins, Byzantine coins continued the placement of the head of the Emperor on the obverse, but with a Christian symbol on the reverse, such as a cross or an image of Christ. Perhaps unique to Byzantine coinage are the scyphate, or cup-shaped coins known as *trachy*, minted in electrum and billon—alloys of gold and silver.

From the Roman silver denarius yielded the Byzantine gold denarius, a forerunner of the Islamic dinar. In the modern era, the dinar is the denomination for Serbia, Bosnia and Herzegovina, Croatia, and the denar for Macedonia—all of these countries were once former republics of Yugoslavia. The remaining former Yugoslav republic, Slovenia, adopted the tolar, a derivate of the German thaler, in 1991 after its independence.

In Eastern Europe, which here geographically takes into account what is traditionally considered Central Europe, ten countries have museums with extensive entries with pictures. Leading the list is the Coin Cabinet of Vienna's Kunsthistorisches (Art History) Museum, considered by many to have one of the five largest and most important coin collections in the world. There are also seven countries represented that have museums whose entries have limited information.

As a major mining town during the Middle Ages, the mint at Kremnica became an important mint for the coins for many of the Hungarian monarchs, who were also emperors of the Holy Roman Empire. Today, the Mint still produces coins and medals for Slovakia plus coins for over 25 countries worldwide. The Numismatic Museum Athens, Greece's national numismatic collection, is one of the world's few major museums that is dedicated solely to the exhibition of numismatics and is housed in the former mansion of Heinrich Schliemann who excavated the ancient city of Troy in the 1870s. The Balkans are also represented by museums of the Bulgarian National Bank Museum Collection in Sofia, the Numismatic

Collection of the Zagreb Archaeological Museum, the Banknote Museum of Ionian Bank on the island of Corfu, the Visitor Center of the National Bank of Serbia in Belgrade, the National Bank of the Republic of Macedonia Museum in Skopje, and two bank museums in Athens: the Museum of the Bank of Greece and the Museum of the National Bank of Greece.

Located on the European side of Istanbul, the Yapi Kredi Bank Vedat Nedim Tör Museum includes Greek, Roman, and Byzantine currencies. Other venues include the countries of Poland, Hungary, Ukraine, Estonia, and Lithuania that were once members of the Warsaw Pact and some republics of the former Soviet Union, but which now are independent nations.

Vienna, Austria	• Kunsthistorisches Museum Coin Cabinet
Sofia, Bulgaria	• Bulgarian National Bank Museum Collection
Zagreb, Croatia	• Numismatic Collection, Zagreb Archaeological Museum
Tallinn, Estonia	• Bank of Estonia Museum
Athens, Greece	• Numismatic Museum, Athens
Corfu	• Banknote Museum of Ionian Bank, Corfu
Budapest, Hungary	• Hungarian National Bank Visitor Center
Vilnius, Lithuania	• Money Museum of the Bank of Lithuania
Warsaw, Poland	• Royal Castle Museum Coin Cabinet
Belgrade, Serbia	• Visitor Center of the National Bank of Serbia
Kremnica, Slovakia	• National Bank of Slovakia, Museums of Coins and Medals in Kremnica: Two Faces of Money

Additional institutions with limited information:

Vienna, Austria	• Austrian National Bank Money Museum
Graz	• Coin Cabinet Schloss Eggenberg
Athens, Greece	• Museum of the Bank of Greece
	• Museum of the National Bank of Greece
Skopje, Macedonia	• National Bank of the Republic of Macedonia Museum
Cracow, Poland	• The National Museum in Cracow/ Emeryk Hutten-Czapski Museum
Moscow, Russia	• A.C. Pushkin Museum of Fine Arts
	• State Historical Museum
Istanbul, Turkey	• Yapi Kredi Bank Vedat Nedim Tör Museum
Feodosia, Ukraine	• Feodosia Money Museum
Odessa	• Odessa Numismatics Museum

Kunsthistorisches Museum
Coin Cabinet
Vienna, Austria

The Coin Cabinet of Vienna's Kunsthistorisches (Art History) Museum is considered to be one of the five largest and most important coin collections in the world. It has been located in the city's Museum Quarter since 1891 and on the building's second floor since 1899. With some 700,000 objects spanning three millennia, the collection contains not only coins, but also paper money, medallions, seals, orders and decorations. Some 2,000 objects can be viewed in the three connected halls housing more than 40 permanent display cases with all text in German.

The front entrance of the Kunsthistorisches Museum located in Vienna's Museum's Quarter.

The Coin Cabinet arose from the collection of the ruling Habsburgs, which had been continuously maintained and expanded. The oldest extant inventory was established around 1547-1550 under Emperor Ferdinand I (1503-1564) and was almost all of ancient Roman origin. His son, Archduke Ferdinand II (1529-1595) even had his own coin collection. The cabinets in which he stored his coins still exist today and are kept in both the Kunsthistorisches Museum Coin Cabinet and at Innsbruck's Ambras Castle. Succeeding Habsburg rulers had their own coin collections and it wasn't until the opening of the Kunsthistorisches Museum that various collections were finally consolidated to one location.

Medallic Art

The first hall offers the history and development of the medal from its origins in Italy from about 1400 AD, with those of Pisanello and Matteo de'Pasti up to the 20th century. Shown are examples of cast medals from the Renaissance period from Austria, Germany, Italy, Spain, and France. The 16th- through 18th-century period is represented by medals from Scandinavia, Poland, and Russia, while those from England cover the 17th and 18th centuries. Medals from Hungary and the former Czechoslovakia round out the 20th century.

A view of the Museum's extensive coin cabinet containing more than 40 display cases.

Orders and Decorations

Several cases of orders and decorations from Austria and other countries are also included in the first hall. The empire's orders include Order of the Golden Fleece badge, the star and badge of the Royal Austrian-Hungarian Order of St. Stephen with collar. Most of the Republic's orders are included, such as the Order of Merit Type II star and badge, and Decoration for Arts and Science badge. Foreign orders include the badge and star of the Vatican's Equestrian Order of the Holy Sepulcher of Jerusalem with black sash and rosette, Portugal's Military Order of St. James of the Sword, and France's Legion of Honor.

Coins and Paper Money

The second hall focuses on the history of coins and paper money, from pre-monetary forms of payment to the electrum coins of the 7th century BC in the region of the Lydian coast. The exhibition continues with those of Greece and Rome, with the silver denarius being the most important Roman coin, first minted in about 211 BC. We often know about Roman emperors who ruled briefly only from evidence supplied from coins.

The Carolingian ruler Charlemagne introduced the silver denier, which later served as the model for many of Europe's currencies.

The birthplace of the first Austrian coins was Krems, with silver pennies during the reign of Leopold III (1095-1136), Margrave of Austria. The first gold coin, a gold gulden minted in Judenburg, was not created until around 1360 and was greatly inspired by the Florentine model.

The displays cover a comprehensive dynastic record of Austria's rulers through its coins up to the breakup of the empire at the end of World War I. The remaining period of the 20th century is illustrated by coins from the two republics (1918-1938, 1945-present) and the period from 1919 to 1945 associated with Nazi Germany and the surrounding countries of Czechoslovakia and Hungary.

The third hall is reserved for special exhibitions.

A 1694 gold 10-facher ducat of Leopold I of the House of Austria (Habsburgs).

Visitor's Checklist

Kunsthistorisches Museum Coin Cabinet, Maria Theresien-Platz, 1010 Vienna, Austria. The Coin Cabinet is on the 2nd Floor.

ℹ ☎ +43 (0)1 525 24 4203

○ Tuesday-Saturday: 10 a.m.-6 p.m.; extended hours Thursday: 9 p.m. Check web site for holiday hours.

● Monday

♿ ⑤ 📷 ⊗ 🎧 🛒 🍴

Public Transportation

Ⓜ U2 (Museumsquartier); U2/U3 (Volkstheater)
🚍 2A/57A (Burgring); 57A (Nibelungengasse)
🚋 D/12 (Burgring)

Internet

✉ info.mk@khm.at
🌐 www.khm.at/en/collections/coin-cabinet/ (also in German, Italian)

Bulgarian National Bank Museum Collection
Българската Народна Банка Музейна Сбирка
Sofia, Bulgaria

The Bulgarian National Bank (BNB) was established in 1879, only one year following its independence from the Ottoman Empire. Although the idea of a museum of the BNB had been discussed since the late 1920s, and after several attempts, it was not until January 1999 that a museum officially opened as part of celebrations that commemorated the Bank's 120th anniversary.

The Bulgarian National Bank building as seen from Knyaz Alexander I Square.

The Museum's collection is located in the Bank's main building, which was completed in 1939. The permanent exhibition, covering an area of over 3,000 square feet (300 square meters), is divided into several sections. It comprises a wealth of antique and medieval coins discovered in Bulgaria and dating from the 5th century BC to the present time. The exhibition also illustrates the coinage organized by the Ministry of Finance and the BNB, and covers BNB money issuing activities from 1885 onward.

There are specially designed table showcases in the style of the original furniture from the 1930s. The exhibition uses 14 large-size and three small-size showcases to display 2,200 coins and 220 banknotes with text in both Bulgarian and English.

Classical Antiquity

Three cases display about 1,000 antique coins that illustrate the intensive monetary circulation in the Balkans—a crossroad between East and West. Visitors see how minting developed as the ancient Greeks colonized the Black Sea coast, trading actively with the Thracians in the hinterland. On display are the iconographic beauty of Macedon's coinage, and the diversity of coins from the Roman period.

A view of the BNB Museum's gallery.

The Middle Ages

Three cases of about 1,300 items showcase the unsettled Balkan Middle Ages, when Byzantium shone and the Second Bulgarian Empire rose. Here, rulers of the First Bulgarian Empire (681-1018) did not mint their own coins but mainly used Byzantine coins. After the Battle of Markeli in 792 AD, Byzantium had to pay tribute in gold and silver coins to Bulgaria. There were imitation Byzantine coins that appeared during the reigns of Tsar Boris II (970-971) and Tsar Roman (977-991).

While Bulgarian coin minting may possibly date back to the reign of Czar Petar (1186-1197), what is beyond dispute is that coins were definitely minted from the reign of Czar Ivan Asen II (1218-1241) onward.

The Modern and Contemporary Periods

The remainder of the nine large and three small cases comprise Turkish coins and the entire collection of Bulgarian coins. The collection also includes supplementary material such as coin and banknote designs that never entered circulation, and tools.

Also included are numismatic specimens from the modern Bulgarian state covering four major political eras: the Principality (1879-1908), the Kingdom (1908-1946), the People's Republic (1946-1990), and the Republic since 1990. The displays include Bulgarian money, designs, mockups, and samples of both coins and banknotes. What makes this section of the collection unique is the Bulgarian National Bank's central role in the issuance of Bulgarian money and the management of its subsequent circulation, including its destruction when no longer legal tender.

There is also a restored bank clerk's office from the late 1930s and a reproduction of manual minting of coins. This allows visitors to participate actively in bringing the historical process of manual minting back to life.

An 1894 gold 100 leva from the Kremnitz Mint (КБ) showing the bust of Ferdinand I.

Visitor's Checklist

Bulgarian National Bank, 1 Knyaz Alexander I Square, 1000 Sofia, Bulgaria. The Museum Collection is located on the first floor.

- ℹ ℂ +359 2 9145 1505, +359 884 322 187, +359 2 9145 6375, +359 887 102 573
- ◯ Monday-Friday: 1 p.m.-3:30 p.m.
- ● Saturday and Sunday; January 1, March 3 (National Day of Liberation), Orthodox Easter*, May 1, 6 (St. George's Day), 24 (Sts. Cyril and Methodius Day), September 6 (Unification of Bulgaria), 22 (Independence Day), November 1 (Day of the Bulgarian Revival Leaders), December 24, 25, and 31.

✋ 📷 🎫 🚫

Public Transportation

Ⓜ M1/M2 (Serdika/Сердика)

Internet

✉ press_office@bnbank.org

🌐 http://www.bnb.bg/AboutUs/AUAboutBNB/AUHistory/AUHMuseumsBNB/index.htm (also in Bulgarian)

Numismatic Collection, Zagreb
Archaeological Museum
Numizmatička Zbirka, Arheološki Muzej u Zagrebu
Zagreb, Croatia

The Archaeological Museum in Zagreb is one of the direct successors to the former National Museum, the oldest museum institution in the Croatian capital. Founded in 1836, this first National Museum was opened to the public with an exhibition held in 1846. The Archaeological Museum today consists of more than 450,000 varied artifacts, and the Numismatic Collection is the largest and most important collection of this type in Croatia. Although metal coins predominate, the collection contains over 270,000 specimens of metal coins, banknotes, medals, certificates, medallions, badges, orders, tags, and tokens. The Numismatic Library that operates in the scope of the department is also important.

Front façade of the Zagreb Archaeological Museum in the Vranyc-zany-Hafner mansion on Zrinski Square.

The collection was displayed for the first time in 1978, and is in its current location in the Vranyczany-Hafner mansion on Zrinski Square. In 2009 it was enlarged and the text in all displays are bilingual: Croatian and English.

The Central Gallery
The central part of the permanent display is represented by coins that are arranged chronologically and geographically: Greek coinage, including the Lydian, Imperial, and

Greek city states, coins from both the Roman Republic (509-27 BC) and Imperial Rome (27 BC-476 AD) periods, Byzantine coins, Medieval and later coinage, as well as some medals. The permanent display represents a review of the most important coins kept in the Museum. Various types of Celtic coinage minted in the territory later occupied by modern Croatia, as well as Greek-Illyrian coins from the Central Dalmatian mints, are especially important.

Partial view of the gallery with many of the coins mounted on swivel-type displays.

Numerous Hoards

There are also quite a number of hoards on display from various periods, accompanied with the very vessels they were found with. These include: silver coins from 3rd-century Imperial Rome which were found in Pitomača (1966); Italian and African 3rd-2nd century BC bronze coins found in Mazin (1896); 17th-century Ottoman-Bosnian copper coins in a small clay pitcher found in Mitrovica (1885); a savings box found in Kneginec (1885) containing a mixture of Austrian, Bohemian, German, and Hungarian coins from the 15th-16th centuries; and a clay pitcher containing 15th-16th century silver coins from Hungary, Poland, Venice, Kotor, and Dobrovnic which was discovered in Valpovo (1897).

The Modern coins of Croatia issued by the Croatian National Bank on display include numerous mint sets and commemorative coins in addition to banknotes currently in circulation.

Additional Greek and Roman Coins

Additional Greek and Roman coins are displayed as part of the ancient Greek and ancient Roman collections on the 2nd floor. A silver denarius with the head of the Roman Empress Plautille (202-211 AD) is on display while groups of coins, mostly dating from the 4th-3rd centuries BC from the ancient Roman and Greek provinces associated with modern day Croatia, such as: Corcyra Melaina, Issa, Far (Pharos), and Heraclea.

Hoard of 17th-century Ottoman-Bosnian copper coins in a small clay pitcher found in Mitrovica in 1885.

Visitor's Checklist

Zagreb Archaeological Museum, 19 Nikola Subic Zrinski Square (Trg Nikole Šubiⵉa Zrinskog 19), 10000 Zagreb, Croatia. The numismatic collection is on the ground floor. Some Greek and Roman coins are also displayed as part of the ancient Greek and ancient Roman collections on the 2nd floor.

🛈 ☽ (+385 1) 48 73 101

◯ Tuesday, Wednesday, Friday, Saturday: 10 a.m.-5 p.m.; Thursday: 10 a.m.-8 p.m.; Sunday: 10 a.m.-1 p.m.

● Monday; January 1, December 24-26.

✋ ♿ 📷 🛒

Public Transportation

Tram 6/13 (Zrinjevac)

Internet

✉ amz@amz.hr

🌐 www.amz.hr/home/departments/collections/the-numismatic-collection.aspx (also in Croatian)

Bank of Estonia Museum
Eesti Panga Muuseum
Tallinn, Estonia

The Neo-Gothic red brick building of the Bank of Estonia Museum is the former building of the bank of the Credit Society of the Estonian Knighthood. Built in 1904, at the time it represented the first modern purpose-built bank in Tallinn. The building is dominated by a corner tower with a lion-shaped weather vane, and above the portal is the coat of arms of the Estonian Province. The tower also bears coats of arms of the County of Harju and towns of Tallinn, Paldiski, Rakvere, Paide and Haapsalu. The building was fully transferred to the Bank of Estonia in 1998.

Corner entrance to the Bank of Estonia Museum with the coats of arms of the County of Harju and towns of Tallinn, Paldiski, Rakvere, Paide, and Haapsalu.

2010 Renovations

Extensive renovations were carried out at the end of 2010 that increased the Museum's size from approximately 1,900 to 4,000 square feet (180 to 370 square meters). There are three exhibition halls: Aadlisaal (Hall of Nobility), Peasant, and Treasury Center. All have a little piece of hidden history in each one which introduces a related field: history of English money, money, production, and operations of the Bank of Estonia.

The new Museum has been extended past the display of the history of English money. The exhibit provides an explanation of the origin of the word "money," what has been its meaning over time, and what monies were in use since ancient times. Computer animation is used to explain the meaning of money and the role of the Viking trade and Estonian participation in world trade in the 9th-10th centuries.

History of Estonian Currency

On display are the currencies that were used in Estonia before it became an independent republic in 1918. The Museum also displays every banknote and coin issued since independence, including the initial promissory and credit notes to the first actual currency banknotes denominated in the original marka system until 1940. This is followed by occupations by the Russians (1940-1941, and 1945-1990) and the Germans (1941-1944), after which independence from the Soviet Bloc allowed the 1992 monetary reform that established the Eesti kroon from 1992 to 2010. Starting in 2011, Estonians traded in their krooni for euros as the 17th member of the euro area.

One display shows printing plates that were carefully buried in 1940, anticipating that they may be needed after the Russians were to leave the country. These were rediscovered in 2000 and used once for a special trial print with the 1940 date.

A 1919 10-marka banknote of the first issue of the newly independent Estonia.

Interactive Games and Multimedia

The displays are accompanied by thematic games that help better realize everything related to the central bank. The new exposition contains a total of 24 various interactive games, animations, exhibitions, and sound and video solutions. Multimedia is displayed in Estonian, English, and Russian, while display texts are both in Estonian and English.

Visitors can also see a historic gold bar of Eesti Pank from 1922 that was part of the reserves backing the kroon during the first Republic of Estonia and also during re-independence. The historic gold bar was delivered to Estonia in December 2011 by the Federal Reserve Bank of New York.

The Museum is located in the heart of Tallinn, a city which gained UNESCO heritage recognition in 1997 as one of Europe's best-preserved medieval towns.

A 1934 Estonia 1-kroon coin made from an aluminum-bronze alloy.

Visitor's Checklist

Bank of Estonia Museum, Estonia piuestee (boulevard) 11, Tallinn, Estonia. The entrance is on Sakala Street.

ℹ ℂ +372 668 0760

○ Tuesday-Friday: 12:00 noon-5 p.m.; Saturday: 11:00 a.m.-4 p.m.

● Sunday; June 24 (St. John's Day/Midsummer Day).

Public Transportation

🚌 17/17A/23/23A/67/68 (Estonia)

🚊 3/4 (Vabaduse väljak); trolleys: 1/3/6 (Vabaduse väljak), 2 (Estonia)

Internet

✉ muuseum@eestipank.ee

🌐 www.bankofestonia.info/pub/en/press/muuseum/ (also in Estonian)

Numismatic Museum Athens
Νομισματικό Μουσείο Αθηνών
Athens, Greece

Founded in 1829, the Numismatic Museum Athens is in a neo-classical mansion once the home of Heinrich Schliemann, a self-taught archaeologist who named it "Iliou Melathron" (Palace of Ilion, or Troy) after the ancient city he excavated in the 1870s. Schliemann also collected coins, and his 1881 home is now the Museum for both Greece's national numismatic collection and his own collection.

There are more than 600,000 coins, lead seals, medallions, and balance weights from ancient Greece, Rome, Byzantium, the European Middle Ages and modern times. About 2,500 coins are exhibited in more than 40 displays in 13 rooms on both floors.

Front façade of the Iliou Melathron as seen from Eleftheriou Venizelou Street.

First Floor Galleries

One of the first floor's galleries is the "Schliemann Hall," where Schliemann's collection of coins of Ithaca, Thera (now Santorini), the Troad, Roman Empire, and coins from his excavations of Troy are in their original wooden table-top cases.

Three of the remaining five first floor galleries are themes of coins of the ancient Greek World.

- Origins and Spread. The large "Hesperides" Hall contains exhibits about the use of coinage as historical sources, the metals and techniques of coin production, and the names of ancient Hellenic coins. Specimens from Lydia from the 7th-century BC are the first coins of standard weight and bearing the stamp of the issuing city. There are also many coin hoards on display. One, from Karditsa where 149 Aeginetan silver staters hidden in an olpe, were thought to have been buried around 440 BC.

- International and Common Coins. Examples are the silver tetradrachm and the gold stater.
- Iconography and Ideology. Many of the exhibits of its ancient Greek coins are displayed in topical fashion, i.e., "monetary iconography," rather as an historical evolution from the earliest coins of Lydia to its last rulers. Shown are the portrait heads—rulers like Ptolemy V, Alexander III, and Antichus I Soter, while the eagle on the shekel of Tyre and the owl on the Athenian tetradrachm are some of the many animals pictured.
- The Great Donors of the Numismatic Museum. What was once the dining room now honors collections by its "Great Donors"—Greek collectors, many from the Diaspora who preserve their ancestral heritage.

The large Hesperides Hall on the first floor of the Iliou Melathron.

The second floor has eight galleries with different themes:
- Coinage in the Roman World. From the 3rd century BC to the 5th century AD.
- Coinage in the Byzantine World. The gold, silver, and copper coins of the solidus monetary system.
- Coinage in the Western and Eastern Medieval World. The development of coins and monetary system of Western Europe and the first Arabic coins.
- Coinage in the Modern and Contemporary World. From the 16th century to the present, highlighting many of the silver and gold crowns of the European states.

- Coinage in the Modern Greek State. From the 1928 silver phoenix and the modern drachm in 1932 to its end with the 2002 euro.
- The World of Medals. In Schliemann's winter office, medallic art that portrays historical events, rulers, buildings, and personalities.
- Money and Society. The relationship between people and money in various time periods is examined in Schliemann's summer office with emphasis on notable coins like the tetradrachm, solidus, dirham, ducat, thaler, pound sterling, dollar, and euro.
- Money and Movies. The relation between man and money in scenes from different time periods.

Numismatic highlights include the Athenian silver decadrachm (475-465 BC) and the denarius of Marcus Junius Brutus with two daggers on the reverse (43-42 BC).

The gold medal of the first modern Olympic Games of 1896.

Visitor's Checklist
Numismatic Museum Athens, 12 Eleftheriou Venizelou Street (aka Panepistimiou Street), GR-106 71 Athens

ⓘ ℂ +30-2103632057, +30-2103612834, and +30-2103612872
◯ Tuesday-Sunday: 8:30 a.m.-3 p.m.
⬤ Monday; January 1, March 25 (Independence Day), Orthodox Easter Sunday*, May 1, December 25 and 26. An asterisk (*) denotes a movable holiday date.
✋ ⓖ ⬚ 🖸 🛒 🍽

Public Transportation
Ⓜ 2-red/3-blue (Syntagma/ ΣΥΝΤΑΓΜΑ); 2-red (Panepistimio/ ΠΑΝΕΠΙΣΤΗΜΙΟ)
 1/12/21 (Kriezotou/ΚΡΙΕΖΩΤΟΥ)

Internet
✉ Use the on-line contact form at: www.nma.gr/contact1_en.htm
🌐 www.nma.gr/index_en.htm (also in Greek)

Banknote Museum of the Ionian Bank, Corfu
Μουσείο Χαρτονομισμάτων Ιονικής Τράπεζής, Κέρκυρα
Corfu, Greece

The Banknote Museum of the Ionian Bank originally opened in 1981. It is located in what was the first branch building of the Ionian Bank in Corfu before its 2000 merger with Greece's second largest bank, Alpha Bank. The Museum was subsequently renovated and reopened in 2005. On display is a nearly complete assembly of Greece's banknotes following the 1821 declaration of independence, starting from 1822 up to Greece's conversion to the euro in 2002.

The Ionian Bank building (ΙΟΝΙΚΗ ΤΡΑΠΕΖΑ) in Corfu's Aghios Spyridon (St. Spyridon) Square.

Revolutionary Bonds of 1822 to the Euro

The exhibition of approximately 1,500 specimens covers four rooms. The first three rooms begin chronologically with the Revolutionary (treasury) Bonds of 1822 and the first editions of the National Bank in 1862, and ends with the latest series of the Democratic Republic before being replaced by the euro.

The National Bank of Greece was established in 1841 and the ancient drachma again became the Greece's official monetary unit. The Museum exhibits the first banknotes printed by the British firms Perkins Bacon and Bradbury Wilkins. The collection also includes the notes printed by the American Banknote Company, which succeeded the British firms at the turn of the century until about 1928. After that, the Bank of Greece undertook the printing of the banknotes itself.

Greece's Largest Banknote Denomination

Banknotes that were issued by the Germans and Italians who occupied Greece during World War II are shown as examples of banknotes issued during 1944, the notorious year of hyperinflation that produced Greece's largest banknote denomination—100 billion (American, 100 trillion) drachmas.

The Museum has a complete series of the last issue of the banknotes of the member countries of the euro area prior to their replacement by the euro. The manufacturing process of banknotes is included among the exhibits as well as the method of adding a watermark. There is also an area that explains the metal plate engraving process for banknotes.

Banknotes issued by the Provisional Democratic Government of Greece's Communist Party are also exhibited, which were valued against the equivalent value of kilograms of wheat.

In addition to actual banknote specimens, the exhibition also includes sketches, essays, and printing plates of Greek banknotes.

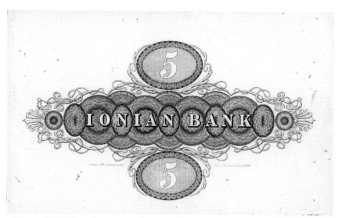

A rare 1860 5-colonata uniface color proof in black of the Ionian Bank, engraved by Perkins, Bacon, & Petch.

Exhibition Highlights

The Museum has several highlights on display that can be seen. One is the rare 1860 "Colonata" banknote. Another is a rare banknote showing Istanbul's (formerly Constantinople) Hagia Sophia without the traditional minarets. Designed in 1920 when functioning as a mosque, the note was released for circulation. Other highlights include the first banknotes issued by first Governor of Greece, Ioannis Kapodistrias, which feature a rose colored phoenix on white background.

The fourth room is dedicated to material pertaining to the history of the Ionian Bank prior to its merger with the Alpha Bank.

Greece's largest denominated banknote – 100 billion (American, 100 trillion) drachmas issued in 1944, with the head of the nymph Deidamia.

Visitor's Checklist

Banknote Museum of the Ionian Bank, Aghios Spyridon (St. Spyridon) Square, 491 00 Corfu, Greece. The Museum is located on the first floor (2nd level, American).

ℹ ℂ +30 266 104 1552

○ Wednesday-Sunday: 8 a.m.-3 p.m. (October 1-March 31); Wednesday and Friday: 9 a.m.-2:00 p.m. and 5:30-8:30 p.m., Thursday: 9 a.m.-3 p.m., Saturday and Sunday: 8:30 a.m.-3 p.m. (April 1-September 30).

● Monday and Thursday (October 1-March 31), Monday and Tuesday (April 1-September 30).

Internet

✉ banknotemuseum@alpha.gr

⊕ www.alpha.gr/page/default.asp?la=2&id=689

Hungarian National Bank Visitor Center
Magyar Nemzeti Bank Látogatóközpontja
Budapest, Hungary

The Hungarian National Bank (*Magyar Nemzeti Bank*), built in 1905, is located on the eastern side of Budapest's historic Freedom Square (*Szabadság tér*). It is one block from the U.S. Embassy and across the square from the former Stock Exchange building that now serves as the headquarters for Hungarian National Television. The building's limestone frieze even features carvings with motifs of smelting ore, designing paper money, industry and trade, banking and mining.

As the country's central bank, it opened its Visitor Center in the spring of 2004 as an interactive museum for adults and children to exhibit the history of money from the earliest times to the euro.

The Hungarian National Bank as seen from Freedom Square in Budapest.

Bank Visitor Center

The Museum uses computer displays and films along with traditional exhibits, in Hungarian only, of its specimens of coins and other articles to show visitors how money developed through history—from the Kaori shell money of the South Pacific islands to today's modern telebanking services. Included are examples from times when bartering was the norm, such as how many chickens were worth one cow.

Interactive Activities

The Visitor Center also features a number of interactive activities. Visitors can stand on a scale, and after a short delay, a printed receipt will indicate how much one weighs as measured in 100-forint coins. Visitors can operate a coin press that was in use from the 14th to the 19th centuries. One can try to lift a 12-kg gold bar and compare it with similar sized bars of lead and iron. Visitors can even print their picture on a banknote, but only if enough quiz questions are answered correctly.

Besides quizzes and games, there are also fascinating facts presented, such as that it takes approximately 1,000 shredded banknotes to make one brick weighing 1.2 kg of outdated or damaged banknotes. There is also a wall panel made up of Hungarian sayings that include the Hungarian word *pénz* (money) and its variations.

A 1539 gold ducat showing St. Ladislas, struck at the Kremnitz Mint during the reign of Ferdinand I.

Hungarian Money and the Euro

Against the back wall visitors can also follow the milestones in both the history of money in Hungary and the Magyar Nemzeti Bank, understanding the Bank's tasks and goals in its role as the nation's central banker.

Although Hungary is not currently a member of the EU's euro area, there are displays that explain the euro, the European Union's common currency, with examples that show the wide range of notes and coins from various periods and euro area countries, including currencies that have not even been issued yet.

Also included is the history of the bank building including such items as scales, wax and seals, and pens. A recreation of an office from a 1920s bank includes a huge Waltheim safe, dating from 1879. There's also a section with coins and banknotes from different countries, and a section on price and stability, and counterfeiting.

Egymillárd billió pengő hyperinflation note of June 3, 1946, having the equivalent of 21 zeros, which was never placed into circulation.

Visitor's Checklist

Magyar Nemzeti Bank, Szabadság tér 8/9, 1854 Budapest, Hungary

❶ ℂ +36 1 428-2752

○ Monday-Friday: 9 a.m.-3:30 p.m.; extended hours: Thursday until 5:30 p.m.

● Saturday and Sunday; national holidays.

✋ 🔒 (lockers) 🛒 (Hungarian Mint Ltd.)

The denar of St. Stephen I (997-1038).

Public Transportation

Ⓜ M3 (Arany János utca)

🚍 72/73/109 (Arany János utca); 15 (Széchenyi utca)

Internet

✉ info@mnb.hu

🌐 english.mnb.hu/Root/ENMNB/A_jegybank/mnben_dummy/mnben_lk_old (also in Hungarian)

Money Museum of the Bank of Lithuania
Lietuvos banko Pinigų muziejus
Vilnius, Lithuania

The Money Museum of the Bank of Lithuania was created in 1999 and is located next to the headquarters of the nation's central bank. The high-technology Museum's exhibition is divided into five galleries on two floors where visitors are introduced to the history of world money, the complicated history of Lithuanian money, and banking in Lithuania.

The telephone, which was in use at the Bank of Lithuania in the pre-war period, rings as visitors stop to take a close look at it. The voice of the Chairman of the Bank of Lithuania welcomes visitors to the Money Museum. Basic information is provided in Lithuanian and English.

Visitors lining up at the Money Museum's entrance at the corner of Totorių gatvė and Gedimino prospektas.

The History of Money Hall

This Hall, located in the basement, presents the development of money from its most primitive forms, like grain, cowrie shells, furs, and amber to electronic money. The exposition is divided into memorable themes and provides the answers to the key questions regarding the history of money: What is money needed for? What was the first money? How are coins minted? Why is gold the most appreciated metal?

The History of Banking Hall

On the ground floor, visitors are introduced to the beginning of banking, the subsequent stages of its development, and its development in Lithuania from the emergence of the first credit institutions to the present day. The role of the Bank of Lithuania in pushing through a currency reform in 1922, stabilizing the country's financial and credit market during the years of the global economic crisis is revealed, and the decline of banking following Lithuania's occupation by the Soviets is highlighted.

The Contemporary Money Hall

Banknotes and coins used in different countries today are on display here. Visitors can view the banknotes put in special drawers after pulling open the drawer with the name of a selected country. The drawers are connected by special sensors to a computer program that activates the screen on a video wall and presents relevant information about the selected country on it. This information for about 200 countries can also be viewed on the wall using a computer terminal.

In this hall, information is presented about the Bank of Lithuania, the nation's central bank. As one of its major functions is to issue currency, exhibits displayed in the showcases tell about the production of contemporary Lithuanian money, its productions materials, and the technological solutions applied by different producers with uncirculated specimen banknotes on display. The cases and computer terminals provide visitors with banknote security features and immediately verify the authenticity of the banknotes in hand by UV detection.

One section of the History of Money Hall.

The Lithuanian Money Hall

Exhibits are able to be seen using a vertical automatic conveyor. Each of the eight conveyors carries plastic cards with the coins of the Grand Duchy of Lithuania, Republic of Lithuania, and other territories which had been in circulation in the country. Pushing a button allow visitors to adjust the height of viewing the cards with the coins, and raise or pull down a lens to view small elements of a coin. In the stationary cases are the commemorative coins of the Republic of Lithuania and in the 20 pull-out cases, the banknotes used in the country from the late 18th century to the present day are on display.

For the consolidation of knowledge, tests for the visitors of age 14 and over have been prepared. Those who give correct answers to the questions will get a prize—their own image on a souvenir banknote.

A display of Lithuanian banknotes, circulation, and commemorative coins in the Lithuanian Money Hall.

Visitor's Checklist

Money Museum of the Bank of Lithuania, Totorių gatvė (Tartar Street) 2, LT-01121 Vilnius, Lithuania. The Museum is at the corner of Totorių gatvė and Gedimino prospektas (Gediminas Avenue).

- ❶ ℂ +370 5 268 0334, +370 5 268 0077
- ◯ Tuesday-Friday: 10 a.m.-7 p.m.; Saturday: 11 a.m.-6 p.m. (April 1 - October 31) and Tuesday-Friday: 9 a.m.-6 p.m.; Saturday: 10 a.m.-5 p.m. (November 1-March 31).
- ● Sunday and Monday; January 1, February16 (Restoration of the State Day-1918), March 11 (Restoration of Independence Day-1990), Easter*, May 1, June 24 (St John's Day/Midsummer's Day), July 6 (Anniversary of the Coronation of King Mindaugas), Assumption Day, November 1, December 25, 26. An asterisk (*) denotes a movable holiday date.

✴ ⑤ ◻ ◯ 🛒

Public Transportation

🚌 2/3/5/6/11/12/14/15/20/21/26/43/53/88/89 (Vinco Kudirkos aikštė/Vincas Kudirka Square)

Internet

✉ muziejus@lb.lt

⊕ http://www.lb.lt/bol_money_museum (also in Lithuanian)

Royal Castle Museum Coin Cabinet
Zamek Królewski Muzeum
Gabinet Numizmatyczny
Warsaw, Poland

The Royal Castle, located in Warsaw's Castle Square, was the home of the Polish monarch. It was built in the years 1589-1619 for Sigmund III Vasa, from the Swedish dynasty of Vasa that ruled Poland at that time. The current structure was rebuilt several times, the last being 1971-1988 as a national monument of Polish history and culture when it was destroyed during World War II.

Arial view of the Royal Castle in Warsaw's Castle Square.

Exhibition of Coins and Medals in Polish History
The Cabinet of the Royal Castle in Warsaw was established in 1981 to continue the tradition of Cabinet des Médailles of the last Polish king, Stanisław II August (1764-1795). The Royal Castle's Numismatic Cabinet has the largest numismatic exhibition in Poland, which opened in September 1985. From its collection, approximately 3,500 items are on display in the permanent exhibit, dating from the 16th century to the present time illustrating the history of Polish minting from the beginnings of the Polish State. In addition to coins, the exhibition includes a selection of banknotes, exchequers, and dies.

Also, the approximate 600 medals are a metallic record of Polish history. The most beautiful medals date from the Baroque period and are the work of famous medallists from Gdańsk such as Sebastian Dadler, and both Jan Höhn the Elder and the Younger.

303

This exhibition is a popular venue for holding museum classes that are conducted for school children. Since 1995 the Numismatic Collection of Bank Handlowy w Warszawie (Commercial Bank of Warsaw) has also formed part of this exhibition and from 2000, so has a selection of 86 medals and gold and gilded plaques from Andrzej Ciechanowiecki's sizeable collection.

The Numismatic Collection of Bank Handlowy w Warszawie

The Numismatic Collection of Bank Handlowy w Warszawie has been on permanent display in the Numismatic Cabinet since 1992 and the collection was donated to the Castle in 2003. It comprises 155 numismatic items of outstanding artistic and historical merit—coins, medals, and banknotes, which are either Polish or connected with Poland.

The coins include very valuable, often unique, medieval issues of the denarii and bracteati of the first Polish kings and dukes. The modern coins include a large number of ducats and their multiples, as well as thalers and their fractions, of nearly all the Polish kings and coins dating to the period of the partitions, as well as the highly sought-after proof coins of the Second Republic (1918-1939). Besides the coins, the collection also contains some very rare banknotes—those dating from the Kościuszko Insurrection to the very first issues of the Bank of Poland, and banknotes and bonds dating from the times of the Polish national uprisings which took place in the 19th century. There are 40 outstanding gold and silver medals, including those from Silesia and Pomerania, commemorating royal coronations and weddings, as well as important events and distinguished people.

A 1611 gold ducat with the image of Sigismund III, from Danzig.

Visitor's Checklist

The Royal Castle in Warsaw, The Numismatic Cabinet (2nd Floor), plac Zamkowy 4, 00-277 Warsaw, Poland

- ❶ ℂ +48 (0)22 35 55 170
- ○ Tuesday-Saturday: 10 a.m.-4 p.m., Sunday: 11 a.m.-4 p.m.
- ● January 1, 6 (Epiphany), Good Friday*, Holy Saturday*, Easter Sunday*, November 1 (All Saints' Day), December 24, 25, and 31. An asterisk (*) denotes a movable date.

✋ (Sundays free) 🍴 📷 (but no flash) ⊗ 🎧

Public Transportation

- Ⓜ Ratusz
- 🚌 100 (Stare Miasto)
- 🚊 13/23/26/32 (Stare Miasto)

Internet

- ✉ informacja@zamek-krolewski.pl
- 🌐 zamek-krolewski.pl/?page=2156

Visitor Center of the National Bank of Serbia
Центар за посетиоце Народна банка Србије
Centar za posetioce Narodna banka Srbije
Belgrade, Serbia

The Visitor Center of the National Bank of Serbia (NBS) opened in July 2004 on the occasion of the 120th anniversary of its creation as the Privileged National Bank of the Kingdom of Serbia. For the first time ever, the NBS presented part of its numismatic collection publically in a standing exhibition entitled, "Money on the Territory of Serbia." Periodically, temporary theme exhibitions have been added as well as a number of interesting interactive displays.

Front entrance of the Visitor Center of the National Bank of Serbia.

Money of the Territory of Serbia

The standing exhibition illustrates the course of development and use of money on the territory of today's Serbia from its earliest appearance to the latest money issues. The oldest money in the exhibition dates to the 4th century BC, coined by Greek city-states. Shown are coins of the Athens city-state and the Macedonian rulers Philip II and Alexander the Great.

In the 2nd and 1st centuries BC, the Roman Republic coined its famous silver money, the denarius. The derivative of its name, the dinar, is still found in the names of national currencies of many countries, including present-day Serbia.

Medieval Serbian Rulers

Display specimens illustrate the tradition of coining money in the medieval Serbian state beginning in the 13th century with such as those by King Stefan, while the Imperial period is represented by numerous issues of Emperor Dušan. His "coronation dinar" stands out by its importance and beauty of the image of two flying angels placing the crown on the emperor's head. The medieval Serbian state together with the Serbian dinar disappeared from use when Serbia fell under domination of the Ottoman Empire in the 15th century.

A view of one section of the gallery, showcasing banknotes.

The New Era

With the its loss of independence, money used in the territory of today's Serbia until the mid-19th century was that of foreign countries, mostly that of Turkey, but also those of Dubrovnik, Venice, Austria, Hungary, and other European monarchies of the time.

After independence from Turkish rule, Serbia took its first steps toward establishing a national monetary system. As of 1868 during the reign of Prince Mihailo Obrenović, the first copper coins were minted; the first silver coins were struck in 1875 when the dinar was introduced; and the first gold coins were issued in 1879. The issuing of paper money began with the foundation of the Privileged National Bank of the Kingdom of Serbia in 1884, when the first Serbian banknote of 100 dinars was printed in Belgium. Examples of all such specimens are on display.

A Changing Serbia

Following World War I, all the issues of banknotes and coins in the changing periods of the Kingdom of Serbs, Croats and Slovenes (1918–1920), the Kingdom of Serbs, Croats and Slovenes (until 1929), the Kingdom of Yugoslavia, and issues following World War II until the last currency issues in Yugoslavia in 2003, are presented in the exhibition. There is a display recalling Yugoslavia's hyperinflation of the 1990s with the largest hyperinflationary banknote—the 500 billion (with 11 zeros) dinara note of 1993 showing the portrait of poet Jovan Zmaj. Following the new State Union of Serbia and Montenegro, the National Bank of Yugoslavia became the National Bank of Serbia, which now issues the money to be used in the territory of the Republic of Serbia.

There are also exhibits on security features of the Serbian, euro, and U.S. paper money. Visitors are able to print a souvenir 1-dinar banknote with their picture as a portrait and watermark.

A Serbian 1882 gold 20 dinara with King Milan Obrenović, minted in Vienna.

Visitor's Checklist
Visitor Center of the National Bank of Serbia, 12 Kralja Petra Street, 11 000 Belgrade (Beograd), Serbia

ℹ ℭ (+381 11) 3027-204, 3027-318, 3027-354

○ Monday-Friday: 10 a.m.-4 p.m.

● Saturday and Sunday.

✋ 🖼 📷

Public Transportation
Tram 19/21/22/28/29/31/41 (Studenski Park/Studenski trg)

Internet
✉ izlozba@nbs.rs

🌐 www.nbs.rs/internet/english/75/75_3/75_3_2.html
(also in Serbian - Latin and Cyrillic)

National Bank of Slovakia – Museum of Coins and Medals in Kremnica
Národná banka Slovenska – Múzeum mincí a medailí v Kremnici
Two Faces of Money - Money and Medal-Making in the History of Slovakia

Kremnica, Slovakia

The Museum of Coins and Medals of the National Bank of Slovakia was founded in 1890. It was originally only concerned with the town of Kremnica and the region but in 1976 it became a specialized museum of numismatics. The town's famous mint, also known by its German name Kremnitz, was established in 1328 under the reign of the Hungarian King Charles I, still turns out coins and medals for Slovakia plus coins for over 25 countries worldwide.

The Museum has various collections, including valuable exhibits in numismatics, medal art, history and plastic arts, all of which comprise around 100,000 items. The exhibition is presented in both Slovak and English.

The main building of the old Kremnica Mint, established in 1328, now serves as an exposition of historical machines.

Two Faces of Money

The exhibition, "Two Faces of Money—Money and Medal-Making in the History of Slovakia," is situated in a gothic civic house in the historical square. It presents the history and evolution of money in Slovakia from ancient times to the present coins and banknotes, as well as the history of medal making. An important part of the exhibition is dedicated to the history of the old mining and minting town of Kremnica with its famous mint.

On the first floor, visitors learn about the complex history of money in the Slovak region from the oldest times to the present with a particular focus on production at the Kremnica Mint. Visitors also learn about the development of coin minting from the Middle Ages, as well as a display of minting machinery and the many rare test specimens.

There is a presentation of the various means of payment that pre-dated coins, and the oldest coins struck in present-day Slovakia region produced by the Celts from the 3rd to 1st centuries BC. This is followed by a display of Roman, Byzantine and western European coins used in Slovakia from the beginning of the Common Era until the 10th century.

The room, "Money in the History of Slovakia," of the Two Faces of Money exhibition.

Minting Methods

On display, the oldest coins were minted manually at Kremnica on a block using a coining die and a hammer up to the 17th century. Gradually the Kremnica Mint introduced machine minting; from 1661 it used a minting rolling machine and from 1710, a minting screw press called a Balancier machine. From the 19th century, automatic minting machines became a part of the technical equipment of the Mint.

In another room, visitors see the various currencies of the multi-national Habsburg monarchy, as well the efforts to establish a monetary union. The history of paper as a means of payment in Hungary dates back to 1762. Visitors can view the inflation money from the Napoleonic wars, the money of revolutionaries in Hungary (1848-1849), the banknotes of the Austro-Hungarian Bank, and the first Czechoslovak banknotes.

Recent Currency

Recent history is brought to life by viewing coins and banknotes after 1948 including specimens of coins that were not put into production. The origins of the 1993 Slovak currency are presented in great detail—from the printing of the Czechoslovak banknotes, to the art designs of coins, to the final version of the Slovak koruna. At the end, visitors view circumstances surrounding the introduction of the euro in Slovakia starting in 2009.

On the second floor, visitors can see the history of making medals in Slovakia.

In a unique installation in the lower basement, examples of individual types of historic mining tunnels have been dug into the andesite. The tunnels date from the oldest times to the present day, and there are also various mining tools, mining carts and other equipment on display.

A 1619 silver thaler, minted in Kremnica, showing the laurel-head bust of Matthias II.

Visitor's Checklist

National Bank of Slovakia Museum of Coins and Medals, Štefánikovo námestie (Štefánik Square) 11/21, 967 01 Kremnica, Slovakia

"Two Faces of Money of the National Bank of Slovakia – Museum of Coins and Medals in Kremnica," numismatic-historical exhibition, Štefánikovo námestie 10/19, 967 01 Kremnica, Slovakia

- ❶ ℂ +421 (0)45-6742696, +421 (0)45-6780308
- ◯ Tuesday-Sunday: 8:30 a.m.-5:30 p.m. (July 1-September 30), or Tuesday-Saturday: 9 a.m.-4:30 p.m. (October 1-June 30).
- ● Every Monday; Sunday (July 1-September 30 only); January 1, 6 (Epiphany), Grand (or Good) Friday*, November 1, December 24, 25, 26, and 31.
- ✋ ♿ (not everywhere) 🪪 (ID required) 📷 📚 🎧 🛒

Public Transportation

🚌 Kremnica Central Bus Station

Internet

✉ muzeum@nbs.sk

🌐 www.muzeumkremnica.sk/en/home (also in Slovak)

Additional Institutions, Eastern Europe

The following east European institutions are known to have numismatic exhibitions of varying degrees that are open to the public. These are listed here, either because sufficient information could not (1) be obtained about the museum, (2) be verified from other sources, (3) the museum did not respond to repeated requests for information, (4) the exhibition is closed due to long-term renovation of the building or other reasons, (5) or I learned about this venue just before the manuscript was to go to the publisher and complete information could not be included.

Austria
Austrian National Bank Money Museum
Österreichische Nationalbank Geldmuseum
Österreichische Nationalbank, Otto-Wagner-Platz 3, A-1090 Vienna
ℹ️ ✆ +43-1 404 20-6644 (for tours)
✉️ geldmuseum@oenb.at
🌐 www.oenb.at/en/ueber_die_oenb/geldmuseum/money_museum_and_ collections. jsp (also in German)

Coin Cabinet Schloss Eggenberg
Münzkabinett Schloss Eggenberg
Schloss Eggenberg (Eggenberg Castle), Eggenberger Allee 90, 8020 Graz
ℹ️ ✆ +43-316/58 32 64-9513
✉️ muenzkabinett@museum-joanneum.at
🌐 www.museum-joanneum.datenkraft.info/en/presse/museum_sites/permanent_ exhibitions/coin-cabinet-schloss-eggenberg (also in German)

Greece
Museum of the Bank of Greece
Μουσείο της Τράπεζας της Ελλάδος
3 Amerikis Street, Athens GR 102 50
ℹ️ ✆ +30 210 320 3555, -5305, -5306
✉️ museum@bankofgreece.gr
🌐 www.bankofgreece.gr/Pages/en/Bank/museum/default.aspx (also in Greek)

Museum of the National Bank of Greece
Μουσείο η Εθνική Τράπεζα της Ελλάδος
Tritis Septemvriou 146, GR 11251 Athens
❶ ℂ +30 210 8807804
⊕ www.greek-coins.net/nbg-museum (unofficial site)
❶ ℂ +39 06 39967700

Macedonia
National Bank of the Republic of Macedonia Museum
Народна банка на Република Македонија
Bulevar Kuzman Josifovski Pitu br 1, Skopje, 1000
❶ ℂ +389 (0)2 3108 108
⊕ www.nbrm.mk/?ItemID=8B62BE8B1342BA49B780D71C5AA36ABB (in Macedonian only)

Poland
The National Museum in Cracow/Emeryk Hutten-Czapski Museum
Muzeum Narodowe w Krakowie/Muzeum im. Emeryka Hutten-Czapskiego
12 Józefa Piłsudskiego Street, Kraków
❶ ℂ +48 12 62 57 310
✉ mwozniak@muzeum.krakow.pl
⊕ www.muzeum.krakow.pl/About-the-museum.88.0.html?&L=1 (also in Polish)

Russia
A.C. Pushkin Museum of Fine Arts
Государственный Музей Изобразительных Искусств Имени А.С. Пушкина
12 Volkhonka Street, Moscow 119019
❶ ℂ +7 (495) 609 9520, +7 (495) 697 7414
⊕ www.coins-and-medals.ru/?en (also in Russian)

State Historical Museum
Государственный Исторический Музей
Red Square 1, Moscow, 109012
❶ ℂ +7 (495) 692-06-68
⊕ www.shm.ru/en/dep_numizmat.html (also in Russian)

Turkey
Yapi Kredi Bank Vedat Nedim Tör Museum
Yapı Kredi Bankası Vedat Nedim Tör Müzesi
⬚stiklal Caddesi No. 285 Kat 1, 34433 Beyo⬚lu, ⬚stanbul
ℹ ℂ +90 212 252 47 00
🌐 www.yapikredi.com.tr/en-US/culture/vedat_nedim_tor_museum.aspx

Ukraine
Feodosia Money Museum
Феодосійський музей грошей
12, Kuybysheva Street, Feodosia, Crimea
ℹ ℂ +38 (06562) 2-14-33
✉ admin@museum-of-money.org, director@museum-of-money.org
🌐 en.museum-of-money.org (also in Ukrainian, Russian)

Odessa Numismatics Museum
Одеський Музей Нумізматики
Catherine's Square 5, Odessa
ℹ ℂ +380 (0)482 725 02 77
✉ loboda@te.net.ua
🌐 www.museum.com.ua/en/o_musee/ab_mus.htm (also in Ukrainian, Russian)

The Middle East

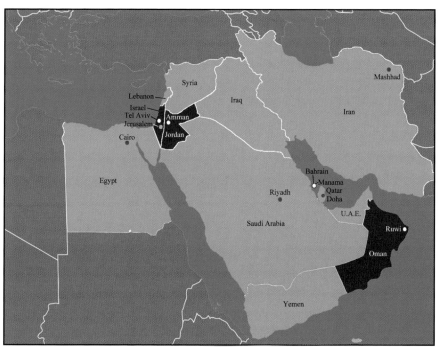

Map of the 13 countries of the Middle East that span across Africa and Asia. The countries having numismatic venues with detailed descriptions are shown in dark blue and their cities indicated by a white dot. A red dot represents cities with limited information while a green dot indicates cities having venues with both detailed and limited information.

The Middle East has long been an important geographical spot for many millennia. First, it was the birthplace of the three major monotheistic religions: Judaism, Christianity, and Islam, and is the spiritual center of many others. Secondly, as a crossroad between Africa, Europe, and Asia on both land and sea, it was on several important trading routes. As such, coins were a very important aspect of trade.

315

Almost since the first coins in Asia Minor, coins were part of everyday life and one need not look any further than the New Testament. Perhaps the most famous, or infamous, of these is the 30 pieces of silver, the price for which Judas betrayed Jesus (Matthew 26:14). Although there is some disagreement as to what coins may have been used, the best theory is that the coins were the Shekels of Tyre–coins that were capable of paying the annual Temple tax in Jerusalem due near Passover. The bronze Greek lepton referred to as the Widow's Mite (Mark 12:42; Luke 21:2) was minted by the Judean king Alexander Jannaeus. Also from the Old Testament, the shekel, from the Hebrew *l'shekul*—meaning to weigh, was the basis for a system of weights which eventually created the coin. Other Hebrew weights mentioned in the Old Testament are: talent, mina, beka, gerah, pim, and kesitah.

The rise of Islam in the seventh century created a new design in coinage that was purely Islamic. No longer were there pictures of animals or persons–a prohibition found in the Qur'an. Instead, Qur'anic verses would now be placed on coins along with the Hijri date.

Visiting some of the countries in this region may pose problems for citizens of certain countries, as not all have full diplomatic relations with each other. Some countries have been known to deny entry if entry/exit markings from some countries (e.g., Israel) are present in one's passport. As a precaution, travelers should always check the visa and entry requirements with that embassy or consulate of the country for which the visit is planned.

In this region there are several excellent museums that exhibit their nation's numismatic heritage. The Central Bank of Bahrain Currency Museum at Manama has on display one of nine known gold dinars with the 77 AH (696 AD) date struck by the Caliph 'Abd al-Malik bin Marwan who introduced a new, purely Islamic coinage. Israel has a quartet of museums that include: the Visitor Center at the Bank of Israel and the Israel Museum, both near each other in Jerusalem, and the well-known Kadman Numismatic Pavilion in Tel Aviv. The Central Bank of Jordan Currency Museum in Amman exhibits its monetary history from the ancient Greek, Nabataean, and Roman coins that circulated in Jordan to the present. The Central Bank of Oman Currency Museum displays a silver dirham minted in 81 AH (700 AD) during the reign of the Ummayad Caliph 'Abd Malik bin Marwan with only two examples known. The earliest Islamic mint in the Arabian Peninsula was in Oman and this is the oldest coin known in Arabia, minted in Oman.

These major venues are supplemented by exhibitions in Cairo's renowned Egyptian Museum, the coin gallery of the Astan e-Quds Museum Complex in Iran's holy city of Mashhad, the Museum of Islamic Art in Doha (Qatar), and the exhibit in the headquarters of the Saudi Arabian Monetary Agency in the capital city of Riyadh.

Manama, Bahrain	• Central Bank of Bahrain Currency Museum
Jerusalem, Israel	• Bank of Israel Visitor Center: Money – A Mirror of Ancient and Modern Times
	• Israel Museum, Samuel and Saidye Bronfman Archaeology Wing
Tel Aviv	• Kadman Numismatic Pavilion, Eretz Israel Museum
Amman, Jordan	• Central Bank of Jordan Currency Museum
Ruwi, Oman	• Central Bank of Oman Currency Museum

Additional institutions with limited information:

Cairo, Egypt	• The Egyptian Museum
Mashhad, Iran	• Astan e-Quds Museum Complex, Coins Gallery
Jerusalem, Israel	• Rockefeller Archaeological Museum
Doha, Qatar	• Museum of Islamic Art
Riyadh, Saudi Arabia	• Saudi Arabian Monetary Agency

Central Bank of Bahrain Currency Museum

مصرف البحرين المركزي متحف العملات

Manama, Bahrain

Opened in February 1999 after four years in development, the Currency Museum is located in the Central Bank of Bahrain (CBB) in the diplomatic area of Manama. The Museum traces the history of the currency in the Kingdom of Bahrain before and after the founding of Islam and the currencies issued by the Bahrain Currency Board, Bahrain Monetary Agency, and the CBB. It also displays Islamic coins as well as some official documents.

Visitors are led through a multi-media tour of the currency history of Bahrain, demonstrating the central role it has played throughout the history of the Gulf.

The first Umayyad gold dinar, 77 AH (696 AD), from the reign of 'Abd al-Malik bin Marwan which set the pattern for centuries to come.

The First Gold Dinar

Caliph 'Abd al-Malik bin Marwan introduced a new, purely Islamic coinage in 696 AD (77 AH). This new gold dinar can be seen at the beginning of the exhibition. It is one of only nine known, and bore only inscriptions from the Qur'an and the date for the first time according to the Islamic Hijri calendar.

Another display cabinet contains examples of very early Islamic coins with examples of the silver drachms struck during the Prophet Muhammad's lifetime (c. 570-632). Visitors can see the development of early Islamic coinage (945-1258 AD/333-656 AH) and the Age of Islamic Empires (1258-1689 AD/656-1100 AH).

Foreign Coins, 550 BC to 1950 AD

Additional cabinets display foreign coins that circulated in the Arabian Peninsula during the 2,500-year period from 550 BC to 1950 AD. These coins were widely used because they carried simple engravings such as pictures of a lion or a bull, or of kings and rulers which helped differentiate them.

Bahrain used the coins of British India as its official currency during the middle of the 18th century. Otherwise, the most widely used coins in the Arab world during that period were the silver Maria Theresa thaler and the Indian copper paisa, examples of which are on display.

World central banks and monetary agencies typically issue gold and silver coins and medals to commemorate local and international events. On display is a 1968 gold medal to mark the opening of Isa Town, and a 1971 gold medal to mark the independence of the State of Bahrain from Great Britain with other medals in the central section.

The face of the first denomination banknote, 100 fils, of the former Bahrain Currency Board, from 1964.

Previous Monetary Authorities

The Museum also has a special gallery concentrating purely on the activities of the previous Bahrain Currency Board, Bahrain Monetary Agency, and the present CBB. The gallery includes cabinets containing specimens of Indian and Gulf banknotes and coins in circulation in Bahrain in addition to official documents issued by the CBB pertaining to the issue of Bahraini coins and banknotes.

Shown are all the Indian and Gulf banknotes and coins which were in circulation between 1947 and 1965. A second cabinet covers the establishment of the Bahrain Currency Board and also a copy of the Amiri Decree announcing the issuance of the Bahraini dinar. There are also historical photographs of the exchange of the Gulf Rupee currency for the new Bahraini dinar at in 1965. The third cabinet relates to the establishment of the Bahrain Monetary Agency in 1973. It contains a copy of the Amiri Decree of 1973 relating to the formation of the Bahrain Monetary Agency.

In addition to its coins and Bahraini banknotes in the Museum, a new permanent stand of the first banknotes and coins issued by the central banks of all the Gulf Cooperation Council countries has been added.

Visitor's Checklist

Central Bank of Bahrain Currency Museum, 96 Road No 1702, Manama, Kingdom of Bahrain

ℹ️ 🕐 +973 17 547700

○ Sunday-Thursday: 8 a.m.-2 p.m.

● Friday; public and bank holidays.

✋ 📷

Internet

✉ currency@cbb.gov.bh

🌐 www.cbb.gov.bh/page.php?p=location_opening

Bank of Israel Visitor Center
Money – A Mirror of Ancient and Modern Times
מרכז המבקרים של בנק ישראל
Jerusalem, Israel

The Bank of Israel has been the country's central bank since 1954, succeeding Bank Leumi Le-Israel B.M. Its Jerusalem headquarters are located among the major governmental buildings, including the Knesset (parliament), Supreme Court, and the office of the Prime Minister across the street.

The headquarters of the Bank of Israel and its Visitor Center.

A Mirror of Ancient and Modern Times

The Visitor Center, whose exhibition is titled, "Money—A Mirror of Ancient and Modern Times," has 18 bilingual displays (Hebrew and English) and nine interactive computer screens. The exhibition serves to familiarize the public with the Bank's main functions as the central bank and its contribution to Israel's economy, along with both a historical development of money in Israel and the reflection of Israel's heritage in the design of its banknotes and coins.

A visit is instructive and interesting, and incorporates three features:

- An exhibition of ancient coins, banknotes and coins issued from pre-state days to the present.
- Interactive stations which explain, by means of computer games, the functions of the Bank of Israel, the history of money, and the contribution of the central bank to the economy.
- Films on the development of the means of payment and the essential role of the Bank—the preservation of price stability.

321

Gallery in the Shape of New Israel Shekel

In the shape of the currency symbol for the new Israel shekel (₪), the gallery's lower level shows the history of means of payment and the conduct of trade during various periods—from the pre-coin periods, via the invention of the first coins in the 7th century BCE up to the present day. The exhibition focuses on coins in circulation in the Land of Israel down the centuries. Visitors see the first coins minted by the Lydians in western Asia Minor and coins from ancient Greece, the civilization that pioneered the widespread use of coins. Alongside these are coins of the Persian Empire—of kings of Persia and of Judean cities from the Persian period in the 4th century BCE. Ancient coins are shown in chronological order, from the Hellenistic, Roman, and Byzantine periods to the Ottoman era, with emphasis on Jewish coins from the Hasmonaean and Herodian periods, and from the time of the Jewish rebellion against Rome and of the Bar Kokhba war.

Alongside ancient coins are two hoards, one found in the wreck of a sunken vessel, and the other, the savings of a wealthy inhabitant of Maresha, unearthed in archaeological excavations near Beth Govrin. The exhibition also displays all of Israel's banknotes and coins from the British Mandate period to the present day. Next to each coin is a photo of the ancient coin on which the motif of the modern coin is based. All Israel's modern coins, from the very first mintage in 1948, are modeled after ancient Jewish coins or other Jewish archeological artifacts.

The lower level gallery is in the shape for the currency symbol of the new Israel shekel (₪).

Emergency Money

A separate display presents emergency money printed in Jerusalem by the British Mandate Government in the early 1940s. Visitors can see trial print runs and original artwork for banknotes that were never put into circulation and were destroyed; these are specimens of the only banknotes ever printed in Jerusalem.

The exhibition covers various other topics, such as money substitutes used in ancient and contemporary civilizations. Many of the 400 items in the exhibition are exclusive to the Bank of Israel collection.

The Archaeology Wing of the Israel Museum is nearby at 10 Ruppin Blvd., and a visit there is highly recommended.

The reverse of the 1954 25-prutot coin, one of Israel's earliest coins.

Visitor's Checklist

Bank of Israel Visitor Center, 2 Kaplan Street, Giv'at Ram, Jerusalem, Israel

ℹ️ ℂ +972 (0)26552828, +972 (0)26552520, +972 (0)26552718

◯ Monday-Thursday: 9 a.m.-4 p.m.

⬤ Friday-Sunday; all Jewish religious and national holidays.

🖐 Prior registration is required. On-line registration is at: www.bankisrael.gov.il/vcenter/visitRequest_en.php

📷 ♿ 📷

Public Transportation

🚌 Egged 9/24/28

Internet

✉️ mevakrim@boi.gov.il

🌐 www.bankisrael.gov.il/vcenter/default_en.html (also in Hebrew)

Israel Museum, Samuel and Saidye Bronfman Archaeology Wing

מוזיאון ישראל, האגף לארכאולוגיה ע"ש שמואל וסיידי ברונפמן

Jerusalem, Israel

Near the southern end of the 20-acre campus of the Israel Museum, the country's largest cultural institution, is the Samuel and Saidye Bronfman Archaeology Wing. The original pavilion opened on May 11, 1965 and had its own numismatic exhibition area. As part of a three-year renovation program, the new archeology wing opened on July 25, 2010. Most of the numismatic specimens are now integrated among the Museum's other historical exhibits with the exception of one specialized numismatic gallery.

The newly transformed wing is organized chronologically from "Dawn of Civilization" to the Ottoman Empire ("Muslims and Crusaders") in seven galleries, or "chapters." All exhibit text is in Hebrew, Arabic, and English. The quote from Deuteronomy 28:6 is seen by every visitor at the Museum's entrance hall: "Blessed shall you be when you arrive and blessed shall you be when you depart."

Main entrance to the Archaeology Wing, one of the many venues on the campus of the Israel Museum.

Israel and the Bible

Of the seven "chapters," the third is the first of any numismatic significance: "Israel and the Bible." On display is an assembly of some of the ancient weights from the 7th to the 6th centuries BCE that were used as monetary units. The shekel comes from the Hebrew *ma'shekal*, meaning weight. Specimens, that look like round balls, include: eight gerah, one, two, four, 40, and 400 shekels, pim, and nezef.

Greeks, Romans and Jews

Here are Greek silver coins from the reign of Alexander the Great (356-323 BCE) who conquered Judea in 332. Coins from the Hasmonian dynasty (142-63 BCE) established by Simon Maccabaeus, plus those of John Hyrancanus (134-104 BCE) and Mattathias Antigonus (40-37 BCE), who was the last Hasmonian king of Judea, are featured.

Under Roman Rule

Included here are silver shekels of the First Jewish Revolt from years 2, 3, 4, and the rare year 5 shekel, plus a hoard of shekels found at the Dead Sea fortress of Masada which was defended against the Romans after Jerusalem had been taken by Titus in 73 CE. Also on display are silver tetradrachm (shekels), denarii (zuzim, one-fourth of a shekel), and bronze coins from the Bar Kokhba revolt (132-135 CE).

The Holy Land, Muslims and Crusaders

This area of the Museum includes some earliest Islamic coins among the historical exhibits such as 7th-century silver dirhams, gold dinars, and copper fals of the Umayyad dynasty (661-750 CE/41-132 AH). This area also includes the first Islamic coin, a gold dinar (676 CE/7 AH) from Damascus, the dynasty's capital.

In the last "chapter"—"Muslims and Crusaders," there is a selection of dinars from 886 to 1035 CE in addition to several hoards of coins and jewelry of the 11th-century Fatimid Period, which were found at Tiberias in the Lower Galilee.

Entrance to the "Coin in Context" circular gallery.

Coins in Context

This is the only gallery solely dedicated to numismatics in the Archaeology Wing. In 10 panels, this exhibit begins with the modern coins of the State of Israel—ordinary coins Israelis carry around in their pockets, but which bear strong links to the past.

Some of the topics in this gallery include: Birth of Coins; The First Local Coins; The Ancient Dollar—the tetradrachm; Propaganda on Coins—Roman suppression of the

First Jewish Revolt 70 CE; Portraits; Coins of the State of Israel.

One additional topic, Israel's Stamps, tells how the design for Israel's first stamps of 1948, *doar Ivri* (Hebrew Post), was taken from the ancient shekels of the First Jewish Revolt of 70 CE. The three highest stamp denominations 250 mils, 500 mils, and 1,000 mils were based on the shekels year 2, year 3, and year 4 respectively.

The Bank of Israel's Visitor Center is nearby at 2 Kaplan Street, Giv'at Ram, and a visit there is highly recommended.

A coin hoard from Masada composed of shekels dating from the First Jewish Revolt. In the front row are the rare year 5 shekels.

Visitor's Checklist
Israel Museum, Samuel and Saidye Bronfman Archaeology Wing, 10 Ruppin Blvd., Jerusalem, Israel

ℹ️ ☏ +972 (0)26708811
◯ Sunday, Monday, Wednesday, Thursday: 10 a.m.-5 p.m.; Tuesday 4 p.m.-9 p.m.; Friday and holiday eves: 10 a.m.-2 p.m.; Saturday and holidays: 10 a.m.-5 p.m.
🖐 ⛐ ⛐ ✉ ⊘ 🎧 🛒 🍴

Public Transportation
🚌 Egged Bus 9/9a/17/17a/24/24a

Internet
✉ info@imj.org.il
⊕ www.english.imjnet.org.il/htmls/Home.aspx   (also in Hebrew, Arabic, Chinese, French, Russian, Spanish)

Kadman Numismatic Pavilion,
Eretz Israel Museum
ובית קדמן לתמטבעו, מוזיאון ארץ לישראל
Tel Aviv, Israel

The Kadman Numismatic Pavilion opened in 1962 from the collection of Israel's foremost numismatist, Leo Kadman, and that of Dr. Walter Moses, forming what is one of the largest and most important coin collections in Israel. The Museum's permanent exhibit runs along the entire inside wall in a counter-clockwise fashion, just as Hebrew is written from right to left.

The entrance to the Kadman Museum Pavilion which is located Ramat Aviv section of the northern edge of Tel Aviv.

Inside, near the Museum's entrance, are Tyrian shekels from the Ussfiyeh Hoard, which is known to have originally contained over 6,000 shekels of Tyre, half shekels, and Augustan denarii. This hoard is thought to represent a delivery of the Temple tax that was intercepted and hidden away due to the Jewish war against Rome that broke out in 66 CE.

With all informational text provided in both Hebrew and English throughout, the permanent exhibit of some 30 cases is divided into five historical periods chronicling the development of payment for goods and services from ancient times to the present, and emphasizes the country's history supported by its coinage.

Before Coinage

This first period shows how various commodities served as means of payment in tribal societies before the development of coins, and metals weighed on scales. Of

327

special interest is a display describing the biblical system of weights. The best known is the shekel, from the Hebrew *l'shekul*, meaning "to weigh."

The Beginning of Coinage-Greek Coins

Shown are the first coins from Lydia, Asia Minor in the 7th century BCE. Also included in this era are coins of the Persian kings, Alexander the Great, the Ptolemaic kings of Egypt, and the Seleucid kings of Syria, all of whom successively conquered and ruled the Land of Israel.

View of the exhibit displays of the museum's permanent exhibit along the outer wall. To the left is the area set aside for the temporary exhibits.

Local Coins

This section comprises coins that were minted in the Land of Israel and used by the Jews between the 4th century BCE and 2nd century CE. These coins of the "Persian" period are the earliest Judean coins which contain the Hebrew *yehud*, the Persian name for this region of Judea. Hasmoneans kings were the first Jewish rulers to strike autonomous coins, and Mattathias Antigonus, the last Hasmonean king, was the only one who struck a coin depicting the seven branched menorah from the Temple in Jerusalem.

The best known coins from ancient Israel that belong to this period—the silver shekels and half-shekels from the Jewish War against Rome (66-70 CE), the Judea Capta coins (70-81 CE) issued by the Roman procurators, and the coins of the Bar Kokhba War from 132 to 135 CE are displayed.

Under Foreign Rule

Under Rome, Jerusalem (called Aelia Capitolina) and 36 other cities of the province of Palestine minted their own coins. Coins following the Arab conquest after the Crusades illustrate how non-Islamic motifs were purged from coins.

From Medieval Times until the Modern Era

By the end of the Ottoman Empire, Turkish and various European monies were used by the population. For their internal dealings, Jews often used tokens issued by the early Zionist settlements.

Following Turkey's defeat in World War I, one display shows Egyptian currency used in Palestine from 1917 until 1927 when the British Mandate then issued its own. Since the establishment of the State of Israel in 1948, many of the designs on Israeli coins have been taken from ancient Jewish coinage. The permanent exhibit is aided with selected antiquities and illustrations, which help reveal the historical-cultural background of coins.

The Ussfiyeh Hoard, which was known to have originally contained over 6,000 shekels of Tyre, half shekels, and Augustan denarii.

The reverse of the shekel of Tyre.

Visitor's Checklist

Kadman Numismatic Pavilion, Eretz Israel Museum, 2 Haim Levanon Street, Ramat Aviv, Tel Aviv, Israel 69975

🛈 ℂ +972 (0)3-641-5244

◯ Sunday-Wednesday: 10 a.m.-4 p.m.; Thursday: 10 a.m.-8p.m.; Friday and Saturday: 10 a.m.-2 p.m.

● All Jewish religious and government holidays.

🖐 ⑤ 📷 🛒 🍴 (at the Entrance Hall)

Public Transportation

🚌 Egged Bus 74, 84, 274 (Ramat Aviv); Dan Bus 7, 24, 25, 27, 45 (Ramat Aviv)

Internet

🌐 www.eretzmuseum.org.il/e/116/ (also in Hebrew)

Central Bank of Jordan Currency Museum
البنك المركزي الأردني متحف النقد
Amman, Jordan

The collection of the Central Bank of Jordan's Currency Museum, although established in the early 1980s, was officially inaugurated by the late King Hussein I in 1988. There are 31 display cases in its collection housing over 2,200 coins, banknotes, and medals spread over more than 4,300 square feet (400 square meters).

Gallery displays featuring coins from the Ayyubid, Selijuk, Mamluk, al-Andalus, Mongol Kahn, and Ottoman periods.

Coins Used in Jordan Through the Ages

On display are old and new coins, which were used in Jordan from the time of the Greeks until the last issue of Jordanian coins and banknotes, notably during the Islamic period. In addition, there are coins and banknotes issued by The Jordanian Currency Board and the Central Bank of Jordan, as well as the commemorative coins and medals issued by the Central Bank.

The 31 cases are arranged in chronological order starting with the coins which had circulated in Jordan before Islam. This includes coins circulated from the 5th century BC to the 7th century AD, starting with Greek, Nabataean, and Roman coins in addition to the coins of the Decapolis, Byzantine and Sassanian periods.

The early Islamic coins (Arab Sassanian and Arab Byzantine coins), in addition to the Islamic coins which were struck from the 7th to the 16th century, are from the periods of the Umayyads, Abbasids, Fatimids, Ayyubids, Selijuks, Mamluks, and the Mongol Khans. The inscriptions were originally verses from the Qur'an, and within a century, they documented the name of the caliph, date, and place of issue.

The obverse and reverse of a 1927 100-mil coin used during the British Mandate of Palestine, in use in Jordan until June 30, 1951.

Ottomans and the Hashemites

Ottoman coins were circulated in this region from the 16th century onwards in addition to the coins and banknotes of the Hashemite in Hejaz, Iraq, and Syria from 1916 to 1958.

Hashemite coinage and banknotes, starting with the issues of Sherif Hussein Bin Ali in Hijaz, through the Syrian issues of Faisal I in 1920, then the Iraqi issues of Faisal I, Ghazi I and Faisal II are on display. These are in addition to Egyptian coins and coins issued by the Palestine Currency Board, which had been circulated in Jordan before 1949.

Also included are Jordanian coins and banknotes, issued by the Jordanian Currency Board in 1949 and the Central Bank of Jordan from 1964 to the present time, and including the commemorative coins and medals which were issued by the bank to commemorate several occasions.

Umayyad gold dinar 90 AH (699/700 AD) from the reign of al-Walid, Damascus Mint.

Visitor's Checklist
Central Bank of Jordan, King Hussein Street 37, Amman 11118, Jordan

- ❶ ☏ +962 6 4630301, ext. 2580
- ○ Sunday-Thursday: 8 a.m.-4 p.m.
- ● Friday and Saturday; January 1, May 1, 25 (Independence Day), Christmas, Birth of Prophet Muhammad (Mawlid an Nabi, 12th of Rabi al-Awwal)*, Eid ul-Fitr (1st of Shawwal, for 4 days)*, Eid al-Adha (Feast of Sacrifice, 10th of Dhu al-Hijja, for 5 days)*. An asterisk (*) denotes a movable holiday date.

✋ ⬤ 🏧 🍽 📷

Public Transportation
🚌 Raghadan bus station

Internet
✉ Museum@cbj.gov.jo

🌐 www.cbj.gov.jo/pages.php?menu_id=203&local_type=0&local_id=0&local_details=0&local_details1=0&localsite_branchname=CBJ (also in Arabic)

Central Bank of Oman Currency Museum
البنك المركزي العماني عملة متحف
Ruwi, Muscat, Oman

The new Currency Museum of the Central Bank of Oman illustrates the history of Oman's coinage in both the pre-Islam and Islamic periods, in addition to the money that circulated before the saidi rial—the nation's first national currency in 1970.

History of Minting Currency in Oman

The Museum contains over 500 coins and 100 banknotes, forming a variety of historical numismatic specimens such as the first Islamic silver dirhams, which are similar to the Sasanian drachma, in addition to Byzantine coins, Islamic gold dinars, and copper fils. Visitors can also see Chinese coins and Indian rupees adorning the walls of the Museum.

The Earliest Islamic Mint

History tells that the earliest Islamic mint in the Arabian Peninsula was in Oman and the oldest coin known in Arabia was minted in Oman. This coin, a silver dirham minted in 81 AH (700 AD) during the reign of the Ummayad Caliph 'Abd Malik bin Marwan, bears the

Headquarters of the Central Bank of Oman.

name of Oman. Only two examples are known; one is in the Central Bank's collection, presented by Sultan Qaboos bin Said, and is on display in the middle of the hall.

The Museum also contains examples of colonial coins and banknotes in circulation in Oman between 1901 and 1970—a time of extensive commercial and economic relations with the outside world. During that period, transactions used Maria Theresa thalers and other foreign currencies.

Banknotes of the Indian Empire

The collection of banknotes on display are banknotes of the Indian Empire which were in circulation in the Sultanate of Muscat and Oman between 1927 and 1948, banknotes of the Republic of India from between 1949 and 1957, and banknotes of the Sultanate of Zanzibar and Pemba. These include the 20-rupees banknote issued in January 1908, as well as 5-, 10-, 50-, and 100-rupees banknotes issued between 1916 and 1920.

Also included are banknotes of both the Reserve Bank of India and the Government of India which were issued for circulation in the Arabian Gulf states after the foreign monetary restrictions were introduced in the Republic of India in 1957.

Muscat Monetary Authority Banknotes

Examples of the five issues of Omani paper currency are on display. The first issue of Muscat Monetary Authority of May 7, 1970 included six denominations from 100 baisas to 10 saidi rials. The second banknote issue of November 18, 1972 changed the denomination to the Omani rial. The third issue on April 1, 1975 was the first under the Central Bank of Oman, which also issued the later fourth and fifth (1982) series.

1394 AH (1974) Omani gold rial of Qaboos bin Said.

Commemorative Coins

Also on display are gold, silver, and bronze commemorative coins issued during the reign of Sultan Qaboos bin Said for achievements of Omani civilization as well as national and international anniversaries and events.

For visitors who wish to know the history of the currencies exhibited in the galleries of the Museum, every display room in the Museum has a panel with buttons and a screen. Pressing the appropriate buttons, visitors can bring up an image of the desired specimen to be viewed on the screen along with details of its history. There is also an exhibition hall which screens films about the history of Omani currency and the operations of the Central Bank of Oman.

1381 AH (1961) gold 15 saidi rials of Said bin Taimur from Muscat & Oman.

Visitor's Checklist

Central Bank of Oman, Markaz Mutrah Al Tijari Street, Ruwi, Muscat, Sultanate of Oman. The Currency Museum is in the head office of the Central Bank of Oman and is opposite the HSBC Headquarters.

❶ ℂ +968 24 796 102

◯ Saturday-Wednesday: 8 a.m.-3 p.m.

● Thursday and Friday.

🖐 🖼

Internet

✉ CCR-Dept@cbo.gov.om

🌐 www.cbo-oman.org

Additional Institutions,
The Middle East

The following Middle East institutions are known to have numismatic exhibitions of varying degrees that are open to the public. These are listed here, either because sufficient information could not (1) be obtained about the museum, (2) be verified from other sources, (3) the museum did not respond to repeated requests for information, (4) the exhibition is closed due to long-term renovation of the building or other reasons, (5) or I learned about this venue just before the manuscript was to go to the publisher and complete information could not be included.

Egypt
The Egyptian Museum
المتحف المصري

al-Mathaf al-Masri, Midan El Tahrir (Tahrir Square), Cairo, 11557

❶ ℂ +20 (0)2 2579 4596

✉ egyptianmuseum@hotmail.com

🌐 www.egyptianmuseum.gov.eg (also in Arabic)

Iran
Astan e-Quds Museum Complex, Coins Gallery
موزه آستان قدس رضوی، گالری عکس سکه

Mashhad, Iran (exact street address unavailable)

🌐 www.aqm.ir/news/news_detail.asp?id=374 (also in Farsi, Arabic)

Israel
Rockefeller Archaeological Museum
27 Sultan Suleiman Street, Jerusalem 91710

✉ fawziib@imj.org.il

🌐 www.english.imjnet.org.il/htmls/page_1684.aspx?c0=15160&bsp=14162 (also in Hebrew, Arabic, Chinese, French, Russian, Spanish)

Qatar
Museum of Islamic Art
متحف الفن الإسلامي
Al Corniche, Doha
🛈 ✆ +974 4422 4444
✉ infomia@qma.org.qa, educationmia@qma.org.qa
🌐 www.mia.org.qa (also in Arabic)

Saudi Arabia
Saudi Arabian Monetary Agency
مؤسسة النقد العربي السعودي متحف العملات
Al-Ma'ather Street, Riyadh
🛈 ✆ +44 (0)20-7323-8299
✉ info@sama.gov.sa
🌐 www.sama.gov.sa/sites/samaen/Museum/Pages/Home.aspx

Entrance to the Kaminarimon (thunder) Gate of the Sensoji Buddhist Temple in the Asakusa section of Tokyo, Japan.

Asia

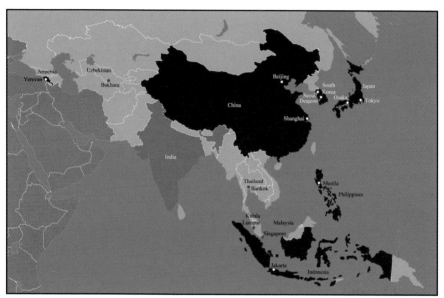

Map highlighting the countries of Asia where those countries having numismatic venues with detailed descriptions are shown in dark blue and their cities indicated by a white dot. A red dot represents cities in those countries with limited information. India has its own individual map in its respective section.

The accepted origin of Western coinage began around 650 BC by the Greeks in Lydia and Ionia in Anatolian Turkey. These first coins were made from electrum, a gold-silver alloy. About the same time, a form of money appeared in both India and China—all three were independent of each other. India's first metallic coins minted by the Mahajanapadas, appeared during India's Vedic Age. These were silver punch-marked coins called *puranas*, which bear neither dates nor the names of rulers, but only symbols.

It is well established that shells were the first primitive form of money in China as far back as the 16th-11th centuries BC during the Shang dynasty. However, anything made from metal used for money first appeared during the Zhou dynasty around the 10th century BC in the form of cast bronze coins resembling farm tools, such as spades and hoes. Those spade coins with definitive mint and denomination markings began to appear around 400 BC and it was not until around 350 BC that the first round coins with round holes appeared. Besides these early coins, the Chinese are recognized as having developed the first form of paper money under the rein of the Emperor Hung-Wu (1328-1398), the founder of the Ming dynasty, although Sweden technically claims the first "banknote" much later in 1661. As for Japan and Korea, they were dependent on China for their coins until the early-8th and mid-10th centuries AD respectively.

In Asia, there are seven countries having museums with extensive entries with pictures in this section for visitors. There are also five countries represented that have museums whose entries have limited information. The History Museum of Armenia exhibits coins from Greek, Achemenian, Hellenistic, Hellenistic Armenian, Roman, Byzantine, Sasanian, Arabian, Medieval Armenian, Crusaders, Seljuk, Georgian, Mongol, late Persian, Ottoman, Russian and European periods, and Armenian banknotes. The People's Republic of China has two major venues: the China Numismatic Museum in Beijing which is across the street from Tiananmen Square and spans three stories, and the Shanghai Museum whose exhibition covers eight chronological eras in China's history supplemented by more than 3,000 specimens.

India has seven listed museums with its central bank's museum, the Reserve Bank of India Monetary Museum in Mumbai leading the way. Over 1,500 items on display in six galleries help explain the evolution of money in India and the Reserve Bank of India's role as the nation's central banker. Visitors to Jakarta, Indonesia will see the top Overall Award for Jakarta's Best Museum in 2012 by the Jakarta Provincial Government and the Jakarta Travel Community for the Museum Bank Indonesia. Among its exhibits is a comprehensive collection of Indonesian coins and paper money, whose displays are arranged chronologically and tell the history of Indonesian money.

The Japan Mint and Museum in Osaka has exhibits of over 4,000 specimens in a renovated three-story building that is the only western-style brick building remaining from the Meiji era on the premises of the Japan Mint. In the capital city of Tokyo, the Bank of Japan Currency Museum displays the first coin minted by a Japanese government—the wado kaichin, a copper coin minted in 708 and modeled after the Chinese kai yuan tong bao coin issued in 621 AD.

Other listed museums in Asia extend from Bukhara, Uzbekistan to Bangkok, Thailand, Singapore, Manila, Philippines, and Kuala Lumpur, Malaysia.

Yerevan, Armenia	• History Museum of Armenia
Beijing, China (PRC)	• China Numismatic Museum
Shanghai	• Shanghai Museum
Mumbai, India	• Reserve Bank of India Monetary Museum
West Jakarta, Indonesia	• Museum Bank Indonesia
Osaka, Japan	• Japan Mint and Museum
Tokyo	• Bank of Japan Currency Museum, Institute for Monetary and Economic Studies
Daejeon, Korea (South)	• Currency Museum of Korea
Seoul	• Bank of Korea Museum
Manila, Philippines	• Museum of the Central Bank of the Philippines

Additional insitutions with limited information:

Guwahati, India	• Assam State Museum
Mumbai	• Chhatrapati Shivaji Maharaj Vastu Museum (formerly Prince of Wales Museum of Western India)
	• Dinesh Mody Numismatics Museum
Udupi	• Corporation Bank Museum
Chennai	• Government Museum Chennai
New Delhi	• National Museum, New Delhi
Kuala Lumpur, Malaysia	• Bank Negara Malaysia Museum and Art Gallery
	• Maybank Money Museum
Singapore, Singapore	• Singapore Coins and Notes Museum
Bangkok, Thailand	• Thailand-Bangkok Pavilion of Regalia, Royal Decorations and Coin-Museum
Bukhara, Uzbekistan	• The Bukhara State Architectural Art Museum-Preserve

History Museum of Armenia
հայաստանի պատմության թանգարան
Yerevan, Armenia

The History Museum of Armenia is the national museum of Armenia and was founded in 1919 as the Ethnographic-Anthropological Museum-Library. However, it was not until August of 1921 the Museum was open for visitors on Republic Square in Yerevan. The Museum's name underwent successive changes from the State Central Museum of Armenia (1922), Cultural-Historical Museum (1931), Historical Museum (1935), and State History Museum of Armenia (1962). In 2003, the Museum's name was changed to its current form.

The front of the History Museum of Armenia.

The Coin Collection

The Museum's coin collection includes a diverse representation from as early as the 5th century BC to the 20th century, covering coins from Greek, Achaemenid, Hellenistic, Hellenistic Armenian, Roman, Byzantine, Sasanian, Arabian, Medieval Armenian, Crusaders, Seljuk, Georgian, Mongol, late Persian, Ottoman, Russian and European periods.

Coins in the collection have been enhanced from three major sources: over 1,700 donated collections from the Armenian diaspora; collections transferred from other Armenian museums and from Moscow; and archeological excavations in Armenia, such as hoards from Dvin and Norashen.

343

Banknote Collection

The first large collections of banknotes were received in the 1920s, when the State Bank and the Central Post Office gave to the Museum the banknotes that were taken out of circulation. The collection also includes issues from the 18th through 20th centuries of numerous countries. Some of these banknotes from the states and governments that ruled in Armenia (Transcaucasia), as well as from the former Russian Empire (1918-1922), are extremely valuable today.

The face of a 1919 250-rubles banknote from the Republic of Armenia.

Stamp Collection

The Museum's stamp collection includes issues from 1918 to 1922 of the First Republic of Armenia, the Soviet Socialist Republic of Armenia (1921-1923), as well as the newest issues of the Republic of Armenia starting from 1992 following the breakup of the Soviet Union. In addition, the collection comprises specimens issued from many countries during the 19th and 20th centuries.

Medals, Decorations, and Badges

The collection includes Armenian and European medals, decorations, and badges, dated from the 17th century to the present. Of special interest are the medals dedicated to memorable events and personalities of Armenian history. Also included in the collection are 900 French silver medals of the 16th-20th centuries, whose copies were made from the original dies at the Monnaie de Paris—the French Mint.

A silver tram of Levon I (1196-1226) seated on throne.

Visitor's Checklist

History Museum of Armenia, Republic Square 4, 375010 Yerevan, Armenia

- ❶ ☾ +374 10 52 06 91
- ◯ Tuesday-Saturday: 11 a.m.-6 p.m. (no entrance after 5:15 p.m.); Sunday: 11 a.m.-5 p.m. (no entrance after 4:15 p.m.).
- ● Monday; National Holidays and Memorial Days as follows: January 1, 2, 6 (Armenian Christmas Day), 28 (Armenian Army Day), March 8 (International Women's Day), April 7 (Motherhood and Beauty Day), 24 (Genocide Remembrance Day), May 1 (Labor Day), 9 (Victory and Peace Day), 28 (First Republic Day), July 5 (Constitution Day), September 21 (Republic Independence Day), December 7 (Spitak Earthquake Remembrance Day), and 31.

♨ 🛒

Public Transportation

 Hanrapetutyan Hraparak (Republic Square)

Internet

⊕ www.historymuseum.am/collections/?id=2&lang=eng (also in Armenian)

China Numismatic Museum

中国钱币博物馆

Beijing, People's Republic of China

The China Numismatic Museum is located across the street from the well-known Tiananmen Square and the mausoleum of Mao Tse-tung. Established in 1992, the Museum's exhibits span three floors and houses a collection of more than 300,000 items covering six categories: ancient money and coins, golden and silver coins, money and coins of minority groups, foreign money and coins, coin molds, and numismatic cultural relics.

Street view of the China Numismatic Museum across from the mausoleum of Mao Tse-tung.

The Museum is under the management of the People's Bank of China and is in the Chinese language only. It traces the evolution of money production in China from the spade-shaped coins of the Spring and Autumn period (722-476 BC) through all the major dynasties that followed to the coinage and paper currency of the present.

The earliest cast coins in China were the spade-shaped coins of the Spring-Autumn period. These were imitations of an ancient farming tool and Chinese characters were usually cast on their surface showing either their weight or names of places. Another example that is shown of the early cast bronze money is the knife coin in the pre-Qin period (before 221 BC). Its shape resembles a knife-like tool called *xiao*, used for cutting meat or wood, and there were generally four types of knife coins used by the four warring states.

Ban Liang Coin Standard

The significant point in Chinese numismatics is illustrated by the ban liang coin. Qin Shi Huang, the first emperor of a unified China of the Qin dynasty (221-207 BC) unified the coinage with a round coin with a square hole as the standard for virtually all the coins that followed. Following the Qin dynasty was the Western Han dynasty. During Emperor Wudi's reign, the ban liang coin for the first time had a ring at its circumference. This was a measure to prevent private casting of coins, and Wudi ordered that the coins should be cast only by the central government. These measures greatly improved the quality of coin casting.

The Tang dynasty (618-907) was a brilliant period in Chinese history. Founding Emperor Gaozu issued a new coin, called kaiyuan *tongbao*, which meant the opening of a new era. And the names of later currencies all carried the character *bao*, meaning "treasure."

Examples of ancient Chinese cast bronze spade money of the Warring States period (475-221 BC).

The Song Dynasties

The Northern and Southern Song dynasties (960-1279) were a prolific numismatic era. During the 320 years of rule of Song, each emperor cast his own coins, many of which are on display. Coins of each reign title had various types and it's said that, if all the coins cast during both Song dynasties were lined up one by one, they could circle the equator of the earth three times.

Perhaps the most notable contribution of this era was the invention of paper currency. Some merchants jointly issued a kind of note, called *jiaozi* which could be transferred or cashed. Furthermore, silver became an official currency, cast in the form of ingots and used by the imperial court, the army and the public, and for war compensations to the Liao and Jin dynasties.

Face of a 1999 50-yuan renminbi banknote with the portrait of Mao Tse-tung.

Yuan Renminbi Banknotes

Of particular interest are the modern Chinese paper *yuan renminbi*, or "people's currency." There are samples of the no-nonsense illustrations of the first series introduced by the People's Bank of China in December 1948 about a year before the establishment of the People's Republic of China, to the far more idealistic with Mao's portrait.

In addition, the Museum has a collection of world coins from more than 100 countries, including gold and silver coins of the countries of the 19th century and modern banknotes.

Visitor's Checklist

China Numismatic Museum, 17 Xijiao Min Xiang, Xicheng (West City) District, Beijing 100031, P.R. China

🛈 🕒 +86 (0)10 66081385 (Museum Office), or +86 (0)10 66081377 (Museum Site)

◯ Tuesday-Sunday: 9 a.m.-4 p.m.; ticket window closes at 3:30 p.m.

● Monday

🖐 📷 🛒

Public Transportation

Ⓜ Red-Line1 (Tiananmen West/天安门广场西); Blue-Line 2 (Qianmen/前门)

🚌 2/5/20/120/126 (Tiananmen Square West/天安门广场西); 9/44/67/212/301/337/608/673/901 (Qianmen West/前门西)

Internet

✉ cnm92@163.com

🌐 www.cnm.com.cn (in Chinese only)

Shanghai Museum
上海博物馆
Shanghai, People's Republic of China

Founded and first open to the public in 1952, the Shanghai Museum opened its doors at its current location in 1996. The building has a unique architectural form of a round top with a square base, symbolizing the ancient Chinese philosophy of the square earth under the round sky. Among the earliest countries to use coins, the Museum provides a historical overview of Chinese money in its 7,850-square foot (730-square meters) gallery.

Shanghai Museum with its round top and square base.

The exhibition area is divided into eight chronological eras in China's history plus two additional themes, all supplemented by more than 3,000 specimens showing a historical development of coins and economic exchange between ancient China and foreign countries.

Primitive Currency
Panels show the first primitive Chinese money, the use of shells, probably starting in the Shang dynasty (16th-11th centuries BC), continuing up through the Western Zhou dynasty period (1046-771 BC) when cast bronze coins appeared.

Many examples of cast bronze coins from the Spring and Autumn period (771-476 BC) during the Zhou dynasty, made in the form of a spade with a hollow handle, are shown. The spade coins cast by the Zhou royal family show two level or bevel shoulders, two arc feet and a hollow handle. These coins continued to be used during the Warring States period (475-221 BC), whose states such as Yan and Qi produced the familiar knife money. Examples of the first round coins with a square hole denominated in hua from the Yan state are shown, which is the ancestor of the familiar cash coin.

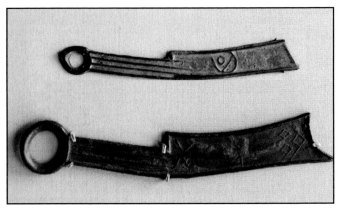

Examples of ancient Chinese cast bronze knife money of the Warring States period (475-221 BC).

Three Kingdoms (220-280), Western Jin (265-420), Eastern Jin (265-420), and Northern and Southern Dynasties (420-589)

Cotton and silk fabric were originally used as currency during the Wei Kingdom. Later they converted to the Wu Zhu system. Both Shu and Wu Kingdoms issued large bills and saw devaluation of their currency. Almost all reigns during this period cast their own coins, sometimes using names other than "Zhu" and "Liang".

Tang, Five Dynasties and Ten States/Kingdoms, and Song Dynasty

Examples are shown for the Tang (618-907) dynasty, using "Wuzhu" coins in its early period, and the Five dynasties and Ten States (907-960). During the period of the Song dynasty (960-1279), the Western Xia dynasty had its own currency systems and cast round coins with a square hole, imitating the shape of the Song coins.

Yuan, Ming, and Qing Dynasties

Bronze coins of the Yuan (Mongol) dynasty, which carried both Chinese and Mongolian inscriptions, are featured along with paper notes that were a main form of currency in the early Ming dynasty (1368-1644). Also shown are silver ingots of various standard sizes that were the main currency from the mid-Ming period and the silver Yin liang widely used during the Qing dynasty (1644-1911).

Highlights of the Exhibition

- The plate used to print the paper notes, *zhen you bao quan*, during the Zhenyou reign of the Jin dynasty (1213-1216).

- Coin of Yongle Tongbao with characters "three qian" cast on the back during the Yongle reign of the Ming dynasty (1368-1644). This specimen is one of two known.
- Of the flat-shouldered, arc-footed and hollow-handled spade coins, one is extraordinarily precious because it has five casting characters. Ordinary hollow-handled spade coins only contain one or two characters.
- Gilt bronze coin of Tian Ce Fu Bao, cast in 119 AD.

Visitor's Checklist

Shanghai Museum, 201 Renmin Avenue, Shanghai, P.R. China 200003. The coin exhibition is on the 4th floor

❶ ☏ +86 (021) 63725300

◯ Daily 9 a.m.-5 p.m.

✋ ⓖ 📷 🎧 🛒 🍴

Public Transportation

Ⓜ Line-1, Line-2 (People's Square)

🚌 46/71/123/574; Tunnel bus 6/934

Internet

✉ webmaster@shanghaimuseum.net

🌐 www.shanghaimuseum.net/en/collection/collection-1.jsp?fl=27&name=Coins (also in Chinese)

Mumbai, India • Reserve Bank of India Monetary
Museum
Additional insitutions with limited information:
Guwahati, India • Assam State Museum
Mumbai • Chhatrapati Shivaji Maharaj Vastu
Museum (formerly Prince of Wales
Museum of Western India)
• Dinesh Mody Numismatics Museum
Udupi • Corporation Bank Museum
Chennai • Government Museum Chennai
New Delhi • National Museum, New Delhi

India

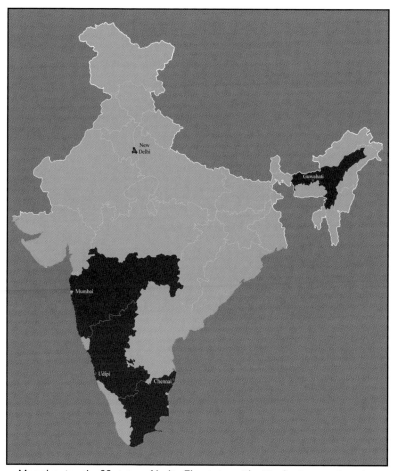

Map showing the 28 states of India. The states with cities having numismatic venues are shown in dark blue. A red dot represents cities with limited information while a green dot indicates that city (Mumbai) having venues with both detailed and limited information.

Reserve Bank of India Monetary Museum
भारतीय रिज़र्व बैंक
Mumbai, India

The Reserve Bank of India (RBI) in 2004 opened its Museum in the nearby Amar Building. The Museum has a collection of over 10,000 items of Indian coins, paper money, financial instruments, and numismatic curiosities. From these, over 1,500 items are on display to provide visitors with a view of India's currencies, their growth, and their emergence of modern day money.

The Amar Building, headquarters for the Reserve Bank of India Monetary Museum.

The Museum is divided into six galleries with graphic panels in English and Hindi that explain the evolution of money in India and the RBI's role as the nation's central banker.

Ideas, Concepts, and Curiosities

This first gallery shows how money has changed in both appearance and substance and evolved from barter to coins to the present-day banknotes and e-money. On display are forms of money in various shapes, sizes, metals, as well as miscellaneous curiosities including some of the world's smallest coins. Exhibits range from a neolithic axe to stored value cards. Here, visitors rediscover the many names of money, some of which are no longer used.

Coinage

Visitors see a glimpse of the ancient punch-marked coins from the Gandhara, Avanti, Mauryan, and Magadhan empires that date from as early as the 6th century BC to coins of the present. Also on display are coins that represent the periods of India's ancient era, Medieval period, Princely States, regional powers, Indo-European companies (Portuguese, Dutch, Danish, French), British India, and the regular and commemorative coins of the Republic. The coins illustrate the rise and fall of empires, the evolution in art forms, and the advances in minting technology. There are also two interactive kiosks that can be used by visitors to check their numismatic knowledge.

A view of the RBI Museum coin gallery.

From Coins to Paper Money

Here, visitors see the journey from coins to paper money. Also demonstrated is how society began accepting tokens of money in lieu of actual money, and how the concept of "Promises to Pay" originated. There is also a section devoted to "hundies"—the equivalent of checks used by India's indigenous bankers.

Know Your Currency

This gallery aims to spread public awareness about how currency is managed in India, the journey of the coins and banknotes from minting or printing to their destruction, and the features of the contemporary Mahatma Gandhi banknotes—the series released starting in 1996.

Also in this area is a large paper money display with India's paper money dating back to the late 18th century. Shown are those notes issued by private banks, like the Bank of Bengal and the Bank of Bombay, British India notes with hand-made paper, and the Bank of Madras. There are also representative notes from the Princely States, like Hyderabad, and other territories, like Goa. In addition, on display are a variety of promissory notes, bills of exchange and checks as well as the entire range of Republic of India banknote issues.

A view of the RBI Museum paper money gallery.

Banking, RBI and You

These last two galleries provide visitors a glimpse of the functions of India's central bank, its role in the economy, and how it touches the day-to-day life of the common man.

The Mumbai branch of the Government of India Mint is located around the corner on Shahid Bhagat Singh Road.

Visitor's Checklist

Reserve Bank of India Monetary Museum, Amar Building, Sir Pherozeshah Mehta Road, Fort, Mumbai 400 001, India. The Museum is located on the ground floor of the Amar Building that adjoins the Reserve Bank of India building on Perin Naniman Street in the Fort area of Mumbai.

ℹ 📞 +91 22 2261 4043, +91 22 2261 0801

◯ Tuesday-Sunday: 10:45 a.m.-5:15 p.m.

● Monday; bank holidays for Maharashtra State.

✋ 📷 (lockers) 🍴 🚫 🚫 🛒

Public Transportation

🚍 2LTD/3/11LTD/111/125/130 (RBI on Shahid Bhagat Singh Rd.)

Internet

✉ museum@rbi.org.in or use the on-line contact form at:
www.rbi.org.in/scripts/helpdesk.aspx

🌐 www.rbi.org.in/scripts/ic_museum.aspx (also in Hindi)

Museum Bank Indonesia
Jakarta, Indonesia

The Museum Bank Indonesia (MBI) is located in the Kota Tua (Old City) section of Jakarta in front of the Beos Kota rail station and adjacent to the Bank Mandiri Museum. The Museum is in a two-story Dutch colonial building constructed in 1909 that was originally a hospital and then transformed as the headquarters of the De Javashe Bank (DJB). After its independence from The Netherlands, DJB became Bank Indonesia, Indonesia's central bank in 1953.

A view of the Museum Bank Indonesia at night.

MBI was established as a follow-up to the mandate from the Governor of Bank Indonesia to build this Museum so that the public will be able to access information on the history, function and responsibility of Bank Indonesia as the country's central bank. The Museum is not only a historical building but it is also a protected cultural heritage, serving as a media to display valuable historical collections from the past.

The process of developing MBI was completed in two stages. The first opening took place on December 15, 2006. The second and final development was officially in-naugurated on July 21, 2009 by the President of the Republic of Indonesia.

MBI displays information about the history of the establishment of Bank Indonesia, the function and roles of Bank Indonesia, the policies issued by Bank Indonesia, and the history of the building as well as numismatic collections. The information is provided using the media such as: panel, multimedia, and diorama with text in both Indonesian and English.

Items of numismatic interest are located in several locations throughout the Museum. On the first floor (lower level), there is the Money Printing and Distribution Room which demonstrates the process of money production from the ignition of an idea, to the printing process, distribution, withdrawal, and shredding of damaged money.

The Museum's Gold Room.

On the second floor (upper level), the Gold Room contains vast displays of monetary gold, including piles of gold ingots. The Numismatic Room comprises a comprehensive collection of Indonesian coins and paper money, whose displays are arranged chronologically and tell the history of Indonesian money.

The Jakarta Provincial Government and the Jakarta Travel Community in 2012 awarded MBI the "Top Overall Award for Jakarta's Best Museum in 2012" in the Old Batavia area. Batavia was Jakarta's original name, and renamed in 1942. "Old Batavia" is the present day part of North and West Jakarta.

A huge replica of a gobog coin from Banten serves as a bench in one of the Museum's break rooms.

Visitor's Checklist

Museum Bank Indonesia, Jalan Pintu Besar Utara No. 3 (No. 3 Pintu Besar Utara Street), Jakarta Barat (West Jakarta), Indonesia

- ℹ ℂ +62 (0)21 2600158, ext. 8111
- ○ Tuesday-Friday: 8 a.m.-3:30 p.m.; Saturday & Sunday: 8 a.m.-4 p.m.
- ● Monday; January 1, Chinese New Year*, Hindu New Year (Hari Raya Nyepi)*, Good Friday*, Waisak Day (Buddha's birthday)*, Ascension Day of Jesus Christ*, August 17 (Indonesian Independence Day), Christmas, Islamic New Year (Ras as-Sanah al-Hijriyah, 1st of Muharram)*, Birth of Muhammad (Mawlid an Nabi, 12th of Rabi' al-Awwal)*, Ascension Day of Muhammad* (Mi'raj, 27th of Rajab)*, Eid-Al-Fitr (1st of Shawwal)*, Feast of the Sacrifice (Eid al-Adha, 10th of Dhu al-Hijja)*. An asterisk (*) denotes a movable holiday date.

✋ ⑤ 🖼 📷 (for non-commercial use only) 🎧 🛒

Public Transportation
🚌 TransJakarta K1-red (Kota)

Internet
✉ museum@bi.go.id
🌐 www.bi.go.id/web/en/Tentang+BI/Museum/Koleksi/Uang/ (also in Indonesian)

Japan Mint and Museum
日本造幣局と博物館
Osaka, Japan

The Mint Museum is the only western-style brick building remaining from the Meiji era (1868-1912) on the premises of the Japan Mint. Originally built in 1869 as a thermal power plant, the building was converted to the Mint Museum. A major renovation was completed in April, 2009 which covers three floors, making the Museum with new exhibits more interesting to visitors.

Entrance to the Japan Mint in Osaka.

The Mint Museum has 4,000 historical items. Visitors can see valuable documents, learn the history of coins, and realize the close relationship between society and coins. Although all explanatory text is in Japanese, multi-language audio-guides are provided free of charge to make the experience an enjoyable one for non-Japanese speakers.

1st-Floor Entry Hall

Here, visitors are first attracted to the Great Clock in front of the factory, made in 1876 to strike on the hour. It has been repaired once, and since then has been marking time as a symbol of the Mint Museum. Also in the hall is a scale model of the Mint at the time of its establishment in 1873, showing the area of 1.9 million square feet (180,000 square meters) to be twice that of what it is today.

2nd-Floor Exhibition Room

The exhibition here features materials used just after the Mint's formation. On display is the balance produced in 1876 by one of the engineers involved in the Mint's founding, and was used to weigh production such as gold coins. This type of balance is still used in the annual coin test.

Also on display are a variety of sample coins and dies; historical documents relating to foreign specialists invited to the Mint; and prize medals from both the 1966 Tokyo Olympics and the 1998 Nagano Winter Olympics, both of which were produced by the Japan Mint.

There are several areas of which visitors can interact with the exhibits. Gold and silver bullion bars can be touched in the "Experience Corner." Visitors can also try to lift a *senryoubako* —originally a chest weighing about 44 lbs (20 kg) used for storing and carrying 1,000 gold koban coins. For the children, the Mint created wooden puzzles featuring a 20-yen gold coin, a 500-yen coin, *kanei tsuho* (square hole copper cash coin), and a miniature model at the time of the Mint's establishment.

A view of the 3rd floor Exhibition Room.

3rd-Floor Exhibition Room

Ancient Japanese coins such as bronze *fuhon-sen* (replica shown), *wado-kaichin*, and *kocho-sen*, which were government issued bronze coins from 708 to 958 AD are shown. Also shown are ancient Chinese coins such as knife money, medieval to modern age coins like the tensho-oban, one of the largest gold coins in the world, and the koban. There is the only existing specimen of *takenagashikin* (gold accumulation) manufactured during the era of Hideyoshi Toyotomi (1536-1598), made by pouring gold into a bamboo-shaped cast, which was found in Osaka's Yodo River in 1935. Also on display are gold and silver coins produced during the Meiji era, other commemorative coins, and foreign coins.

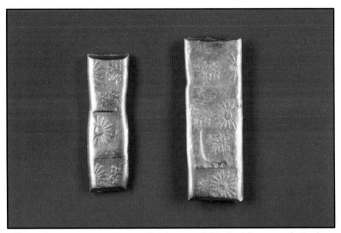

The only existing specimen of *takenagashikin* (gold accumulation), made by pouring gold into a bamboo-shaped cast.

Visitor's Checklist

Japan Mint and Museum, 1-1-79, Temma 1-chome, kita-ku, Osaka 530-0043, Japan

ⓘ Ⓒ +81 6 6351 8509

○ Monday-Friday: 9 a.m.-4:45 p.m.; visitors should enter the Museum before 4 p.m.

● Saturday and Sunday; January 1, national holidays, and during the Cherry Blossom viewing week.

✋ Ⓖ ☃ (Japanese only) 🎨 🎧 🛒

Public Transportation

Ⓜ JR Tozai Line JR 東西線 (Osaka Temmangu Station 大阪天満宮駅); Osaka Loop Line 大阪環状線 (Sakuranomiya Station 桜ノ宮駅, or Kyobashi Station 京橋駅); Keihan Railway 京阪電気鉄道株式会社, or Tanimachi Subway Line/Purple-T22 谷町線 (Temmabashi Station 天満橋駅); Tanimachi Subway Line/Purple-T21 谷町線, or Sakaisuji Subway Line/Brown-K13 堺筋線 (Miami-morimachi Station 南森町駅). The Japan Mint and Museum is about a 10-15 minute walk from all the above listed stations.

Internet

✉ pub@mint.go.jp

🌐 www.mint.go.jp/eng/plant/index.html (also in Japanese)

Bank of Japan Currency Museum
Institute for Monetary and Economic Studies
日本銀行金融研究所貨幣博物館
Tokyo, Japan

The Currency Museum of the Bank of Japan was founded in 1982 to commemorate the Bank's centenary and opened in November 1985. The Museum belongs to the Institute for Monetary and Economic Studies of the Bank. At the heart of the Museum's collection is the Sempeikan Collection acquired from renowned numismatist Keibun Tanaka at the close of World War II.

Front entrance of the Institute for Monetary and Economic Studies. The Bank of Japan Currency Museum is on the second floor.

Currency of Japan

For the currency of Japan, the exhibition is arranged in chronological historical periods:

- Ancient Times: This section on the Early Days of Japanese Coinage includes the metal coins of ancient China with examples of bronze spade money (8th- 5th centuries BC), bronze knife money (7th-4th centuries BC), bronze round coins with round holes (5th-3rd centuries BC), and bronze round coins with square holes (c. 210 BC). Also, examples of the first Japanese coins (*wado kaichin*) made of silver and copper from the 7th and 8th centuries AD are on display.
- Medieval Times: Documents the use of imported Chinese coins (12th-16th centuries) primarily those of the Song dynasty (960-1127) , e.g., the huang song tong

363

bao, but some coins from the Ming dynasty (1368-1644), e.g., the yong le yong bao and hong wu tong bao.

- Early Modern Times: Displays the emerging of the currency system of the Edo Period (16th century), and the birth of a unique currency system when Tokugawa Iyeyasu began to establish a unified currency system when he minted the keicho gold and silver coins in 1601. In the meanwhile, examples of paper money known as *yamada hagaki* are shown which came to be used in the Ise-Yamada region (near Nara) at the beginning of the 17th century. Later on, feudal notes for use within their domains were issued by many lords. In this way, a currency system unique to Japan came into existence, with the nationwide coins of gold, silver and copper of the Shogunate and the local paper money both circulating together.
- Modern Times: This area includes coins and paper money from the early Meiji era, the origin of the yen in 1871. The first note, 10 yen, issued by the Bank of Japan on May 9, 1885 after its founding in 1882, is also shown.

The major section of the Museum gallery that traces the origin and evolution of currencies in Japan.

Other Sections of the Exhibition

Another section of the exhibition focuses on various types of world currencies, unique notes, and coins, including large stone money on display. Commodity money used as barter with examples of arrow heads, rice, gold dust, and cowrie shells from ancient China (16th-8th centuries BC) are shown.

Highlights of exhibition are considered to be the wado kaichin copper coin, the first coin minted by a Japanese government in 708 and modeled after the kai yuan tong bao Chinese coin issued in 621; the oban and koban gold coins, which were usually presented as gifts; *yamada-hagaki*, the first paper money in Japan issued around 1600; *fundo-kin* gold ingots issued in the legacy of Ieyasu; and the first Bank of Japan banknote. After viewing the first Bank of Japan banknote issued in the Meiji period, visitors can learn about the latest anti-counterfeiting technologies of Bank of Japan notes through interactive exhibits.

Most of the displays are in Japanese although, some captions and panels are written in English.

A 1592 Tensho Naga Oban made of 74 percent gold on the orders of Toyotomi Hideyoshi.

Visitor's Checklist
Bank of Japan Annex Building, 1-3-1, Nihonbashi-Hongokucho, Chuo-ku, Tokyo 103-0021 Japan. The exhibition is on the second floor.

🛈 🕓 +81- 03-3277-3037

◯ Tuesday-Sunday: 9:30 a.m.-4:30 p.m.; last admission 4 p.m.

● Monday; national holidays (except Saturday and Sunday), January 1-4, December 29-31.

✋ ♿ 📷 🚫

Public Transportation
Ⓜ Hanzomon Line-Z09 (半蔵門駅), A5 Exit; Ginza Line-G12 (東京地下鉄銀座線), B1 Exit (Mitsukoshimae Station 三越前駅)

Internet
✉ c_museum_mail@boj.or.jp

🌐 www.imes.boj.or.jp/cm/english_htmls/index.htm (also in Japanese)

Currency Museum of Korea
한국 화폐 박물관
Daejeon, Republic of Korea

The Currency Museum of Korea was established June 1988 by the Korea Minting and Security Printing Corporation (KOMSCO), a government-owned corporation which prints the country's banknotes and mints the coins. The Museum provides a systematic exhibition of both Korean and foreign currencies that span more than a millennium. In addition, there are displays that trace KOMSCO's history since its beginning in 1951. All exhibits are in Korean with display titles only given in both Korean and English.

Front entrance to the Currency Museum of Korea.

Coin Gallery
As one of the Museum's two major galleries, the Coin Gallery has a section explaining the history of currency. In prehistoric times, barter allowed commodities like grain, livestock, agricultural implements, and trinkets as currency for exchange purposes.

Korean Coins
On display are coins from China's Song dynasty (960-1279 AD) and from when Korea first began to use money during its Goryeo dynasty (936-1392). Prior to this time, barter was the principal means of exchange. The first coins actually minted in Korea occurred during the reign of King Songjong. Examples on display show this coin

was cast in both bronze and iron and was based on the standard Chinese cash coin which was round with a square hole in the center.

Gallery with a coining press on display.

Joseon Dynasty Coins

Sangpyong tongbo was the representative coin of the era of the Joseon dynasty (1392-1897). However, it was not until 1633 during the reign of King Ingo that the most representative coinage of Korea was first cast. A round coin with a square hole in the center made of copper or bronze, it has the obverse inscription: *sang pyong tong bo* (常平通寶). The reverse of these coins can display a number, an astronomical symbol like a star, moon or sun, a character from the ancient Chinese text "The Thousand Character Classic," or a character of the five elements: metal (*kum* 金), wood (*mok* 木), water (*su* 水), fire (*hwa* 火), and earth (*to* 土). The sangpyong tongbo coins were used for more than 250 years (1633-1891) and has an estimated 5,000 varieties of this coin characterized by mint, style of calligraphy, *Cheonjamun* order, Chinese numeral order, and symbolic mark.

There is a three-dimensional full-size showcase, or diorama, illustrating the various stages of making jeon coins at the mint of a later period of the Joseon dynasty. Also on display are a number of coining presses, abacuses, scales, weights, and large wooden money boxes, which were forerunners of safes.

Banknote Gallery

The other major section of the Museum is its banknote gallery. On display are notes from the 1st currency reform from the Bank of Joseon, the central bank of Korea until 1950, for the new Bank of Korea notes, released on August 28, 1950. Inflation pressures due to payments from the war between the two Koreas forced a 2nd Currency Reform in February 1953, devaluing the old won 100:1, and instituting the hwan as the new currency.

367

Succeeding currency reforms required changes in the currency, which are all on display. One of the most noted changes in Korea's currency was the change in its denomination from hwan (환) to won (원) by the 3rd Currency Reform in June 1962.

One section of the gallery about ancient coins.

Visitor's Checklist

Currency Museum of Korea, 80-67 Gwahang-no, Yuseong-gu, Daejeon, Republic of Korea 042 870-1000

❶ ℂ +82 042 870 1200

◯ Tuesday-Sunday: 10 a.m.-5 p.m.

● Monday; January 1, Harvest Day (Chuseok, on 15th day of the 8th lunar month around the Autumn equinox)*, and other contemporary Korean holidays. An asterisk (*) denotes a movable holiday date.

Public Transportation

🚌 604 (KAIST), 606 (Expo Science Park)

Internet

✉ young@mall.co.kr (webmaster)

🌐 museum.komsco.com/kor/index (also in Korean)

Bank of Korea Museum
한국은행 화폐금융박물관
Seoul, Republic of Korea

Opened in 2001 to commemorate the Bank of Korea's golden anniversary, the Museum is housed in what was once the Bank of Korea's head office and is a designated historical structure that was built in 1912. The Museum's exhibition is spread over two floors and a mezzanine. The text of the exhibits is primarily in Korean although some English is used. Brochures are available in Korean, English, Japanese, and Chinese.

The eclectic Bank of Korea Museum building sits among Seoul's modern architecture.

1st-Floor Exhibits

There are five major exhibits in addition to a library and book shop on the 1st (ground) floor. In the "About the Bank of Korea" exhibit, visitors learn about the Bank of Korea, established in 1950, what happens in the Bank, and how the Bank is organized and managed. The original zinc plates used for printing the first banknotes issued by the Bank of Korea are on display.

The Currency Exhibition Hall has on display Korean currencies from its various periods in chronological order where Hangul wasn't used on Korean banknotes until 1962, plus historical currencies from around the world. Even banknotes from North Korea are shown with their propaganda themes.

The "Life of Currency" exhibit explains the manufacturing, circulating, and redemption process for damaged currency. When Korean banknotes are unfit, they're shredded up and turned into sound insulation for cars. The security measures on banknotes and how counterfeits are identified is explained. Interactive computer screens allow visitors to examine various security features of Korea's 10,000-won banknote.

As the nation's central bank, the "Money and the National Economy" exhibit emphasizes the importance of price stabilization and monetary and credit policies using video clips, models, and computer games.

A view of the Currency Hall on the Museum's first floor.

Mezzanine

One area of the mezzanine represents donated currencies from a variety of people since its opening. An exhibition promotes these donations, paying tribute to the donors.

The "Currency Handling Equipment" exhibit showcases equipment and machines that the Bank uses to handle money and eventually to shred unusable banknotes. This includes machines for identification, counting, bundling, packaging in vinyl for storage and sorting of coins and banknotes.

2nd-Floor Exhibits

The top floor is perhaps the Museum's most popular area. The "Replica Vault" simulates a real vault filed with stacks of banknotes on pallets behind a security glass.

Currencies from 170 nations in the "Currencies From Around the World" exhibit illustrate banknotes having the same design, different materials used for coins and banknotes, unusual denominations of banknotes and coins, sizes of banknotes that vary with denomination or same size for all denominations, and banknotes with different themes. There are slide out panels with banknotes from these countries so visitors can see both sides of the banknotes, and scenes of the country appear on an adjoining video screen.

For a small fee, visitors can have their face printed on a 50,000-won banknote. There is also an impressive touch-screen simulated waterfall of money where visitors can touch any given banknote and learn about both it and its country of origin.

Several activities that appeal to children and adults are in the "Play and Learn with Money" exhibit area. A two-player game requires matching the currency to the country. Another tests if you can match currency symbols, such as ¥, with their correct countries. Visitors can also make their own coin using a replica coin press.

Visitor's Checklist

Bank of Korea Museum, 110 Namdaemunno 3-ga, Jun-gu, Seoul, Republic of Korea

- ℹ ℂ +82 (0)2 759 4881 (in Korean), +82 (0)2 1330 (Korean, English, Japanese, Chinese)
- ○ Tuesday-Sunday: 10 a.m.-5 p.m.
- ● Monday; Harvest Day (Chuseok, on 14 th-16th days of the 8th lunar month around the Autumn equinox)*, December 29-January 2. An asterisk (*) denotes a movable holiday date.

✋ 🅟 🍽 📷 🎧 🛒

Public Transportation

Ⓜ Line 1 (City Hall Station, Exit 7), Line 2 (Euljiro Station, Exit 7), Line 4 (Hoehyeon Station, Exit 7)

Internet

✉ museum@bok.or.kr

🌐 museum.bok.or.kr/english/main/index.jsp (also in Korean)

Museum of the Central Bank of the Philippines
Museo ng Bangko Sentral ng Pilipinas
Manila, Philippines

The Museum of the Central Bank of the Philippines was inaugurated in 1999. In seven galleries with texts in English and Filipino, the Museum presents its story of money, from the earliest trading times in the Philippines when primitive money was used and barter was practiced, to the creation of modern coins and banknotes.

The building of the Central Bank of the Philippines.

Pre-Hispanic Era

For at least 2,000 years prior to the arrival of the Spaniards, the chief means of trading throughout the Philippine Archipelago was barter. On display are unearthed *piloncitos*—gold ingots which were the country's first recognized form of coinage. Also shown are different sized barter rings, gold ornaments, beads, and other objects used as mediums of exchange.

Spanish Era

Exhibited here are gold, silver, and copper coins: the four reales brought by Magellan in 1521; the *dos mundos*, or pillar dollars used during the galleon trade; odd-shaped silver and gold coins called *cobs*, or *macuquinas*; fractional coins, or *barrilla*; and the Isabelinas and Alfonsinos, the first locally produced gold and silver coins starting in 1861 and inscribed with the word "Filipinas," named after Spanish monarchs Isabel II and Alfonso XII. Also shown are *pesos fuertes*, the first banknotes issued in 1852.

Revolutionary Period

A small section is devoted to the Malolos Republic currencies. When the Philippines declared independence from Spain in 1899, the Aguinaldo government issued its own money. Shown are the rare 2-centavo copper coin and banknotes in denominations of 1, 2, 10, 20, 25, 50, and 100 pesos.

Back of a 1944 2-pesos banknote counter-stamped with "Victory" to mark Japan's defeat.

The American Regime

This gallery features currencies from when the United States took control of the Philippines in 1901. The colonial government organized the country's monetary system through the Philippine Coinage Act of 1903, for which coins and banknotes were issued. Shown are Silver Certificate banknotes (1903-1918) and the replacement Treasury Certificates (1918-1935).

World War II

In this gallery are banknotes that circulated during the Japanese Occupation from 1941 to 1944: Japanese Invasion Money issued by the Japanese government and the resistance currencies issued by Filipino guerrillas. When World War II ended, existing pre-World War II banknotes were counter-stamped "Victory" on the back to mark Japan's defeat.

Republic Period

This gallery shows currencies in use after the establishment of the Philippine Republic in 1946 and the formation of the Central Bank of the Philippines in 1949. It features the English series (1958-1966), the Filipino series (1967-1974), the *Ang Bagong Lipunan* (The New Society) series (1975-1982), succeeded by the Flora and Fauna series coins (1983-1990), the New Design series (1985-1991), the 1987 500-piso and 1991 1,000-piso banknotes.

Foreign Currencies

A timeline highlighting the history of central banking in the Philippines plus a colorful array of international currencies, featuring the latest issues of banknotes and coins from countries worldwide are also on display. These include foreign money with historical designs and themes.

Face of 1-centavo Japanese Invasion Money used in the Philippines.

Visitor's Checklist
Museum of the Central Bank of the Philippines, Bangko Sentral ng Pilipinas Complex, A. Mabini St. (corner Pablo Ocampo St.), Malate, Manila 1004 Philippines
- ❶ ℂ +632 5167499
- ○ Monday-Friday: 9 a.m.-4 p.m.
- ● January 1, Maundy Thursday*, Good Friday*, April 9 (Araw ng Kagitingan/Day of Valor), May 1 (Labor Day), June 12 (Independence Day), August 21 (Ninoy Aquino Day), National Heroes Day (last Monday of August), November 1 (All Saints' Day), 30 (Bonifacio Day), December 25, 30 (Rizal Day), and 31. Holidays falling on the weekend are observed the next working day. An asterisk (*) denotes a movable holiday date.
- ✋ ⑤ ♿ (photo ID required) ♻ 📷 ⊗ 🎧
- 🛒 At the Economic and Financial Learning Center (EFLC) near the Museum

Public Transportation
- 🚍 Jeepney: A. Mabini-Baclaran route
- 🚊 LRT: Taft Avenue corner Pablo Ocampo St. (formerly Vito Cruz) Station stop

Internet
- ✉ bsppmail@bsp.gov.ph
- 🌐 www.bsp.gov.ph/about/facilities_money.asp

Additional Institutions, Asia

The following Asian institutions are known to have numismatic exhibitions of varying degrees that are open to the public. These are listed here, either because sufficient information could not (1) be obtained about the museum, (2) be verified from other sources, (3) the museum did not respond to repeated requests for information, (4) the exhibition is closed due to long-term renovation of the building or other reasons, (5) or I learned about this venue just before the manuscript was to go to the publisher and complete information could not be included.

India
Assam State Museum
Gopinath Bordoloi Road, Ambari, Guwahati, Assam 781001
❶ ℂ +91 0361 2540651, +91 0361 2550245.
⊕ www.cointalk.com/t68920/ (unofficial site)

Chhatrapati Shivaji Maharaj Vastu Museum
(formerly Prince of Wales Museum of Western India)
159/161 Mahatma Gandhi Rd, Fort, Mumbai (Bombay) 400 023
❶ ℂ +91 22 284 4519
✉ csmvsmumbai@gmail.com, csmvs@hathway.com
⊕ themuseummumbai.com/Collection_category.aspx?link=Indian Coins

Corporation Bank Museum
Haji Abdulla Saheb Memorial Building (Rajaji Marg), Udupi, Karnataka 576101
❶ ℂ +91 (0)820 2520321 (corporate branch)
✉ query@corpbank.co.in

Dinesh Mody Numismatics Museum
Saroj Sadan, Mumbai University, Kalina Campus, Santacruz East, Mumbai
❶ ℂ (+91) 22 22998587
⊕ No official website

Government Museum Chennai
அரசு அருங்காட்சியகம் சென்னை
Pantheon Road, Egmore, Chennai - 600 008, Tamil Nadu
🛈 📞 +91 (0)44 2819 3238
✉ govtmuse@tn.gov.in
🌐 www.chennaimuseum.org/draft/gallery/04/num.htm (also in Tamil)

National Museum, New Delhi
राष्ट्रीय संग्रहालय, नई दिल्ली
Maulana Azad Road, New Delhi
🛈 📞 +91 (0)11 2301 9272
🌐 www.nationalmuseumindia.gov.in/collection.htm (also in Hindi)

Malaysia
Bank Negara Malaysia Museum and Art Gallery
Muzium dan Galeri Seni Bank Negara Malaysia
2 Jalan Dato Onn, Kuala Lumpur (located at the Sasana Kijang complex)
🛈 📞 +60 (0)3 9179 2888
✉ infomuseum@bnm.gov.my
🌐 museum.bnm.gov.my/teaser/index.html (also in Malay)

Maybank Money Museum
1st Floor, Menara Maybank, 100 Jalan Tun Perak, 50050 Kuala Lumpur
🛈 📞 +60 3-2070 8833
🌐 www.malaysia-traveller.com/maybank-numismatic-museum.html (unofficial site)

Singapore
Singapore Coins and Notes Museum
2 Trengganu Street, Level 3, Singapore 059199. Entrance is at 40 Pagoda Street.
🛈 📞 +65 6222 2486
🌐 www.singaporecoinsandnotesmuseum.com/index1.php

Thailand
Thailand-Bangkok Pavilion of Regalia, Royal Decorations and Coin-Museum
The Grand Palace, Th Na Phra Lan Road, Maharaj Pier, Bangkok 10200
🛈 📞 +66 (0)2 224 1833
🌐 bangkokforvisitors.com/ratanakosin/grand-palace/palace-buildings/regalia-and-coins.php (unofficial site)

Uzbekistan
The Bukhara State Architectural Art Museum-Preserve
Бухарский государственный архитектурно-художественный музей-заповедник
2 Afrasiyab Street, Registan Square, Bukhara
❶ ℂ +998 65 224 13 78
🌐 bukhara-museum.narod.ru/English/E_Skl3_0/e_skl3_1.html (also in Russian)

An honor guard stands watch in front of the mausoleum of King Mohammad V and his two sons, King Hassan II and Prince Abdallah, in Rabat.

Africa

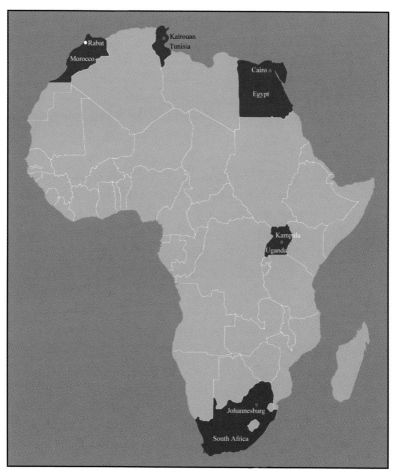

Map highlighting the countries of Africa with those having numismatic venues with detailed descriptions are shown in dark blue and their cities indicated by a white dot. A red dot represents cities with limited information while a green dot indicates cities having venues with both detailed and limited information. Information for Egypt is given in The Middle East section.

The numismatic history of Africa can be considered in four major periods. The first coins used in Africa were those of the empires of ancient Greece and Rome, mainly confined to the northern edges of the continent. The second period occurred with the rise of Islam. The gold dinars struck by the many dynasties that ruled the Islamic world were a design in coinage that was purely Islamic. Only verses from the Qur'an were placed on these coins along with the Hijri date.

The third and most important period concerned itself with European colonial rule. This historically begins with the Muslim defeat at the Moroccan city of Ceuta in August, 1415 by the Portuguese. From this time until after World War II when the former African colonies, one by one, obtained their independence. During the final period, virtually the entire continent was ruled by seven major European powers. In order of the total land area of their colonies, they are: France, Great Britain, Germany, Belgium, Italy, Portugal, and Spain.

Apart from primitive money used by the indigenous tribes, the first metal colonial coins for regular commercial trade were those of the Portuguese in the 14th century. The first French coins specifically earmarked for use in Africa were bronze 5- and 10-centimes coins with 1824 and 1825 dates struck during the reign of Charles X and had the *Colonies Française* legend on the reverse.

The British set up the British West Africa Currency Board in 1912 for its West African territories of Nigeria, the Gold Coast (now Ghana), Sierra Leone and Gambia, which authorized the issue of both coins and banknotes. A similar agency, the East African Currency Board, was formed in 1919 by England for its East African colonies of Uganda, Kenya, and Tanzania, with Zanzibar being included in 1936. Germany, despite having several African colonies, only minted coins for German East Africa. Despite its close proximity to Africa, Spain did not have the level of colonization as it did in the Western Hemisphere.

Visitors to the Bank Al-Maghrib Museum in Rabat, Morocco have the opportunity to view approximately 1,200 coins, items, monetary instruments and banknotes dedicated to the monetary history of Morocco. In South Africa, the Absa Money Museum is in Johannesburg while tours of the South African Mint are held at Centurion.

Located near Kairouan, which lies southwest of Tunis, Tunisia is the Raqqada National Museum of Islamic Art. Finally, the Money Museum of the Bank of Uganda is located inside the headquarters of the central bank in Kampala.

Rabat, Morocco • Bank Al-Maghrib Museum

Additional institutions with limited information:

Johannesburg, South Africa • Absa Money Museum

Centurion • South African Mint

near Kairouan, Tunisia • The Raqqada National Museum of Islamic Art

Kampala, Uganda • Money Museum of the Bank of Uganda

Bank Al-Maghrib Museum

بنك المغرب متحف

Musée de Bank Al-Maghrib

Rabat, Morocco

Bank Al-Maghrib is the central bank of Morocco and was founded in 1959. The Bank Al-Maghrib Museum was inaugurated on June 19, 2002 by King Mohammed VI and houses a unique collection of coins. The very core of the collection was acquired in 1947 and, throughout the years, the Museum's collection has been constantly enhanced to over 30,000 monetary documents.

Entrance to the Museum of Bank Al-Maghrib.

In 2009, on the occasion of the fiftieth anniversary of Bank Al-Maghrib, a new scenographic project was born with the creation of the Museum of Bank Al-Maghrib. This new Museum is meant to be an educational, timeless, space concept which attracts visitors to share the history and heritage of an institution, beyond those of a people and a country.

This concept spans three areas:

- The history of money through an outstanding numismatic collection, which relates the stories of civilizations from antiquity to the present.
- The art gallery accommodates a permanent collection and temporary exhibitions of paintings by artists of all stripes.
- The space devoted to the bank activities describes the missions of the Central Bank and relates its evolution over the past 50 years.
- On two floors, the new Museum spans almost 21,500 square feet (2,000 square

meters) and finds its unity in contemporary architecture unfolding in the heart of the historic Bank headquarters, which was renovated and converted to accommodate the new Museum space.

A gold dinar of Yûsuf ibn Tâshfîn, Aghmât, 498 AH, the first king of the Almoravid dynasty.

The History of Money

The Museum has a wing dedicated to the monetary history of Morocco. Approximately 1,200 coins, items, monetary instruments and banknotes are on display. Exhibited coins transcend borders and time to reflect different eras and civilizations: Greece and the Hellenistic world, Carthage and Rome, Oriental and Occidental Muslims. Morocco, aka Maghreb (meaning "West," or "Occident"), also occupies a privileged place from antiquity up to the present in the Museum. Each time period has its share of the collection and is organized by sets and display units.

- 7th-1st centuries BC: Beginning with the birth of money and its introduction in Morocco.
- 1st century BC-4th century AD: The Kingdom of Mauretania. Here visitors can discover how the currency was introduced in the Maghreb and Andalusia of present-day southern Spain, when part of the Roman Empire. After the collapse of Roman rule at the hands of the Vandal invasion, North Africa was conquered by the Byzantine fleet. At that time, two monetary systems characterized the major economies of the Mediterranean world and the Orient: the Sassanid coinage which was based on the silver drachma and that of Byzantium, based primarily on the gold solidus and the bronze folis. One highlight is an aureus of Juba II and Cleopatra, 25 BC-23 AD.
- 5th-7th centuries: Umayyads. Dinars with Arabic inscriptions were similar in both size and weight to the Byzantine solidus.
- 8th-12th centuries: Isrisid and Almoravid dynasties. As the first Muslim dynasty in Morocco, the Isissides were the first dynasty to strike coins.
- 12th-15th centuries: Almohad and Merinid dynasties. Coinage production increases due to the influx of Sudanese gold.

- 16th-19th centuries: Saadi and Alaouite dynasties.
- The period of Moulay Al Hassan to the present.

The Museum also features a beautiful collection of banknotes which relates the overall history of banknotes in Morocco.

The gold dinar of Abû al-'Ulâ Idrîss (1229-1232 AD).

Visitor's Checklist

Museum of Bank Al-Maghrib, Angle Avenue Allal Ben Abdellah Street and Rue Al-Qahira, Rabat, Morocco. The Museum is on the third floor.

🛈 ☾ +212 (05) 37 70 26 26, +212(05) 37 21 64 72

◯ Tuesday-Friday: 9 a.m.-5:30 p.m.; Saturday: 9 a.m.-12 noon, 3 p.m.-6 p.m.; Sunday: 9 a.m.-1 p.m.

⬤ Monday

✋ (free on Friday) ♿ 🔀 💳 ⊗ 🎧 🛒

Public Transportation

Tram 1 and 2 (Joulane Place, Rabat-Ville)

Internet

✉ musee@bkam.ma

🌐 www.bkam.ma/wps/musee/default.html (in French only)

Additional Institutions, Africa

The following African institutions are known to have numismatic exhibitions of varying degrees that are open to the public. These are listed here, either because sufficient information could not (1) be obtained about the museum, (2) be verified from other sources, (3) the museum did not respond to repeated requests for information, (4) the exhibition is closed due to long-term renovation of the building or other reasons, (5) or I learned about this venue just before the manuscript was to go to the publisher and complete information could not be included.

South Africa
Absa Money Museum
160 Main Street, Johannesburg, Gauteng
❶ ℂ +27 (0) 11 350 4684
✉ money.museum@absa.co.za
🌐 www.absa.co.za/Absacoza/About-Absa/Corporate-Citizenship/ Attractions/ Absa-Money-Museum

South African Mint
Old Johannesburg Road, Gateway, Centurion
❶ ℂ +27 (0)12 677 2777
✉ numismatics@samint.co.za
🌐 www.samint.co.za

Tunisia
The Raqqada National Museum of Islamic Art
المتحف الوطني للفن الإسلامي برقادة
Musée national d'art islamique de Raqqâda
Exact address unavailable. This former presidential palace is 10 km southwest of Kairouan.
✉ contact@patrimoinedetunisie.com.tn (Ministry of Culture)
🌐 www.patrimoinedetunisie.com.tn/eng/musees/raqqada.php (also in Arabic, French)

Uganda
Money Museum of the Bank of Uganda
Plot 45 Kampala Road, Kampala
✉ info@bou.or.ug
🌐 www.bou.or.ug/bou/services/museum/about_the_museum.html

Oceania and Pacific

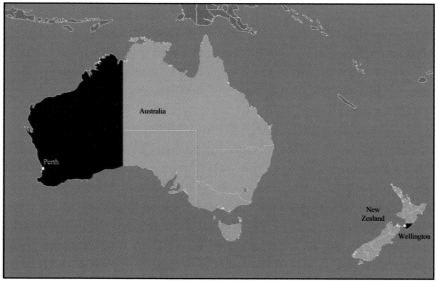

The highlighted regions of Australia and New Zealand, which are part of the continental region known as Oceania and Pacific that have detailed numismatic information and are indicated by a white dot.

The arrival of the first European explorers initially resorted to the age-old barter system with the Aboriginal Australians and the New Zealand Maoris and among themselves. In time, a mixture of British and other European coinage, mainly from Spain, Portugal, The Netherlands, and India, became the norm for commerce.

One of the most prized Australian coins is the "Holey Dollar." This came about by coins leaving the country resulting in a shortage of coins of small denominations. In 1813 the government's solution was to have a known forger cut out a circular center from each section of about 40,000 Spanish silver dollars. This center section was known as the "dump" and the remaining coin with the hole, i.e., the "Holey Dollar," was worthless outside the country. Today, considered as Australia's first coins, they command very high prices.

Just as California's 1849 gold rush had a major impact on that region's numismatic history, so did the 1851 discovery of gold at Mount Alexander in Australia. The country's first gold coin was the Adelaide Pound, minted in 1852, and after that Australia minted gold sovereigns at the Sydney, Perth, and Melbourne mints.

Prior to 1897, coins that were accepted in trade in New Zealand were from a number of countries. The United Kingdom's Imperial Coinage Act of 1870 declared that only British currency was legal tender, although Australian sovereigns and half-sovereigns were permitted. However the withdrawal of gold coins started in 1914 just before the start of World War I. In 1935 British currency ceased to become legal tender and New Zealand became the British Commonwealth's most distant dominion to issue its own currency.

Visitors to "down under" will enjoy a visit to The Perth Mint in Western Australia. Here, one can marvel at the world's largest, heaviest, and most valuable gold coin, weighting 2,230 lbs (1,012 kg) of 0.9999 gold. Also, one can watch a traditional gold pour, where pure gold is transformed into a solid gold bar weighing 200 troy ounces (6 kg), and see the second largest gold nugget in existence, weighing a massive 820 ounces (25.5 kg). Over at the Reserve Bank of New Zealand Museum in Wellington, visitors can see the numismatic exhibition of New Zealand's central bank as well as its economic and banking history.

Perth, Australia	• The Perth Mint
Wellington, New Zealand	• Reserve Bank of New Zealand Museum

The Perth Mint
East Perth, Australia

One of Western Australia's leading tourist venues, The Perth Mint was established in June 1899 as a branch of Britain's Royal Mint to refine the gold from Western Australia's newly discovered eastern goldfields and to turn it into British sovereigns and half sovereigns for the British Empire. It remained under British control until 1970, when ownership was transferred to the government of the State of Western Australia.

The Perth Mint on Hay Street.

Historic Perth Mint Coin Exhibition
There are approximately 300 coins on display from the Mint's collection, all of which were struck by The Perth Mint. The issuing authorities of the coins in the exhibit include the Commonwealth of Australia and the Governments of the Cook Islands and Tuvalu.
Among the historic coins struck by The Perth Mint are:
- An 1899 gold sovereign—the very first coin produced in Perth.
- The first copper decimal coin made in Australia—a 1966-dated 1-cent piece.
- Two of the largest legal tender coins in the world—the 10-kg Australian Lunar gold ($A30,000 face value) and silver ($A300 face value) bullion coins.
In October 2011, the Perth Mint created the world's largest, heaviest, and most valuable gold coin, breaking the record of a C$1 million Canadian coin, weighing 220.5

lbs (100 kg), previously held by the Royal Canadian Mint. The Perth Mint coin is 31.5 inches (80 cm) in diameter, 4.7 inches (12 cm) thick, and is made of 2,230 lbs (1,012 kg) of 99.99 percent pure gold. It is legal tender in Australia with a face value of A$1 million; at time of minting, its value was US$57.34 million.

Visitors examine the Mint's gold bar exhibition.

Guided Talk

Visitors to The Perth Mint can join one of the regular hourly guided talks. The grand heritage building, the heavily secured vault, and the original melting house provide many extraordinary stories about Western Australia's golden history and the Mint's prolific output of priceless gold bars and coins.

Watch a Gold Pour

A visit includes the amazing spectacle of a traditional gold pour, during which pure gold is heated to molten temperatures of approximately 1,200 degrees Celsius and transformed into a solid gold bar weighing 200 troy ounces (6 kg). The 19th-century brick walls of the melting house are literally embedded with gold dust, accumulated over many decades of continuous refining.

World's Largest Gold Bar Exhibition

The world's greatest collection of investment gold bars permanently resides at the The Perth Mint. Although the complete collection comprises more than 1,000 bars from 135 manufacturers and issuers in 35 countries, space limits a selection of 200 gold bars currently on display. Unique bars are Roman gold bars from 378 AD, rainbow bars from Japan which give a multi-colored effect, and hologram bars from Switzerland and Germany.

Australia's Largest Natural Nugget Collection

It has been said that early prospectors endured years of back-breaking labor in the bone dry Australia outback in search of gold nuggets. On display is a breathtaking collection of approximately 150 natural gold nuggets plus wafers and crystals, including Newmont's Normandy Nugget, the second largest gold nugget in existence—a massive 820 ounces (25.5 kg). The second largest nugget on display, called The Golden Beauty, weighs 11.5 kg.

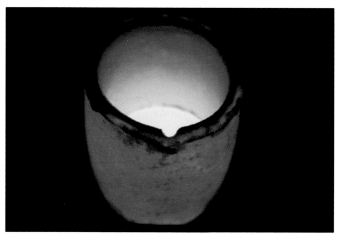

Visitors can watch a gold pour, during which pure gold is transformed into a solid gold bar weighing 6 kg.

Visitor's Checklist
The Perth Mint, 310 Hay Street, East Perth, WA 6004, Australia. The Mint is located at the corner of Hill and Hay Streets.

- ❶ ℂ +61 (0)8 9421 7376, 1300 366 520 (toll free)
- ○ Daily: 9 a.m.-5 p.m.; guided tours start on the half hour beginning at 9:30 a.m. with the last tour at 3:30 p.m.; the gold pour tours start on the hour beginning at 10 a.m. with the last tour at 4 p.m.
- ● January 1, Good Friday*, April 25 (Anzac Day), December 25, and 26.

Public Transportation
- 🚌 24/25/27/103/111/158 (Hay Street before Hill Street); 28 (Goderich Street After Hill Street); Red CAT bus (Hay Street Perth Mint-Free)

Internet
- ✉ tourism@perthmint.com.au
- ⊕ www.perthmint.com.au

Reserve Bank of New Zealand Museum
Wellington, New Zealand

The Reserve Bank Museum, opened in September 2006, is the only specialized economic and central banking museum in New Zealand, and is designed to educate and inform, highlighting New Zealand's economic and banking history, as well as the origins and role of the central bank.

The Reserve Bank of New Zealand as seen at the corner of The Terrace and Bowen Street.

Numismatic Collection
The Reserve Bank of New Zealand owns a small collection of paper money and coins, some of which are on display in the Museum. Although the Bank has been the sole producer of New Zealand's banknotes since 1934 and coins since the late 1980s, the collection also includes a range of other banknotes and coins, such as £1-banknotes issued in the 1860s and 1870s by the Bank of Otago, Bank of Auckland, and Bank of New Zealand, some of which are on display.

Commemorative Coins
Other rare and important examples of New Zealand's numismatic history include a selection of coins issued by the Bank to commemorate various events. These include one dollar collectors' coins from 1970, 1974, 1978, 1983 and 1986; a "Benz" gold coin from 1998; and a complete 1937 proof set.

Merchants' tokens

In the early colonial period there was no formal New Zealand currency, and British currency was commonly used. Promissory notes and merchants' tokens were redeemable from the issuing merchant. The collection includes examples by Jones and Williamson, J. Caro & Co., Edward Reece, and Milner and Thompson.

Reserve Banknotes

The first series of Reserve Banknotes were issued 1934 on a temporary basis until a more permanent series could be developed. A complete set of 1940 Series 2 Reserve Banknotes, the intended lasting design, is also on display. These banknotes remained in circulation until decimalization in 1967. On display are a set of printing plates, and draft sketches of the third series decimal banknotes.

One of the Museum's gallery displays.

Bank of Aotearoa £1-Banknote

Tukaroto Matutaera Potatau Te Wherowhero Tawhaio (d.1894) was the second Maori king and in the 1880s he founded the Bank of Aotearoa, which issued a £1-banknote. The banknote was never circulated, and this specimen is one of three known to exist, which is a highlight of the collection.

Counterfeit Banknotes and Polymer Security Features

A few of the counterfeits the Bank has collected over the years are on display, along with details of some of the security features in the current banknote series. New Zealand was one of the first countries in the world to adopt polymer for its banknotes, being more durable and offering superior security features. Displays highlight some of the security features of New Zealand's modern banknotes.

The Balancing Act

The rear wall of the Museum has been dubbed the "Balancing Act" and is designed to highlight the wide range of tasks and functions performed by the Bank under the Reserve Bank Act 1989. The Bank has roles that range from formulating monetary policy to monitoring and supervising the health of the financial system, maintaining foreign reserves, operating in the financial markets if necessary, and issuing currency as required. It is very much a balancing act, symbolized by scales from the Bank's collection.

The New Zealand 1935 proof Waitangi Crown with a mintage of 1,128 – 468 of which are proofs. This is not as rare as the almost similar looking 1935 pattern with three known specimens, one of which is on display in at the RBNZ Museum.

Visitor's Checklist

Reserve Bank New Zealand Museum, The Terrace, Wellington, New Zealand
The building is at the corner of The Terrace and Bowen Street and the Museum is located on the ground floor.

- ❶ ☏ +64 (04) 471 3682
- ○ Monday-Friday: 9:30 a.m.-4 p.m.
- ● Saturday and Sunday; January 1, February 6 (Waitangi Day), Good Friday,* Easter Monday,* April 25 (Anzac Day), Queen's Birthday (1st Monday in June), Labor Day (4th Monday in October), December 25, and 26; and for special events.

✋ ⑤ 📷

Public Transportation

🚌 Metlink 17/20/22/23 (The Terrace at Bolton Street); 3/3S/3W/13/21 (Bowen Street/Ministry of Justice)

Internet

- ✉ museum@rbnz.govt.nz
- 🌐 www.rbnzmuseum.govt.nz

Picture Credits

The following suffixes are added to the page number to indicate the position of that picture when more than one picture appears on a page: t= top; tr=top right; tl=top left; c=center; cr=center right; cl=center left; b=bottom; bl=bottom left; br=bottom right; l=left; r=right

All pictures or digital images were provided by a number of sources. Both the author and publisher are grateful to the following photographers, museums, and other institutions for their permission to reproduce their pictures.

© Bank of Japan Currency Museum
364, 365
© Historisches Museum Basel, Peter Portner
221
© Sunflower Foundation
230, 231, 232t, 232c
A. H. Baldwin & Sons Ltd.
318
ANA Edward C. Rochette Money Museum
80, 81, 82
Yigal Arkin
110, 111t
Chris Backe
370

Bank Al-Maghrib, Inventory #1134
383
Bank Al-Maghrib, Inventory #1148
384
Bank of Estonia Museum
288
The Banknote Book (www.banknotenews.com)
125b, 141, 289, 296, 319
Howard M. Berlin
45, 63, 64, 65, 66, 67, 68, 72, 73, 74, 97, 98, 99, 100, 101, 103,
111b, 136, 137, 138t, 142, 143, 144, 145, 146, 147, 148, 149, 153,
154, 155, 156, 157, 158, 159, 161t, 161c, 162, 163, 164, 165, 166,
168, 169, 170, 172, 174, 175, 176, 177, 178, 179, 180, 181, 182,
183, 184, 185, 186, 187, 188, 189, 192, 193, 194cl, 194cr, 195,
196, 197, 201, 202, 203t, 203b, 204, 205, 206t, 206c, 207, 208,
211, 213, 214, 239, 240, 241, 242, 243, 244, 245, 246, 247, 248,
249, 250, 251, 252, 253, 254, 255, 258, 259, 260, 262, 263, 264c,
264b, 266c, 266b, 267, 279, 280, 281, 285, 286, 287, 299t, 306,
307, 321, 322, 323, 324, 327, 328, 329cl, 329cr, 331t, 338, 347,
350, 363, 373, 374, 378
Bernisches Historisches Museum, Bern. Photograph Alexander
Gempeler, Bern
224
Bernisches Historisches Museum, Bern. Photograph Stefan
Rebsamen
225, 226
Bulgarian National Bank
282, 283
Central Bank of Brazil, Photo: David Borges
119, 120
Central Bank of Jordan
330
Courtesy Museum on the Mound. Photography by Antonia Reeve
261c, 261b
Courtesy of Heritage Auctions
58, 102, 105t, 105b, 112, 125c, 138c, 199, 200, 209, 284, 290, 295,
298, 299c, 304, 308, 331b, 334, 335, 345, 394

Courtesy Reserve Bank of India Monetary Museum
354, 355, 356
Johnny Cuppens
346
Danmarks Nationalbank
140
Federal Reserve Bank of Atlanta
54, 55
Federal Reserve Bank of Kansas City
70, 71
Federal Reserve Bank of Kansas City, Denver Branch
84, 85
Federal Reserve Bank of New York
39, 40, 41
Federal Reserve Bank of Philadelphia
42, 43, 44
Federal Reserve Bank of San Francisco
89, 90, 91, 92, 93, 94
Alex Feldstein
48
Tammy Young Heck
75
Historisches Museum Basel, Photo: Alwin Seiler
223
Historisches Museum Basel, Photo: Philippe Emmel
222
Image Courtesy of The Perth Mint
390, 391
Japan Mint & Museum
360, 361, 362
José Luis López Iglesias
333
Ursula Kampmann; first published in *CoinsWeekly* 2012
325, 326
Fritz Rudolf Künker GmbH & Co. KG, Osnabrück and Lübke &
Wiedemann, Stuttgart, image owner
167

Swiss National Museum, Inventory Number SLM-.DA 9744
234
United States Mint
46, 47, 87, 88t
University of Oxford Ashmolean Museum
257c, 257bl
Uppsala University Coin Cabinet
216, 217, 218
Ömer Yalçinkaya
344, 348

The following images were obtained from the Wikipedia/Wikimedia Commons repositories and are reproduced in accordance with the indicated GNU Free Documentation License (Version 1.2), and Creative Commons Attribution-Share Alike (CCSA) version Generic licenses for each author or user name. Every effort has been made to properly attribute and identify the correct license(s), author or owner of the original image and we would be pleased to insert the appropriate acknowledgements in any subsequent editions of this book if an unintentional omission or an error in attribution has been made.

ACrush (GNU1.2, CCSA3.0Un) 118
Atlantacitizen (GNU1.2, CCSA3.0Un) 53
Eddie Chen (CCSA2.0G) 349
ChrisO (GNU1.2, CCSA3.0Un) 237
Chronus (GNU1.2, CCSA3.0Un) 116
Merlin Cooper (CCSA2.5G) 256
Sebastian Dubiel (CCSA3.0Un) 210
EvgenyGenkin (CCSA1.0G, CCSA2.0G, CCSA2.5G, CCSA3.0Un)
343
Habanero36 (CCSA3.0Un) 108
Ham (CCSA3.0Un) 265
Jleon (CCSA3.0UN) 26
Jleon and Mcshadypl (CCSA3.0Un) 60
Szeder László (CCSA1.0G, CCSA2.0G, CCSA2.5G, CCSA3.0Un)
309

David Liuzzo (CCSA2.0G) 151
mmann1988 (CCSA3.0Un) 50
Moody 75 (CCSA2.0G) 369
Nichalp (CCSA1.0G, CCSA2.0G, CCSA2.5G, CCSA3.0Un) 353
Onetwo1 (GNU1.2, CCSA3.0Un) 86
Otourly (CCSA1.0G, CCSA2.0G, CCSA2.5G, CCSA3.0Un) 191
Andreas Praefcke (GNU1.2, CCSA3.0Un) 33
Lokal_Profil (CCSA2.5G) 95
Pymouss44 (CCSA1.0G, CCSA2.0G, CCSA2.5G, CCSA3.0Un) 219
Enrique Íñiguez Rodríguez (CCSA3.0Un) 294
Roland zh (CCSA3.0Un) 233
Alberto Salguero (GNU1.2) 212
Camilo Sanchez (CCSA3.0Un) 115
Sceptre (GNU1.2, CCSA3.0Un) 130
Ssolbergj (GNU1.2, CCSA3.0Un) 129, 275
Kaihsu Tai (CCSA1.0G, CCSA2.0G, CCSA2.5G, CCSA3.0Un) 392
Taifarious1,Matthiew Field, Adrian104, Oreos and Nserrano
   (CCSA3.0Un) 78
Tango7174 (CCSA1.0G, CCSA2.0G, CCSA2.5G, CCSA3.0Un) 96
Theshibboleth (GNU1.2) 23, 27, 51, 61, 77
TodorBozhinov (GNU1.2, CCSA1.0G, CCSA2.0G, CCSA2.5G,
   CCSA3.0Un) 274
Ramon F. Velasquez (CCSA3.0Un) 372
Davide Cesare Veniani (CCSA2.5G, CCSA3.0Un) 382
Kali Wisła (CCSA2.0G) 303

The images on the following pages were stated as being in the
public domain by its author or owner.
   40, 69, 83, 86, 88b, 104, 107, 139, 171, 198, 238, 297, 315, 339,
   379, 387, 389

Index

V

W

Y

Z

About the Author

Following his retirement from teaching college after twelve years with the Department of Defense, Howard had written the "World Destinations" column for *WorldWide Coins* about his visits to museums around the world that feature exhibits about coins, banknotes and medals, and travel articles for Delaware's *Jewish Voice* as part of the "Jewish Traveler" column. To date, he has visited more than 50 countries on five continents.

As a collector for many years of British Mandate of Palestine coins and banknotes, along with National Banknotes of towns with the name of "Berlin" or its variation, he had many times exhibited parts of his collection at national and regional shows, often being awarded the "best of show" prize. In addition, he has written many articles on coins and banknotes for *Coin World, WorldWide Coins, Paper Money Values, The Banknote Reporter, World Coin News, The Shekel,* and the *Jewish Voice.*

A writer with varied interests, Dr. Berlin has written more than 30 books on electronic circuit design, financial markets, numismatics, and the cinema in addition to his articles about numismatics and travel. Some of his books, articles, photographs, web sites, and columns have won "best of" awards by both the Delaware Press Association and the Numismatic Literary Guild. Besides memberships in the Authors Guild, Delaware Press Association, and the Numismatic Literary Guild, he served two years as an ex-officio member of the Community Advisory Board of *The News Journal,* writing periodic editorials on various issues.

When not writing or traveling, in his spare time he enjoys playing folk guitar and 5-string bluegrass banjo. He has also been a licensed ham radio operator for over 50 years since age 14.

He received bachelor degrees in both electrical engineering and arts and science from the University of Delaware; an M.S. degree in electrical/biomedical engineering from Washington University in St. Louis; an M.Ed. degree in computer science and an Ed.D. concentrating on educational statistics, both from Widener University. For his scientific and academic efforts, Dr. Berlin had been elected to several honor societies and awarded several U.S. patents.